D1610933

THE PRIVATE LIFE
OF
POLAR EXPLORATION

FICTION BY J. M. SCOTT

The Private Life
of
Polar Exploration

J. M. SCOTT

William Blackwood
Edinburgh

William Blackwood
32 Thistle Street
Edinburgh EH2 1HA

First published 1982
© J. M. Scott 1982

ISBN 0 85158 153 6

Printed by William Blackwood & Sons Ltd

Acknowledgements

I am very much indebted to Harry King, Librarian of the Scott Polar Research Institute, Cambridge; Mrs G. A. Cooke, Librarian of the Boreal Institute for Northern Studies, Alberta; Dr Charles Swithinbank of the Antarctic Survey; Dr Gertrude Nobile and the Centro Documentazione 'Umberto Nobile' at the Museo Aeronautico, Rome; also Pat Baird; surviving comrades of the British Arctic Air-Route Expedition; and many other people alive or now dead who told me first-hand stories. All important book references I hope have been acknowledged in the text.

J. M. Scott

Contents

Illustrations

Preface

Edward Pellham, writing in the early seventeenth century, tells of a group of malefactors who had been condemned to death for heinous crimes but who – whaling crews being hard to find – were offered pardon, food, clothing and a reward if they would spend a year in Greenland. They accepted, and sailed to the Arctic shore. After one look at it they besought the captain to take them back to England and execution.

Yet many people without need of legal remission or thought of material reward, but with a bit of imagination and adventurous urge, jump at an opportunity to experience life in the polar regions.

Their spoken excuses may be scientific, professional, commercial. The reason is that they see a tide in their affairs that leads to something quite different from anything else in the rest of the world and they are of the type that dives straight in, whatever the water.

This book is about the classic discomforts, obstacles, dangers they may find – that have been encountered by explorers. The interesting point is that the bigger these are the better. That makes it all the more worth while, all the more pleasant afterwards. The traveller broadens his experience, discovers something about himself and earns a life pension of memories. The quest rewards.

That is why men explore.

J. M. S.

1

Fifty Years Back

Organising and leading an expedition to the polar regions is similar to writing a play and getting it staged. The would-be explorer must have a good idea and set it down convincingly on paper. With this and his powers of persuasion he must obtain financial backing.

First he should win the approval of the Royal Geographical Society. Materially the R.G.S. can only lend instruments and make a small grant. But its blessing is like that of the church in marriage – it makes what he wants to do respectable in the eyes of the world. In this case it is the monied world – the media, the makers of warm clothing, nourishing foods, sports equipment. Only if he is exceptionally lucky is there an altruistic patron.

Whatever strain and difficulties are involved in his plans, they are nothing compared to what he must go through to get his expedition launched. With the first sign of success he starts on the props and cast – rations, equipment, ship, personnel. He is worried and hectically busy for months and relaxes only when he is actually off on his adventure. That sigh of relief soothes the melancholy of personal partings.

Gino Watkins had a brilliant idea. It came to him when we were travelling together in Labrador in the winter of 1928-29. We were both hooked on exploring and Greenland was an obvious next field. But how to justify the considerable expense? The British Arctic Air-Route was the answer.

Lindberg's flight from the United States to France was a spectacular success because few people had conceived of the possibility of flying non-stop as far as that. He, of course, had not been able to carry anything except fuel, so the 3,000 miles of Atlantic continued to be crossed by ship after his flight. But if one followed the great circle route from the British Isles – the land bridge of Faroe Islands, Iceland, East Greenland, over the icecap to West Greenland, and then via Baffin Island and Hudson Bay to Winnipeg – the hops would be less than 500 miles. So there were commercial possibilities.

The least known section of the route was East Greenland. We would go there and map it by boat, on land and by aerial photography. We would make journeys on the icecap, determining its altitude. We would keep year-long weather observations both at its highest levels and at our coastal base. And if possible we would fly in our two little Moth aeroplanes to Canada.

Gino put up his plans to the R.G.S. which approved them, trusting in the reputation he had gained on two previous expeditions although he was only twenty-two. He found an altruistic sponsor, and a number of firms promised equipment and stores. When Shackleton's old ship, the *Quest*, had been chartered, all was set – barring detailed preparations and choice of personnel – to start the following year, 1930.

I saw nothing of the final preparations, for I left before the summer to buy dogs; but I was involved in the preparation of sledging rations. Expecting very cold conditions Gino was determined that the daily ration should have a calorific value of 6,000, and not exceed 35 oz. in weight. He achieved this concentration by including 8 oz. of pemmican, which was 40 per cent fat, 8 oz. of margarine, and by cutting down the biscuits to four. The rest was mainly sugar, chocolate, oats and peaflour, plus a little concentrated lemon juice and a spoonful of cod liver oil. Dr Zilva of the Lister Institute said it was an excellent ration, with carbohydrate, fat and protein in suitable proportions and all the necessary vitamins. Its only shortcoming was that we would not be able to stomach it.

Gino said he would prove we could actually eat it and roped me in for the experiment. It was a warm early May. We ran round and round Hyde Park at night and slept almost naked. We got the sickly stuff down – just. I can say now that on the icecap it proved to be exactly what we all wanted. Thus do conditions alter tastes. I do not think the ration could be improved on today. Fads change but not food values.

I did not meet the party until 11th July when the *Quest* reached the Faroe Islands where I had been waiting with the dogs. It would not help the reader to be introduced to Gino's twelve men all at once; they will make their individual entrances in due course. There were two

R.A.F. and two Army officers and a Surgeon Lieutenant, R.N. The rest, bar one, were just down from Cambridge and had not yet worked in jobs. All except one were under thirty, most in their early twenties, the leader youngest of all.

I have recently asked all who are still available why they wanted to go on the expedition. For Alfred Stephenson, the chief surveyor, it was an adventurous follow-up to a geographical tripos. Martin Lindsay, Royal Scots Fusiliers, whose previous travel experience had been a remarkable crossing of Africa, simply said that he happened to have been a fellow guest with Gino at a weekend house party. Ted Bingham heard of it while at supper on his ship and instantly applied. Another doctor had put his name in first but somehow Ted overcame that. To all, this was an opportunity not to be missed. August Courtauld never admitted *wanting* to go on any expedition, yet somehow he frequently did. He had made two university summer trips to Greenland and had travelled by camel in the Sahara. Only he, Gino and I had been in the Arctic before. Only Wager and Stephenson had scientific degrees.

We soon got to know each other, being almost as tightly packed together as the dogs in their pen. The first adventure was barging through the pack ice which impenetrably guards East Greenland except during two or three summer months, and which too often nips ships and sinks them. But the Norwegian captain and crew of the sealer (as the *Quest* then was) knew their job. Only the occasional bump and involuntary clang of the ship's bell disturbed the calm, which was a relief after the initially stormy Iceland sea.

Then came the first glimpse of Greenland's mountains. The man who wrote the hymn could never have seen them. They are starkly black or brown, much too steep to be 'icy'. It is only through gaps at the head of fjords that the snowy icecap appears like sugar piled to capacity in a jagged-edged bowl, spilling over to the sea here and there in the white cliffs of a glacier face. But on a bright summer's day the effect is not grim, quite the reverse. It is a contrast of colours – the brilliantly blue sea studded with brown islands and white floes, the aquamarine of icebergs with the purple shadows of their waterworn caverns.

I wish I could give with authority the reactions of all those who saw this for the first time. I suspect that most reactions were practical. The aviators, Flight-Lieutenants D'Aeth and Cozens and engineer Wilfred Hampton, must have worried about runways littered with

3

floes and with high mountains to windward. Lawrence Wager, though he loved mountains, certainly scratched his head as to how he would assess the geology. And Stephenson admits that the scene scared him. His practical surveying had been done on the Pennines and the smooth little Gog-Magog hills of Cambridge. My main interest was in the steep approaches to the icecap where the dogs and I would principally have to go. Only Freddie Spencer Chapman who had read English at Cambridge, was an ornithologist by hobby, and was a poet and romantic at heart recorded differently:

> Some Eskimos brought in a number of eider and long-tailed ducks which they had just got with their bird-spears; while near some low islands a terrific commotion was caused by a snowy falcon being mobbed by a lot of squawkingly angry Arctic terns for approaching too near the ternery. It was a blazing hot day, and this enchanting place seemed almost too good to be true.

For the next three weeks, having found a site for our base, we worked too hard for any reactions except physical, and a vague and dreamy sense of satisfaction. It was the end of July. With the summer ending and a vast amount to be done before winter set in, we worked like the slaves who built the pyramids – and enjoyed it in a masochistic, self-discovering sort of way. We worked in twelve-hour shifts day and night, unloading from the *Quest*, rowing to the shore and carrying to the site timber for the hut (which had to be built); sections for the wireless masts (which had to be erected); parts of the aeroplanes (which had to be assembled); the light-generating plant; all the rations for sledging and the base for a year; whale meat for the dogs prepared in the Faroes; fifteen tons of coal which had to be shovelled out of the hold and many other miscellaneous items. What was pleasant about that? Yet in many ways it was the happiest part of the expedition.

After that, drawing breath before the exploring work started, we only worked by day, taking by whaleboat about 4,000 lb, of stores plus sledges to the head of the fjord and carrying loads up 500 feet of rock to the glacier foot for the first icecap journey. There was a sense of competition in this. Lieutenant Martin Lindsay, who had 'seldom previously carried anything heavier than a message', learned that he could shoulder 120 lb. John Rymill, our Australian giant, could shrug on and off 160 lb. Quintin Riley, a Leander cox, and Surgeon

4

Lieutenant Ted Bingham did their stints, and I hope I did. With our last loads we had dogs twining their leads about our legs.

The other members of the expedition helped in this, of course. Then they went north in the *Quest* to make a coastal survey. Imagine them pushing whaleboats through brash ice, climbing rocky hills with a plane table, or flying over a mountain wilderness uncertain of finding open water to land on when each flight was done. We five who have been mentioned by name set off up the glacier (for the icecap) to establish the central weather station.

I had driven dogs before – though never in these conditions. It must have been a disconcerting introduction for the others. The glacier by which we approached the icecap was dead – it was no longer moving and therefore had no crevasses. But that was its only virtue. In this season all the snow had melted at that level, leaving slippery undulations on which the ski-runner sledges skidded wildly. And the ice surface had been eroded by dust and thaw-water into chisels and needles. The dogs had to be fitted with boots, and made more fuss than any customer in a shoe shop. When a sledge swung sideways and overturned they lay down to chew their shoes off, and got their feet cut. The men worked frantically to urge them on. I, ashamed of their behaviour, hauled with them. John Rymill, accustomed to herding steers, swung a stock whip and managed to wind the lash round my neck. 'Sorry, Number One', he said laconically. I specify these discomforts because we truly enjoyed what we were doing – or enjoyed being able to do it.

This glacier was the beginning and end of all our icecap journeys, so however farcically it made us behave on this occasion it must have some description. It protruded seaward like a bare foot, the toes amongst the rocks of the coastal hills. In the course of the first day we got up the lower slopes. Then the instep rose before us, and it was a high instep. It took us several days to mount it, with loads of 700 lb. on each of our five sledges, although the distance was no more than half a mile. Captain Lemon at the base signalled frequently to the *Quest* that we were still in sight.

In our despatches to *The Times* we always referred to this instep as Bugbear Bank. The author of the recent biography of Augustine Courtauld (not on the expedition), called it what we actually called it from this first occasion. But, bugbear it, it was always Bugbear Bank in print and so it shall here remain.

Inland lay a zone of crevasses and we flagged out a safe way.

Beyond the last crevasse we planted the Big Flag which later became a depot. It was not so then, of course; we needed to carry in all we could. But, safely above the level of thawing temperatures, we saved a little weight by taking all the perishable food out of tins which we scattered about. (Litter, a sign of humanity, is a delightful sight on the icecap.) We did not dispose of all the cans, however. An empty tin is a very useful article on a sledge journey. It saves you going out of the tent into the cold.

The icecap, any icecap, once you are fairly on it, is like an ocean – of a smaller world than ours for the curvature is such that, although you scarcely notice it as you advance, the coastal mountains drop below the horizon. Beyond is nothing but whiteness and the sky which in calm weather may be blue.

There is a tremendous frozen swell, its crests a mile or more apart, but this may be unnoticed unless you spot a man, dog, tent or sledge at that distance, and see it truncated. There are no other objects to observe.

The waves that corrugate the swell are snowdrifts. These may be virtually non-existent after snowfall and a long calm (a rare condition), or large enough to overturn or even break a sledge. But, unlike water, snow can be soft or hard, sticky or crusted – different in a dozen ways. This governs good or bad going quite apart from the wind blowing at the time.

Yet it is the wind that rules. If strong enough, it can whip up any surface in no time, creating a swift stream of choking, blinding particles – and often increasing the effect of cold to danger levels. It is an awesome place, the icecap. Not even the ocean can make you feel so fragile and insignificant. In any case you generally venture on the ocean in a largish vessel. On the icecap you go by foot and have to set up shelter for the night. Besides, the ocean is crowded with life, more so than is the land. On the icecap there is no living thing at all, animal or vegetable. It is inimical to life – in Greenland a lump of ice 1,500 miles long, on average 350 miles across (it is pear shaped) and up to 9,000 feet thick, completely smothers the rocky topography beneath except for the coastal mountains just as the Ice Age once smothered most of the Europe we know. I once picked up a dead snow bunting on the icecap. Poor little twerp, it had had its own bright idea about an Arctic air route.

It was through this neither-land-nor-sea that we travelled after the Big Flag. We went cheerfully, hopefully, adventurously, and not

6

uncomfortably for it was summer. In the book he wrote directly afterwards, Martin Lindsay spoke of a day when the wind blew fresh in our faces and caused superficial frostbites. That was as exciting as a bullet graze. We went slowly, holding precisely to a compass course, marking each half mile with a small red flag. Every twenty or thirty miles John Rymill took theodolite observations to ensure that our dead reckoning was correct, the flags exactly placed. We were not aware that the course we were so carefully tracing was a line drawn on water.

Our object was to set up the weather station on or near the highest contour of the icecap. On the eighteenth day we were at an altitude of 8,600 feet, and the slope had flattened out. We were 130 miles inland. That was good enough, for since the place would have to be maintained and relieved in all weathers we did not want to go further than necessary to obtain a year-long record of the central conditions.

So we stopped and set up the station, a double-skinned dome-shaped tent ten feet across at the base and nine feet high at the apex where a one-inch brass vent protruded. The tent was to be entered through a snow tunnel on the thermodynamic principle of the Eskimo igloo, slightly improved (cold air lay low in the tunnel, spent air went out of the vent). It was brilliantly designed by Gino. The enormous umbrella with curved ribs withstood all gales. The two skins with air between provided as good insulation as was practicable. The little brass tube proved to have a significance besides ventilation. There was just one thing wrong, which we did not realise at the time – the tent protruded above snow level and would annoy the omnipotent wind when it woke from its summer sleep.

Four of us spent the next day erecting the tent and fiddling about while John in his large, slow, methodical way fixed the longitude and latitude to within 100 yards. Thank God he did! We then had a farewell supper in what seemed the Pantheon and said goodbye to Martin Lindsay and Quintin Riley who were to do the first stint.

Doc Bingham, John and I set off light loaded, extra dogged and flat out for the base, covering up to forty miles in a day. Only one incident sticks in my memory. While breaking the third camp the doctor found a blind puppy shivering in the snow. This was quite a surprise, for its mother, Unalit, had been pulling with the best the day before. We made a nest for them on a sledge, and drove on – four more puppies were born.

We reached the Big Flag at dusk. We should have camped there, but we were only fifteen miles from the coast, eighteen from the base. We smelt the stable. So on we went, dodging the open crevasses and taking the bridged ones on trust. One let us down – or rather the dogs of the leading sledge. They went through a snow bridge, fell the length of their traces and hung there supported by the sledge which had bridged the gap.

We could not pull them up, stooping from a slippery perch, for the traces were tangled and the weight of eight huskies was too much to lift. John said, 'A Spanish windlass'. The essential parts of this mysterious apparatus were two skis lashed at right angles. At this we laboured like sailors at a capstan, but the plaited traces only cut deep into the snow lip and stuck.

So I claimed the right to go down on a rope. It was dark apart from the glimmer of the ice walls. I could not untangle the dogs. Finally I called for another line, tied it to a dog's collar, slipped him from his harness and had him hauled up, half strangled – and so with the rest. When I emerged the pups were fast asleep on the sledge, surrounded by their mother who gave me that pathetic half snarl, half 'please don't hurt them' look. For safety's sake we camped where we were till daylight. Even so John's fifteen stone – or two thirds of it – went through another snow bridge and he saved himself (he was not roped) only by grasping his sledge.

Thus the first icecap journey was a great success. With just enough hardship and danger, we had set up the weather station.

With today's techniques we might have done it by motor sledge. I am told by Dr Charles Swithinbank that the modern motor sledge, or snowmobile, could climb even the rocky coastal fringe by its own power, could tow reduced loads up Bugbear in relays, and cover the remaining distance to our weather station in two or three days. No doubt he is right for he has much experience of them, and motor sledges recently crossed the Antarctic. But men like Dr Smithinbank would have to have driven them. I picture myself arguing with an inanimate object that refuses to start on a cold morning and eventually having to kick it. It seems to me that as mechanical things have developed they have modified human temperament. Anyway, this book is about the days before snow was successfully ploughed by tractors. We reached the coast behind galloping dogs, sharing their exhilaration.

We were greeted by Gino and D'Aeth who had flown home ahead of the *Quest* from Kangardlugsuak 300 miles up the coast. (We did

8

mechanically plough the sky and the sea according to our resources – Gino was a modern man, up to the minute in anything usefully available.) Lemon was also at the base as he had been throughout, getting his wireless communications going and turning the hut into a home with three Eskimo girls and a boy as domestic staff. They waited on us at table, offering the dishes from the left, then threw the tin plates out of doors to be washed up by the dogs. This was all great fun, something to tell of.

Captain P. H. M. Lemon, R.E., was not only the oldest of us by several years (he was thirty-two; he had entered the First World War just in time to be made a prisoner), he also had the best brain, the most experience of life. From scratch, without a book, he had acquired a working knowledge of the language and had established a – still limited – authority over our wayward staff. He was a first class wireless operator. For balanced thinking, general usefulness and stability, he was probably the strongest member of the party.

I must interject a paragraph on names, which were then *not* automatically first names – except Gino. For a year in Labrador I could never bring myself to call him Gino. (Nor did he call me Jamie.) Equally, we could not be as formal as the old explorers and use surnames. So we called each other nothing, but since we were usually alone that did not matter. In crowded Greenland he was Gino to everyone at once. Most of us soon had first names, or abbreviations like Steve (Stephenson) and Ham (Hampton). But two or three were known by surnames throughout. This had nothing to do with popularity – they were quite as well liked and as good mixers as any. But Lemon was Lemon throughout (his Christian name was Percy); Iliffe Cozens was Cozens; and D'Aeth was D'Aeth, possibly because nobody then knew his other name which was Narborough.

The *Quest* returned from the coastal journey. All of us were briefly at the base except for the weather station couple. We were in the best of spirits, thoroughly pleased with ourselves. The airmen, D'Aeth, Iliffe Cozens, Ham and Gino had managed the aerial survey (Iliffe was also, in fact primarily, in charge of ordinary photography). A range of mountains that proved to be the highest in the Arctic had been sighted. Steve, aided by August and Freddie Chapman had found the small-boat surveying not too overpowering. Wager (another surnamer, his first name was Lawrence) had geologised and helped with the small boats.

We dined and slept and then were off again, Gino and I to make a southern icecap journey from the weather station, John and Freddie to carry up stores, Doc and D'Aeth to relieve Quintin and Martin. Naturally we all joined up and arrived at the station together, having followed the flagged route without much difficulty. It was September, still summer weather.

We found Martin and Quintin in fine form. They had done their stint excellently. It would be wrong to belittle the achievement of the first parties at the station in comparison with that of the man who finally held it alone – he was strong on that point himself. Martin and Quintin had set up their instruments and maintained a series of three-hourly meteorological observations. They had improved the structure – or so we all thought – by building two igloos and an eight-foot snow wall round the 'courtyard'. They had lived sparingly on sledging rations and made the most of such luxuries as an evening cup of tea. Though utterly different in temperament and tastes, in ideas about religion and recreation – everything – they had shared life like the winners of the Dunmow Flitch.

They returned to the base with Freddie and John. Gino and I, leaving Doc and D'Aeth at the station, set out on our southern journey.

We had talked a lot about this trip since the days of trotting round Hyde Park – being greeted with, 'Run home with me, darling' by the ladies who in those days wandered alone – trying to digest our experimental sledging ration. The official object of our sledge journey was to trace the profile of the icecap as far south as possible, thus gaining useful information for future flights from coast to coast. But the truth is that we, the two 'experts', were determined to cover a spectacular sledging distance *pour encourager les autres*, at the start of the expedition.

We left the station with six weeks' rations, half to be used in travelling south, half for the return to the Big Flag. Fifteen miles a day – a safe estimate, surely – would get us 300 miles, near enough to the sharp end of Greenland. As it turned out the journey proved that the icecap upsets even the best calculations. It also demonstrated that the bone-headed husky knew more about icecap meteorology than our weather station ever discovered.

After a fairly good start the dogs began to go slow, for no apparent reason. We were not climbing. The surface was average – sticky after snowfall, drifted and therefore apt to upset the sledges after wind. The dogs looked in good condition and had been on full rations since

10

leaving the base where they had been well fed. It was not really cold, the lowest day temperature −36°F. But after the first couple of days we could not get a trot out of the teams, which stopped at the slightest excuse or none at all.

We tried everything from beating to petting, curses to encouragement. We gave them extra pemmican, biscuits and margarine from our own rations. Gino went out in front to make a trail and give them something to look at. The only difference was that I had two sledges to right and re-start after every check.

I think I was even more upset than Gino, for I had known the dogs for two months before the expedition sailed from England. I had selected them in West Greenland from where the best sledge dogs in the world come, conveyed the fifty of them to the Faroe Islands where, since dogs were not permitted because of the sheep, I had kept them on a lighter anchored in a fjord. Since I could not speak Danish, Eskimo or Viking they had effectively been my only companions. I had scrubbed them out daily, exercised them with tugs-of-war on whale blubber, broken up their battles (I still bear scars), done what I could to soothe their love affairs. I knew not only all their outlandish names but their individual characters. When it came to making up teams I had, humanly, given the best to Gino and myself. And here they were sitting down every fifty yards.

Instead of progressing 300 miles south or even 200 we had to change course for the Big Flag and home, having covered only ninety-five miles from the station.

It was at noon that we set the new course – a quite different course, not back along the old trail for the journey was triangular. The dogs started at a trot and kept it up. In three days we covered thirty miles – nothing to be proud of but far more than we had been managing. We were exasperated. The dogs had made fools of us. How would we explain getting back to the base from a futile journey with plenty of food in hand?

The third evening was absolutely still. We had just blown out the candle and settled down in our sleeping bags when something that felt like a breaking wave struck the tent. There was a moment of complete silence. Then another wave, and another and another struck until the storm settled down to blow in earnest. The canvas crackled and flapped deafeningly, frighteningly. The four bamboo poles of the pyramid tent creaked and groaned. Our shelter was the only obstacle in the path of a semi-solid wind heavy with drift. Next morning,

11

peeping out, all we could see was this flood of snow, a great bank to leeward of the tent and a few of the wretched dogs creeping about with their tails between their trembling legs looking for non-existent shelter. The holes we had dug for them had soon filled up and the wise or lucky had been buried.

The storm blew for two nights and days, then stopped as suddenly as it had come. We spent five hours digging out, then hurried on until the next storm broke. They came more and more frequently, from the middle of the icecap and therefore across our line of advance. We tried travelling while one was blowing but it was futile. The sledges were sent skidding round. This frightened the dogs and swung them upwind. Their eyes were filled with snow so they turned about and ran before the storm. We had a hard fight pitching the tent, holding onto the precious canvas with numbed hands.

After that we lay up during the storms and travelling as hard as we could when they lulled, night or day. The intervals varied. Once we managed to cover nearly fifteen miles, but on the next advance only 200 yards. We were converging on the mountainous coast and crossed a deep, wide ice valley that ran down to a big fjord. Evidently this funnelled the wind, increasing its speed to an estimated 80 m.p.h. There were also crevasses.

We did not doubt that we would reach the base. But we realised that if the dogs had gone at normal speed while we were travelling south we would not have got back. So we owed our lives to their strange behaviour.

Most of our food having been eaten by this time we jettisoned a sledge and travelled on with one, both teams hitched to it. There was no talking while we hurried forward but whenever we were laid up we discussed the chances of Freddie Chapman's party. He had left the station for the base when we started south. The plan was that he should come in again with a relief couple for Doc and D'Aeth, sufficient stores for their wintering, and a wireless transmitting set which would enable contact to be maintained and, by weather reports, facilitate supply, perhaps relief, by air. If Freddie had made a rapid journey out (his loads were light) and done a quick turn-around he should have been fairly near to the station before the weather broke. And coming out again he would have the wind behind him. So we argued, but we were worried. We had learned to respect the icecap.

We could never have anticipated what actually happened. As we

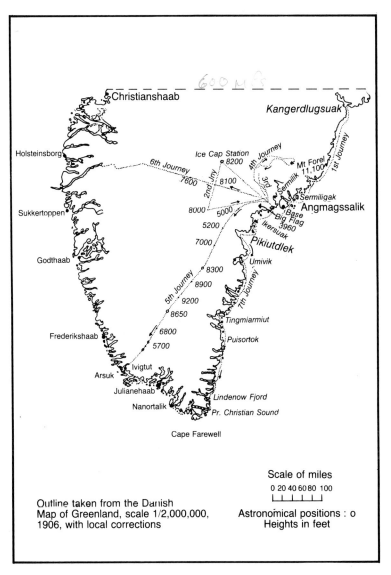

Christianshaab

Kangerdlugsuak

Holsteinsborg

Ice Cap Station
8200

4th Journey

Mt Forel
11,100

1st Journey

6th Journey
7600

2nd Jrny

8100

3rd

Sermilik

Sermiligak

Sukkertoppen

8000

5000

Angmagssalik

Base
Big Flag
3960

5200

Ikersuak

7000

Pikiutdlek

Godthaab

Umivik

5th Journey

8300

8900

7th Journey

9200

8650

Tingmiarmiut

Frederikshaab

6800

5700

Puisortok

Ivigtut

Arsuk

Julianehaab

Lindenow Fjord

Nanortalik

Pr. Christian Sound

Cape Farewell

Scale of miles

0 20 40 60 80 100

Outline taken from the Danish
Map of Greenland, scale 1/2,000,000,
1906, with local corrections

Astronomical positions : o
Heights in feet

Southern Greenland, showing the seven journeys of
The British Arctic Air Route Expedition, 1930-31

The base in summer. Watkins hand on hip. Courtauld in the boat, right. D'Aeth, left. Bugbear Bank is behind the masthead

The start of the first Ice Cap journey. Bingham, Riley, Lindsey, Rymill, Scott

Personal relationships were often acrimonious, but the reproduction line
was kept rolling

After a storm. It took five hours to break camp. The aeroplane took longer to mend

The Ice Cap Station in autumn and as found next May

Watkins cutting through the top of the tent

Courtauld emerging, having put on dark glasses

Relaxation at the base

approached the Big Flag we saw a group of figures – black dots in the snow. They had seen us and stopped so we could not tell which way they were heading. . . . It was too good to be true if they had finished their job, too bad if they had scarcely begun it. We hurried towards them.

Travelling on courses almost at right angles it was a remarkable coincidence that we should have met. But I doubt that the outcome would have differed if we had not. Circumstances and August Courtauld saw to that. When Gino had asked Freddie to lead this party he had requested what he wanted done. Freddie, enthusiastic, boundlessly energetic, bold almost to the point of foolhardiness, had thrown himself into the details of performance. But his journey out after our parting at the station had been hampered by bad weather; his turn-around had taken ten days; then he and his five companions with a supporting party as far as Bugbear had spent fifteen exhausting days covering fifteen miles.

Freddie's five men stood round him looking tired and cold. This was their baptism of ice. They were Steve, the chief surveyor who could scarcely survey this featureless desert though he could take astronomical observations if the astronomy was visible; August Courtauld who was also a surveyor; Ham, the aeroplane engineer, who looked like a sturdy Duke of Wellington; Wager, mountaineer, introvert, geologist without rocks; and Lemon who was not intended for sledging but had come to get the wireless working. Everyone had to be prepared to do anything. Gino was ruthless.

When he had learned the position in a few words he was for once taken aback. 'But, Good Lord, you'll never get there!'

'Oh, I know,' Freddie answered, cheerful, irrepressible. We all laughed. Life was bloody but it was funny too.

Then Gino spoke seriously and briefly (I noted it down that night). 'Never mind about the wireless. Take its weight in food and concentrate entirely on getting in and bringing out Doc and D'Aeth. You may have to abandon the station. I don't know. You'll just have to use your own judgment and do the best you can.'

After that we went our opposite ways. It was no place for standing about. A dead spot had already appeared on Steve's face. That night Gino was long silent but finally said, 'One of us should have gone with them, but we've had such a mouthful already I doubt if we'd have been much use. They are north of the big valley, but they will have a bad time till they get through the windy zone.'

Gino and I got back to the base on armistice night, with one day's

13

food on the sledge, thinking of them sweating with heavy loads. Literally sweating. Working like that you perspire profusely however low the temperature. That is one of the troubles.

That same night they decided to split their party – three turn back and three go on. Chapman wrote, 'Lemon and I spent most of the night discussing plans and working out loads. It is good to share a tent with a man of his age and organising experience.' The result of their deliberations was that half the party (Freddie, August and Wager) should go on carrying food and fuel, not the wireless equipment which in those days weighed 600 lb. and required a signals officer to operate it. Besides rations for three men for the return journey, they would take stores to last three months for the couple (presumably August and Wager) who would take over the station from Doc and D'Aeth. The other half of the party (Lemon, Ham and Steve) would return to the base at once, travelling light. The balance of the party's stores, amounting to seven 50-lb. ration boxes, would be cached with the wireless for use or recovery next season.

Freddie and Lemon were breakfasting after a brief sleep when August came into their tent and suggested that he should stay alone at the station. He pointed out that they might take so long to get to the station that they would have to encroach on the 300 lb. of food and five gallons of paraffin intended to be left there. They did not know how long the worst of the winter would last. But one man would have twice as much to eat as two and should easily see it out. He, August, was used to being alone (I don't know when he had been alone, except in thought) and was 'very keen to try the experiment in such conditions'. With plenty of books, food and baccy he would be perfectly happy.

Freddie, clearly from his diary, was tempted but funked the responsibility of leaving a man alone. So the matter was left unresolved. 'Anyway, we can't decide anything yet: we've got to find the station first.'

The two parties of three made their large, expensive cache, marked it well, and parted. It was never seen again. That considerable excrescence obviously annoyed the wind.

'Find' the station, not 'reach' it, Freddie had written in his diary. They were on the line of flags but had considerable difficulty in following it. 'We now go on for a mile (by sledge wheel) after we miss a flag. . . .' All the flags were damaged, some tattered to pieces, some never sighted.

They arrived at the station on 2nd December – after twenty-two more days, many spent tent bound. They went into the courtyard shouting '*Evening Standard, Star, News!*' They dived into the tunnel, came up in the tent where, said August, 'We found D'Aeth and Doc sitting there as warm and comfortable as could be, smoking their pipes. Being three weeks overdue they were naturally jolly pleased to see us'.

Wager, who slept alone in one of the igloos, wrote next morning: 'D'Aeth and Doc have been here nine weeks. They got a certain amount of exercise throwing snow over the wall of the courtyard.' Doc's diary reveals that he did this practically every day, and thereby kept himself fit for the journey out. Their exercise of clearing the nearby flags was important but not physically exacting. The three-hourly weather readings and maintaining the station in good order, fit for inspection and handover, was Service discipline.

Wager went on:

> They have read all the books, written a good few letters, told each other all their stories and smoked all their cigarettes, but they have tobacco. They do not look fit.
>
> We on our side who have taken five weeks getting here have found the last part somewhat of a strain – tempers have been worse and disappointments more keen. Being cramped up in small tents has been less bearable, and the cold has sometimes almost made us weep.

Comfort is comparative. At the station they rested, talked and feasted prematurely on a Christmas dinner that had been brought for two – though whom? This question, after the exchange of news, dominated conversation.

The debate as recorded was whether the station should be abandoned or maintained by one man alone. From this distance in time I feel there was a less dramatic alternative. The 6,000-calories-a-day sledging ration lasted two or three times as long in sedentary conditions. Doc and D'Aeth, though they had been at the station three weeks more than expected, handed over two full 50-lb. ration boxes plus some pemmican, paraffin and odds and ends. There was surely enough for two men for the three months expected, even subsistence for the five months that the period proved to be – if they had looked after themselves, the rations and the station with meticulously disciplined care.

What I have to say may appear in some points a criticism of August. So I state at the start that during the expedition he became, and remained, one of my closest friends. I analyse the story only from interest and for value to possible imitators. One such imitator was Admiral Byrd in the Antarctic. His 'Alone' makes an interesting comparison. I will point out the key factor at once so that it may be followed throughout. A temperament that accepts – welcomes – a winter alone in inimical surroundings is not a temperament for meticulously disciplined care.

The debate was between August and everybody else – as to a certain extent it was throughout his life – with Freddie, the temporary leader, a divided chairman. There was no hierarchy in the expedition below Gino. August had never assumed any authority. He was on the Committee, cousin of Stephen Courtauld who was chairman and had put up nearly all the money. But he did not use this in the argument, only his mule-like obstinacy.

Wager confided to his diary (I don't know if he expressed it aloud) that he himself would not like to remain there alone for more than a month. Doc Bingham was quite definite. 'Courtauld wants to stay alone, but I have given a very decided opinion against it.'

Chapman recorded, 'The Doctor and D'Aeth are dead against one man staying alone. They say they have experienced it and they know.'

If anything was needed to strengthen August's resolve it was total opposition. Freddie concluded: 'However, Courtauld is determined to stay and eventually we gave in. I must say it would be a thousand pities to abandon the station now, since it has been established and maintained with so much trouble.'

It has often been asked why August wanted to remain at the station alone. I don't think the reason was any more complicated or subtle than why people want to go exploring – adventure, self-discovery, an opportunity not to be missed. He saw a tide in his affairs and took it at the flood.

Did he do it well? He came out of it five months later, having latterly been entombed in the dark, perfectly balanced in mind. This can be explained by temperament. He was able to lose himself as completely as he might have in a smoking-room armchair in thinking philosophically, gastronomically, and in writing a long diary which was largely a letter to his fiancée and family. He was a very human, unascetic hermit.

16

But that is not the temperament of the practical do-it-yourself young man. Let us be clear on the facts. It was not August's fault that the station was finally buried. The only way to beat an icecap winter wind is to keep out of its way. I, we, should have pitched the tent under the snow, dug out a sub-glacial station with no excrescences thicker than the ventilating tube. But no one had thought of that and even if they had we lacked the rations and programme time to make the changes. The courtyard wall, the snowhouses, the tent itself upon the surface only infuriated the omnipotent wind which finally snow-drifted over everything as smoothly as a plasterer except for the thin projections of two weather instruments and the ventilating tube.

Professor Wegener's much larger German expedition which was in Greenland at the same time excavated their icecap station, and although the garrison – two active men during the winter – had to dig and dig to keep their entrance clear they had less drift to remove and attended to it as a daily discipline. August, because he was above the surface at first and because he was alone throughout faced much greater odds. But he might have kept his eye on the shovel.

And he might have made the station less difficult to find. He could get out until the last six weeks and saw that the place was being obliterated. Certainly he dug and dug (finally with a sheath knife). He seems continually to have been filling tins with snow and emptying them outside, or at the last moment searching and scrabbling for a ration box or a case of paraffin. But he also spent a lot of time reading, writing and pondering, and he sometimes forgot to close the entrance.

If I had been with him I would have been scared enough to think (as I have) of the pyramid tent we left when we set up the station. It was valueless as shelter, it was buried, but it contained four stout eight-foot bamboos. If he had set these up all around at some distance the place would have been reasonably marked. Or he might have lashed them together and made a beacon visible for miles through binoculars. The wind would scarcely have noticed it, but we would. And there were other ways in which he might have marked his grave. His feet were painful but his life was at stake.

August never seems to have considered his own safety. He trusted implicitly in God and 'the chaps'. No doubt this mentality kept him sane but it might have left him dead.

He had a streak of let-happen-what-will in his make-up. It came out even in his yachting at which he was expert and dedicated. On the icecap he felt that his fate was in other hands, divine and less so. He would give me hell if he were alive to read this. He gave me hell looking for him.

There was a good deal more to the expedition than the Courtauld affair but I will continue with that to its climax before sketching what else was done.

When Lemon, Steve and Ham returned to the base without an ounce of food on their sledges (three days after Gino and I did) we heard of August's suggestion that he should remain in the station alone. None of us really knew him then so we were not quite sure that his will would prevail. But we expected so, and this was confirmed when Freddie and Wager, Doc and D'Aeth arrived on 19th September.

They were all very tired, but fit – except for D'Aeth whose hands were badly frostbitten. The fingers were black, a frightening sight. But Doc boldly decided against amputating any joints, merely keeping the fingers sterilised with gauze soaked in surgical spirit. He wrote:

A definite line of demarcation developed between the healthy tissue and the coal black dead portions. This separation gradually deepened until nothing held the dry – I emphasise dry – dead tissue in position but the chalk-like dead tips of the terminal phalanges. One morning, asking D'Aeth to notice something taking place outside, I snipped off the dead pieces quite painlessly and in due course the finger tissue grew over the powdery bone ends, and D'Aeth was left with quite functional if slightly shortened fingers. So the calculated risk of spreading gangrene proved worth while taking.

This may be compared with the horrific description of toe amputations in the chapter on Wegener's expedition.

The gales by this time were fairly frequent. They had not yet worked up to full force but they were already stronger than any of us had experienced elsewhere. They blew all the new ice out of the fjord as soon as it formed; that was why the aeroplanes, which had been fitted with skis, could not fly in to the icecap – or anywhere else. They kept one or other of the machines out of commission in spite of valiant ingenious repairs by Hampton. Ham later became a B.O.A.C. pilot. I wonder if any of his passengers knew that he had once passed as airworthy a Moth with a tail made from the root stump of a Siberian pine that had drifted over the North Pole to Angmagssalik, the carpentry covered with stuff the Eskimo women used for blouses. That was as near as we actually came to launching an Arctic air-route. The wind trundled into the ocean anything left loose, whatever its weight. The hut jumped under the stout wire stays which anchored it to the rocks. Wager, lying flat, saw the anemometer register 130 m.p.h. before it blew away. The Eskimos called these things *anosta ankaiou*, the superlative of 'wind'. 'Our name is unfortunately unprintable!' Chapman wrote in *Northern Lights*.

Our name was 'fornicators'. Our delicacy was such in those days – I call them gales now only because fornicator was such an inaccurate and inadequate description of their character. But Polar explorers have always been most strict and pious in their prose. Read the early stories of exploration. They are tracts. As for conversation I don't know – historically.

Regarding Courtauld's safety, which was much discussed, we were not primarily worried about gales – so long as he managed to keep the place in something like the state of orderliness that the Service officers had done.

There were worse dangers for a man alone. Certainly August would not catch a cold and was unlikely to break a leg. But in thick weather he might lose his head and his direction even in the few yards to the met. instruments. Cold soon numbs the brain. As for warmth which one longed for as for a drug, I, on the southern journey, kneeling over the primus stove to cook, had been knocked out by carbon monoxide as if by a bullet. I came to painfully on the snow outside where Gino, who had been lying flat in the tent, had dragged me. That might happen to August (he did block up the ventilation tube to keep the place warmer at least once). Or he might get stuck in the tunnel (he did, for a short time). A man alone was fatally vulnerable to accidents from which a companion would have saved him.

The practical question was when we would be able to relieve him. There had always been talk of this being done by aeroplane. Freddie had sent with his returning party a code of noughts or crosses written on the snow signifying whether it was possible to land or not. They might fly in and out within two or three hours on a fine day. If they could not land they could drop staple food and luxuries and *see* the man at the station. If a healthy-looking man had waved that would be something, for they were getting anxious at home.

Two flights were made, on 8th and 25th February, the first by D'Aeth and Freddie, the other by Iliffe Cozens and me. Goodness knows where we got to, certainly not the station. We did not even see any flags. Iliffe tells me that at one stage we were almost stationary against the wind, and drift could not be measured above that featureless desert. It was unbelievably cold in an open cockpit. After the first flight one Moth was wrecked by a storm, and after the second the other hit a snow-hidden ice hummock while landing and would be out of commission for some time. So that was that.

Gino's orders were inclined to sound more like suggestions, and if they involved something unpleasant he sugared them with compliments. He said to me, 'I'm afraid someone will have to go and fetch August while the weather is still bad. I'd like it to be you, for you know far the most about winter travel.'

I don't think I was taken in. I knew Gino pretty well. I knew I had to do it yet felt bound to point out my limitations. This was not a case of travelling hopefully, even doggedly. I *had* to arrive – at a particular point in a featureless desert – and I lacked the skills of astronomical navigation to do this neatly. I could find a latitude – the altitude of the sun at noon – but I had never done a longitude, a much more complicated observation which depends in effect on determining the difference in local time from that of the meridian of Greenwich. We possessed time signal wireless sets, of course, to check our half-chronometer watches. But I could not master the necessary skill with sextant or theodolite (which latter I had never used) within a few days. Therefore I would have to fall back on the old sea captains' method – aim definitely to one side, say east, of the station and when I found myself on the latitude, turn west along it. This seemed laborious, but Gino said it would be all right and repeated that I was the best man for the job.

I have often tried to fathom Gino's reasoning in picking on me, with the whole party, bar August, at the base. I might have been the most experienced cold weather traveller but I was not by a long way the best fitted to find an exact spot. There were the chief surveyor, Steve, and John Rymill who could navigate with scientific accuracy. I was only the dogsbody. But by my old-world reckoning and an exact latitude (one sure dimension) I should have been able to get very near the spot, and keep going. There was (by signal) anxiety at home, therefore urgency that something be done at once. I think Gino saw these alternatives: If August was alive, the station should be visible from a mile as it had been when Chapman's party left it. In that case I would certainly find it and further anxiety would be avoided. If he was not alive that melancholy fact could be established later. An obliterated station would take months rather than weeks to locate by any means and in the best of weather.

I asked Gino what I should do when I reached the place. He said the prime object was to bring August out but he did not want the station abandoned unless it was necessary. He would like Quintin Riley, our meteorologist, to take it over. Only if conditions were such that it was more unpleasant to stay than to travel back would he prefer that I stayed and send the others home.

Quintin and I set off a few days later, on 1st March. Our Eskimo staff gave us a tearful farewell, not expecting to see us return.

We came back the next day. The evil spirits of the icecap in the form of huge hard snowdrifts had broken one sledge in half just beyond the Big Flag. Gino then added Martin Lindsay to the party so that if a similar misfortune occurred there would still be two men to go on.

I was better off with Martin included because he, being practised with a theodolite, could provide a check to my sextant observations. But we still did not take a time signal set which would have allowed him to fix longitude – if the set still worked after 130 miles of rough going. Having capsized scores of times and broken one sledge in a single day it seemed that the delicate thing would be useless weight, so I stuck to the original plan.

We set off again in perfect weather, taking only a biscuit lunch, for we could stock up for the extra man at the Big Flag depot and could climb Bugbear and cross the crevasses fast if we were light.

A couple of miles short of the Big Flag we were blinded by a blizzard, visibility only a few yards. For three days we lived on our lunch, nothing to drink except snow melted over a candle. Then by compass and on snowshoes we waded downwind to the coast and found our way to the base late at night.

On the third attempt we got right away. For three-quarters of the distance we followed the line of flags by compass, making slight zigzags to compensate for error and checking our latitude now and then. We found no flags at all. Then we aimed well to the east of the station.

There were difficulties in both stages. Our compasses had been filled with a liquid which, the firm assured us, would not freeze above −50°F. That may have been true. We only experienced −46° by day. But the needle became so sluggish that it took a full minute to decide about magnetic north; we had to carry the compasses inside our double mitts to bribe them into doing that. We had a spare compass with no steadying liquid but it could never make up its mind, shivering as we were.

Observations were difficult. Martin's theodolite stood on a tripod and one leg always wanted to sink deeper into the snow than the other two. It took ages to level. With a sextant on land as opposed to sea, where there is a true horizon, I depended on measuring the vertical angle of the sun as seen reflected in a bowl of mercury. The mercury froze and ceased to reflect. Once when I had scraped off the ice I saw not the image of the sun but what looked like the moon – a white frozen chin. My breath froze on the verniers and soon stuck them. All I could do was follow the sun up to its highest point, then clamp the instrument and carry it into the comparative warmth of the tent to thaw out and be read. These are diary-recorded incidents. I do not remember the physical discomforts at all, only the mental strain that followed.

Martin's and my observations finally concurred – we were on the latitude of the station to within a fraction of a mile. That being established, we travelled due west for sixteen miles – eight miles each side of its believed position by dead reckoning. Then we went a mile north and travelled back east a similar distance. Then we went a mile south of our original latitude and travelled west again. We made three traverses of the maximum possible area. Every half mile or so I stood on the sledge and looked all round with binoculars, and we took frequent observations. We spent twenty-one days in the vicinity of the station, and saw nothing.

> So lonely 'twas that God himself
> Scarce seemed there to be

– let alone another human being.

The search was not followed continuously, of course. On average only one day in three permitted travel or offered sufficient visibility. At the start we had a six-day blizzard, the one that finally sealed in Courtauld as we later discovered. I believe now that the few bright days were scarcely better, being deceptive. We could see a distance of a mile or so – one did not really know. But under the oblique sun the snowscape was a zebra pattern of bright snow-drift crests and dark shadowed troughs. A lot must have been hidden or camouflaged. It was like looking for a man overboard in a rough sea.

Gordon Hayes in *The Conquest of the North Pole* adjudged this

22

journey from our met. records to be one on which 'the conditions approached the limits of human endurance'. We endured physically. We were young. But the mental strain remains – something you do not usually associate with the Arctic. It followed me into my dreams in the ice-rimmed tent – a man drowning nearby.

On Easter Sunday, 5th April, Quintin read the Communion Service to himself. I killed a dog. We were as short of food as that. In my diary is the calculation that we could spend three more days searching before beginning systematically to kill the lot. It was also considered that all the good dogs at the base would have been taken on the Kangardlusuak journey. So our dogs would be vital for any other search.

Quintin suggested that August might have tried to walk out. That would explain why there was nothing to be seen. He and Martin remembered the place as a considerable establishment with adjoining igloos and snow wall. His suggestion was a possibility but not a consideration. You tack up and down searching for a man overboard thinking of him drowning, not drowned. There is hope until you find proof of death. We had evidently missed the place but did not know where and when. So our choice was to search the same area again by the same or similar parallel lines for as much as another three weeks, living on the dogs; or race out and give Gino a chance to bring in a fully equipped party which could fix the position exactly, longitude as well as latitude. They might have better weather. Winter ought to be over.

We made a final gambler's throw until 10th April (without losing more than one more dog) and then raced out all the quicker, travelling by compass in any weather. At the Big Flag we found ration boxes left by Steve, Freddie and Wager, who had evidently turned back from their Kangardlugsuak journey. This was a relief, for there would be dogs at the base. But it was something of a shock that we had hit on the Big Flag almost exactly. It suggested that we had started from where we ought to have been, very near the station. All the more need to hurry.

We ran the crevasses blind in darkness. By tradition we paused at the top of Bugbear. That was a mistake after forty days of drive and strain. The coast, the position of the base, was dimly visible. It was warm, zero, and enervating. I remember fiddling about with the sledges, doing unnecessary things. Then we slid down the old bank drawn by gravity.

On the gentler slopes below, the wretched dogs, after all their splendid effort, suddenly could no longer haul the pathetically light loads. So we let them loose, left the sledges and walked the remaining few miles through deep snow.

Martin and Quintin were magnificent. They went in front to break the trail – without ever suggesting I should take my turn. I trailed behind. I dreaded the base, people vaulting from their bunks and asking questions. Memory of that abysmal state of mind and body is painful even after fifty years.

Our dogs were too weak and tired to pull a sledge but they could still fight. There was a hullabaloo as we arrived. Gino came out in pyjamas – it was as warm as that in this other world. In his quiet, unhurried voice he asked about the weather we had had and what plan we had followed. He said I had done the right thing, that August must still have food and would be all right if he, Freddie and John Rymill could reach him quickly as they should be able to do now that the last *anosta ankaiou* seemed to have blown.

We fed the dogs, talking in a leisurely way, he asking *my* advice about details. He was a great leader.

We went inside. It was the small hours of the morning but everyone was quietly busy getting us food and drink, making us comfortable. Gino sat down to work out the loads for his journey, his fingers playing scales on the table as they always did when calculating. Steve went through the mathematics of our observations. John and Freddie gathered their kit. The rest were gently welcoming, solicitous, hiding the anxiety they must all have felt.

One or two of those still alive, whom I spoke to before starting this long-view account of the expedition, remarked on the bond that still binds us after half a century. It was forged by occasions like this, but also by everyday life that was not *everyday* life. It is impossible to avoid sentiment – thank God.

At the time we were not sentimental but aggressive – or we pretended to be. From early times in the expedition self-sufficiency had been the party line. When we sailed from England, we had been given a painted board that read:

> The power of man is as his hopes.
> In darkest night, the cocks are crowing.
> With the sea roaring and the wind blowing;
> Adventure. Man the ropes.

That might have been considered appropriate to the occasion. But, long before, someone had turned this to the wall and idiotically written, 'Damn you, I'm all right'.

When Gino had finished working out loads he packed his personal kit. He was always careful to cut this down to the last ounce – sheer necessities only. He was seen to put in a prayer book.

Chapman and Rymill had been preparing for a second attempt to reach Kangardlugsuak, a dash with two large teams, but had fortunately been held up by the weather. So their dogs were re-divided to draw three sledges. Gino's party was ready to start at dawn – if there had been a dawn. But thick cloud had come down on the icecap like the solid safety curtain which used to interrupt cinema dramas. They had to find the Big Flag depot to pick up rations. It was three days before they could start.

That delay allowed Gino to send a wireless message to England saying that my party had failed to find Courtauld but owing to the severe conditions might have passed within a quarter of a mile of him. Courtauld still had food and another party of three was starting immediately. But, 'There is always the possibility that Courtauld is not alive or unwell in which case station is probably completely covered'. That, one can see now, was asking for trouble – or help.

On 21st April they got away. The curtain had lifted on summer, the other icecap season. Freddie wrote: 'We had clear skies and little wind. The heat of the sun was terrific. Our faces peeled and our lips became open sores.'

In other words they had the best possible icecap conditions. They travelled fast and efficiently without their sledges ever upsetting or being delayed by storms. There is in fact nothing to record about their 130-mile journey. On 3rd May they pitched their tent within an estimated two or three miles of the station. But the next day was windy, with drift, and the scrupulous navigator, John, insisted on waiting for an exact fix. In the evening of the 4th it cleared and they went out on skis in different directions. They found nothing. John came back late. 'With characteristic thoroughness he had quartered the ground for about 20 miles.' Freddie never underestimated anything except danger.

'May 5 dawned a wonderful day. . . . With a theodolite and time signal set it is possible to fix your position to within a few hundred yards. Our calculations proved us to be about a mile north-west of the station.'

25

They set off in a widely open order, each with a dog on a lead. 'From the summit of a long undulation we made out a black speck. . . .'

Freddie's description of what they saw as they approached, and of their emotions, is vivid. There is no other first-hand account. But, for me, the photographs he had the wit to take are still more telling. Apart from two bored dogs they show a snowscape flat as a dead-calm sea with only the tops of two weather instruments, the tattered remains of a Union Jack and the handle of a shovel protruding. It is generally the sexton, if anyone, who leaves a spade about. A more dead scene it is impossible to imagine.

What is not distinguishable in the photograph is the inch or two of ventillating tube projecting through the snow from the apex of the tent. Above this Gino knelt and shouted, and received an answer. 'The voice was tremulous, but it was the voice of a normal man.'

They shovelled away the snow, cut through the roof, dropped into the tent. 'It was in a state of great chaos and everything was covered with a delicate tracing of ice-crystals. Courtauld was in his sleeping bag with the remains of his food supplies spread around him. We helped him out through the hole in the roof and were surprised to find that he could walk. . . . The lowest temperature recorded by the minimum thermometer outside was −64°F., 96° of frost.'

That temperature – at some time during the final six weeks when he had been entombed with a bare minimum of paraffin for melting snow – sufficiently stresses August's feat of physical endurance. But his normality, his modesty and complete freedom from heroics was still more striking. His first remark to me when they reached the base five days later was, 'I'm frightfully sorry to have given you so much trouble, starting at the beginning of March! It was too bloody even to go out of doors.' If I noticed any change in him it was that he was better socially. He had always been well mannered but he was more forthcoming. He invited me to go out with him and look for ptarmigan. We were alone together for an hour or two, talking away, absolutely at ease.

Much had happened in the outside world since Gino had signalled, 'There is always the possibility . . .'. Had we been more mature we would have realised the inevitable result. Perhaps Gino did, for he told Lemon, whom he left in charge, to do his utmost to prevent any rescue attempts. 'Rescue' is a dirty word for a self-sufficient expedition, and in truth nobody could help materially. But naturally the Committee and August's family had to do anything that might help and could not hinder. A Junkers monoplane, large by the standard of those days, was chartered from the Swedish Aero-Transport Company. It was piloted by Captain Ahrenberg, with a mechanic and wireless operator.

The difficulties of this courageous trio were a sardonic joke on the British Arctic Air-Route Expedition which justified its existence by exploring part of the land bridge between Europe and America. In Iceland there was water to come down on but in Greenland at that season little except ice. We heard by wireless that they had left Reykjavik – on floats. Lemon kept in close touch. They passed the point of no return over pack ice on which nothing could have landed. Clouds were coming down fast. Ham and I raced out on a sledge to the limit of the fjord's ice and made a great smoke signal with petrol and oil. When we got back to the base we heard that they had landed in an open lead at Angmagssalik just before the clouds sank to ground level.

Captain Ahrenberg forced his seaplane up onto the ice, changed to skis, and in better weather flew to our frozen fjord. He was an impressive gentleman, elegant in spats. We fitted him out in more suitable clothes and he made two flights over the icecap with D'Aeth as passenger. The first was negative in result. The second saw *four* men sledging out.

Lemon had been working twenty hours a day – transmitting and receiving in morse, transcribing, changing his batteries. When he shouted 'August's O.K.', I think we all went mad. The tension snapped with a twang. When Ahrenberg, his crew and D'Aeth landed, we gave them our rare whisky laced with concentrated lemon juice antiscorbutic. I remember their faces twisting like whirpools round the citric acid. The whisky scarcely diluted it at all. We laughed our heads off from sheer relief.

A different acid taste came when we read or heard about the press reports. Our contract was with *The Times* which kept our despatches to itself to the extent that it published them. But that lit the fuse for an explosion of speculation or sheer imaginative journalism. I don't want to bash the Press. I became a sort of journalist myself. I don't think they told any – or not many – actual lies. But a young man of well-known family, and with a fiancée, to be 'Lost Alone in the Arctic' – it was news. 'Great Arctic Mystery' and 'Snow Hunt for

Rich Young Explorer' lasted from 23rd April when Gino's first signal was made public until 10th May when they got back. It must have been hell for relatives and close friends. But the public evidently loved it. However little they knew about the Arctic they came to know the names of Gino, August, our expedition. Our fame spread beyond the British Isles. A French paper reported that Mlle Augustine Courtauld, the only female member, was alone in an ice cavern with the rest of the party feverishly searching for her. The poor girl, it seemed, had the choice of immolation or worse than death from thirteen brutal and licentious explorers. We catered for all tastes.

The expedition actually achieved substantial exploratory work. In the spring and summer Steve, Doc and Wager sledged to Mount Forel and although they did not quite reach the summit – which was annoying but did not matter for we were *not* a mountaineering expedition – they climbed high enough for a very useful survey point, and Wager did geological work. Thus, when combined with the previous season's survey by ship, whaleboat and aeroplane, a great deal was learned about the wide and lofty strip of east coast mountains which contains the highest peaks in the Arctic.

Our party broke up with a final explosion of journeys. Only six went home 'like gentlemen' on the Danish supply ship, *Gertrud Rask*, when she made her annual Angmagssalik call in August. Steve, Martin and I had by then already travelled via Ivigtut on the south-west coast which meant a 430-mile crossing of the icecap. It was a treat of a sledge trip made by night because it was too warm by day. We skied at speed with Viking sails on the sledges. The icecap said goodbye to us very politely.

It was less than polite to John and Ham who crossed almost due west to Holsteinborg. They could not start until the *Gertrud Rask* had called on 9th August, for she brought them their dog pemmican. By that time the snow had melted from Bugbear, leaving bare ice and opening up the crevasses. They fell into a couple of chasms. The first stage to the Big Flag was hard and dangerous. From there they made the actual icecap crossing well enough though the last forty miles were complicated by soft snow, enormous crevasses, thaw rivers and lakes – not good going for heavyweights. They did not reach the mountainous hinterland – of which there was 100 miles before Holsteinborg – until 30th September, by which time they were very short of food.

They had brought kayaks but the waterways were generally

frozen. Once both kayaks were upset in a rapid and John was swept under the ice upside down. He came up, however, in open water while still holding his breath. The imperturbable pair had a number of near fatal adventures.

Most of the way they had to back-pack, and consequently dropped weeks behind their scheduled time. They were finally picked up by a boatload of Eskimos sent out to look for them. Shameful! From Holsteinborg they sent an irritated wireless signal: 'Can't understand fuss.' They did not actually say, 'Damn you we're all right', but those of us who were home by then got the message.

Gino, Lemon and August – who had vowed never to go on another journey – set off by whaleboat with pensionable outboard motors for Julianehaab, not far from Ivigtut. This meant, of course, rounding the southern end of Greenland, a 600-mile journey. Their object was to survey the sketchily charted coast. This they did successfully for 100 miles. Then they got into trouble – storms, mixed snow and rain, rocks, ice, mist – all the old bugbears plus exhausted engines.

They had taken a wireless but felt it was not worth its weight so decided to dump it but sent a final message: 'Owing to engine trouble due to rough conditions may cross icecap to Igalico or winter at Umivik.'

As Martin put it, 'Marooned in the Arctic again made its melancholy appearance'. Neither of these places was on any ordinary map. But those who knew the men decoded their signal as 'D.Y.Y.O.K.'.

In fact they pushed on – just about literally. Their major hazard was Puisortok, a glacier face whose name means 'that thing which comes up'. This extensive ice cliff has the reputation of calving under water, and to be hit by a new born iceberg from underneath is a terminal experience. 'Do not eat and do not speak till Puisortok is passed,' say the Eskimos.

Twice the trio tried and failed to pass. On the third attempt they broke down half way; but concentrated juggling got the engine going again. They reached Julianehaab in good time to hear that John and Ham were still unreported. So they continued up the coast to look for them – and found them safely arrived. 'Damn you, you're all right,' they said very cheerfully to each other, and just caught the last west coast supply ship to Copenhagen.

This last group was back in November. We were of course very happy to be in England, but I think we all found it a little difficult to settle down in what had become – for all our homesick thoughts – a strange soil. This estrangement showed when we came together from our families to some lecture or other gathering. We tended to hang together like fruits of the same transplanted tree. The other trees were as kind, interested and complimentary as could be but only we shared roots. I don't think this is too exaggerated a metaphor for the first phase of homecoming. The feeling wore off with time, but not entirely.

Lemon was the first apple to fall. He killed himself. There was no evident reason. I have heard it said that the best brains find readjustment most difficult. But I have also heard the opposite.

Then Gino died. He had been encouraged in a major plan – crossing the Antarctic continent. He had every sort of backing – except financial. In 1931-32, during the depths of the Depression, there was no big money to be had. He went back to Greenland on a minor expedition connected with the Arctic air route. Nothing compelled him to go away again at once except that he had heard 'the call of the North' which he had once mentioned in his diary. He had become engaged to be married while in England. He was drowned while hunting in his kayak. His trousers were found on a small floe close to a glacier that frequently calved, throwing up great waves. His kayak, half-full of water, was drifting a mile away. It was a mysterious tragedy.

His companions were Quintin Riley, John Rymill and Freddie Chapman. John Rymill led a successful Antarctic expedition in which Quintin, Stevenson, Doc Bingham and Hampton took part. John later died following a car accident in Australia. Quintin also died after a car accident.

Martin Lindsay followed up our icecap crossing to Ivigtut with a much longer one on an expedition of his own – 1,180 miles, a record – and made it valuable with a survey of the inland side of the east coast mountains. He won a D.S.O. in the war, and became an M.P. and a baronet.

Freddie Spencer Chapman survived the Himalayas, the war and *The Jungle is Neutral* adventure. He won a D.S.O. and seemed indestructible in his amazing enthusiasm. But he died by his own hand. Lawrence Wager died as F.R.S. after distinguishing himself academically as a professor of geology, and on Mount Everest. The last time I saw August Courtauld was in the King Edward VII

Hospital for Officers. He said truculently, 'Lots of famous admirals and generals have died here.'

The rest keep in touch, at least go to each other's funerals – except D'Aeth. My last news of Air Vice Marshal Narborough D'Aeth was at his farewell dinner as Senior Air Staff Officer, Home Command, at White Waltham. He began his speech, 'For thirty-five years I have served my King. Now I shall serve my God. I am going into the Church. . . .' He did, and was never seen again by any of us.

Not only those who went on other Polar expeditions but everybody, I think, found that their Greenland experience gave them something in later life, however hard to define. They feel richer for it.

Certainly we had a touch of glory at the time. Our expedition was considered the most fruitful for fifty years. Gino was awarded the gold medals of the British and Danish Royal Geographical Societies – and passed the compliments on to his companions. Lined up in Buckingham Palace we heard August, the stoutest of monarchists, say 'No' to his King three times.

> 'I am sure you were very cold, Mr Courtauld.'
> 'No, sir.'
> 'You were hungry, though.'
> 'No, sir.'
> 'You must have felt desperately lonely.'
> 'No, sir.'
> 'I am very glad to give you the Polar Medal!'

That the expedition was applauded by geographers was not particularly surprising for we had fulfilled most of an exacting programme. The unusual thing was that the many more non-geographers knew the essential points. 'You don't mean to say you were with August Courtauld? Really!' We could have dined out on it for months. Everybody had read enough in the newspapers to want to ask questions. The expedition was famous.

I have often thought, though I have never stated it before, that this was mainly due to me. If my party had found August and brought him out, it would have been noted as a creditable achievement – in the R.G.S. lecture, the expedition book and one *Times* article. No other paper or the wireless would have mentioned it. It would certainly not have been news. But as it happened, millions of people knew about the lost explorer and most of those old enough still remember.

2

General Nobile and the Italia

Umberto Nobile flew over the North Pole twice, on both occasions in semi-rigid airships he had built himself. The first flight, the Amundsen-Ellsworth-Nobile Expedition of 1926, was international. The American amateur adventurer Lincoln Ellsworth put up most of the money. Roald Amundsen lent the prestige of his reputation and added half a dozen Norwegians to the Italian crew, thus claiming the right to name the airship *Norge*.

In his and Ellsworth's opinion Nobile was little more than pilot, but the Italian Government had no doubt who was in command whatever the order of names in the title of the expedition. King Victor Emmanuel stated by royal decree that:

> At the proposal of the Head of Government, Prime Minister, Secretary of State, and Minister and Secretary of Air [all of whom were Mussolini] Umberto Nobile, Colonel of the Corps of Aeronautical Engineers, is entrusted with the task of commanding the airship N1 during the time necessary to achieve the aerial expedition to the North Pole.

The *Norge* flew from Spitsbergen to Alaska in May 1926. Flags of the three nations were dropped at the North Pole and, according to the Press, the Polar Ocean was discovered. There were a number of adventures, largely owing to fog and icing. But the flight, covering 3,400 miles and taking seventy-two hours, was accomplished without mishap.

It is easy to understand how during those three sleepless days and nights tension built up within the pilot cabin. Ellsworth and Amundsen had nothing to do. The reaction to nervous strain was

32

criticism. Amundsen accused Nobile of emotional behaviour during a crisis and of deception when at the end of the flight he appeared in a fine uniform which he must have secreted in spite of the extra weight. Nobile replied that the most explicit language for orders to the mixed crew was Italian with gestures. As for the uniform, being on duty he had worn it throughout the flight but only disclosed it when he took off his Arctic clothing on landing. It was a silly quarrel and would not deserve mention except for the manner of Amundsen's death two years later. But it also spurred Nobile, a touchy romantic, into deciding to lead a wider-ranging, more scientifically valuable expedition all his own.

He dreamed in a hut in Alaska while the *Norge* was being dismantled. He dreamed throughout a triumphant sweep through the United States, marred only by Amundsen's criticisms. In Rome he was fortified by a hero's welcome.

Mussolini made one of his speeches from the balcony of the Palazzo Chigi:

> In the name of the Facist Government – in your name, O Romans! – in the name of all Italians – I tender to the valiant General Nobile and his companions in the flight enthusiastic greetings, and the expression of our admiration, affection and gratitude. . . . Millions and millions of hearts all over the world followed the flight that sped from Rome – Immortal Rome, whose very name thrills all civilisation – straight for the goal. . . .
>
> General Nobile, my comrade! In one of your speeches in America you recalled that I was certain you would return. Yes! I remember. I was sure you would return and I said so. I had seen in your look that methodical tenacity and unswerving pluck which ought to become fundamental attitudes of the Italian race. I well knew what enormous difficulties you would have to encounter, but I also knew that you and your companions had the essential quality for overcoming them – courage.

The dictator sent a bunch of red roses to Signora Nobile, 'as a token', he said, 'of my esteem and my profound admiration of your husband's heroism. He has written an indelible page in the history of Italy'.

Italy's new favourite son was of humble origin. He was a *meridionale*, a southerner, born in the little town of Lauro near Naples, fifth of the seven children of an official of the Ministero della Finanza. The family made great sacrifices for his education. He studied engineering, finally specialising in airship construction. He was a civilian until 1923 when the Corps of Aeronautical Engineers was formed. Then he became a Lieutenant-Colonel; that was his first military rank. In 1925, the year before the *Norge* expedition, he was made a full colonel and, after the flight, a general. But he was not a fully qualified pilot, holding only a licence to test newly constructed airships, and he had little experience of commanding men. He was not a natural leader. He was gentle by nature, a dreamer by temperament (perhaps also something of a schemer), conventionally religious, a family man devoted to his wife, his daughter, and to the cheeky little dog, Titina, he took on all his flights and carried in his arms even when presented to the President of the United States.

Now he was on the crest of a wave with every prospect of being able to make his dreams come true. His own expedition would do much more than the *Norge*. Not only would he fly to the North Pole but he would moor there for three weeks and land a party to make scientific observations. There would also be a flight eastwards over the seas north of Russia and Siberia, one or more westwards beyond Greenland and the Canadian Arctic archipelago, and finally a flight of at least a week's duration, in whichever direction the wind might blow.

The airship, a sister of the *Norge*, was already under construction and would be named *Italia*. She would be provided by the Government together with an all-Italian crew. And 'three young and valiant scientists' were chosen: Dr Aldo Pontremoli, Professor of Physics at the University of Milan; Dr Finn Malmgren, Professor of Meteorology at the University of Uppsala, who had been on the *Norge*; and Dr Francis Behounek, Director of the Prague Wireless Institute and a Professor of the University. The Italian navy provided a base ship, *Città di Milano*, and the city of Milan put up the necessary money. The Italian Geographical Society sponsored the project. There was a hangar available at King's Bay, Spitsbergen.

The *Italia* reached Spitsbergen at the beginning of May 1928, having completed a long uneventful flight from Rome. Now Nobile had to prove himself as a commander. 'There could be no failure,' he recorded.

Besides his three scientists and a journalist, he had an airship crew of thirteen, most of them in their early thirties. This included three naval officers who could be trusted for navigation, taking turns to avoid fatigue; two petty officers to maintain wireless contact with the *Città di Milano*; and first-class mechanics with specialist qualifications. Everything was provided for so long as the airship remained in the air. But Nobile himself had set foot in the Arctic only in Spitsbergen and Alaska, at the beginning and end of a flight, and he had no one with practical experience of ice or snow – except his Swedish scientist, Dr Malmgren. He had shown his appreciation of this lack by taking advice on Arctic equipment and carrying concentrated rations in case of an emergency. He had also asked the Under Secretary for Air, Balbo, that two seaplanes should be sent to Spitsbergen to be available for instant rescue. He was hurt when the request was refused.

He had another early hint that behind the smiling faces at his send-off from Rome there had been unfriendly feelings against the hero of the hour. The Commander of the *Città di Milano* declined to provide sailors to pull the *Italia* down on her arrival and tuck her into the hangar at King's Bay. This was left to Norwegian coal miners.

Nobile had decided that the order in which he made his four or five flights should depend upon the reports received from the weather station at Tromsø with which Malmgren had made close contact. In the event, the first flight was eastwards and adequately successful if not spectacular – meaning that no new land was found as Nobile had hoped. A distance of 2,400 miles was covered in sixty-nine hours.

Next, on 23rd May, came the Polar flight. But the scientific high spot of the expedition, the landing and stay at the Pole, was abandoned. Nobile wrote only: 'The strong wind, although it helped us on our way to the Pole, made me regretfully consider that I should have to give up the descent we had planned'.

However, a solemn little ceremony was performed. The *Italia*, which had been flying high to allow the navigator to fix their position by the sun, now descended through the fog and circled slowly at 450 feet above the pack ice while a cross sent by the Pope and the Italian flag were dropped. It was then early in the morning of 24th May.

The outward route from Spitsbergen had led first to the northernmost point of Greenland and then true north. The return course was set direct for Spitsbergen. But a headwind blew for twenty-four hours, reducing almost by half the normal ground speed of about 40 m.p.h. It was foggy all the way, a damp grey air. They flew low above the endless pattern of floes and leads, and the sun never penetrated the cloud cover. Astronomical observations were of course impossible. The wireless gave them no more than the direction to the

Città di Milano at King's Bay; they did not know the distance, and due to the long struggle with the wind, fuel was running low. Ice sheathed the ship; ice even formed on the propeller-blades and flew off, striking and often puncturing the gas envelope. There could be no moment of relaxation. Nobile, passing between the navigation table and the wireless cabin glanced at a photograph of his daughter and had the impression that her eyes were full of tears.

He well knew the strain upon the airship – motors, frame and fabric – of battling for long against the wind. When the airspeed with all three engines running was 60 m.p.h., he decided to reduce it. But Dr Malmgren came to him and said, 'We aren't going ahead. It is dangerous to stop here. The weather might grow still worse. We must get out of this zone as quickly as possible.' Nobile at once reverted to their former speed.

Much earlier, at the Pole, he had considered running on to the Mackenzie Delta instead of turning back against the wind, but Malmgren had dissuaded him. Throughout the flight the young Swedish professor was a dominant personality, definitely affecting the decisions of his commander.

At 9.25 a.m. on 25th May (they had left the Pole more than thirty hours before) the *Italia* began to fly downwards. She was tilted bow down, the ice was only 750 feet below and the elevator had stuck. Nobile had the engines stopped.

At 250 feet from the pack the airship began to rise like a balloon. She rose gradually through the fog into clear sunlight. The naval officers quickly took observations. They were 180 miles from King's Bay, less than half that distance from the nearest point of the Spitsbergen archipelago. But they could not yet see land.

The elevator, which had become clogged with ice, was cleared by a sharp blow. The *Italia* continued to rise – to 3,300 feet – the pressure of the expanding gas beginning to increase alarmingly. Nobile had two engines restarted and they drove down again through the cloud to 900 feet. Cecioni, chief technician, the oldest and heaviest of the crew (he was forty-one and more than fifteen stones), had at the start of the emergency wakened from sleep and at Nobile's orders paid out the heavy ballast chain, holding it looped by a rope and ready to be dropped.

By now everyone was wide awake and at his post with the exception of Dr Pontremoli and the journalist Lago, who for some hours had been asleep in the stern.

The *Italia* flew on towards the land, which they expected to reach quite soon, for the headwind had dropped. It was necessary to keep the pack ice in sight, about 750 feet below, to check speed and drift. Nobile was measuring altitude by dropping glass balls full of red aniline dye, timing the fall by stop-watch, when Cecioni shouted excitedly, 'We are heavy!'

The nose of the airship was pointing eight degrees upwards, but she was descending.

Nobile ordered that the two running engines should be accelerated and the third started. This was promptly done. *Italia* went faster, now with an upward tilt of fifteen to twenty degrees. Yet she continued to descend.

'Stop the engines! Cast loose the ballast chain!' was the only possible order.

Cecioni fumbled with the rope that looped up the heavy chain. Two of the engines were stopped at once. Nobile leaned out of a porthole to yell a repeat order to switch off the stern engine. As he did so he saw the jumbled pack ice rapidly approaching. He dodged back into the cabin and grasped the wheel which Malmgren, with a startled expression, had flung up. But it was too late for steering. The stern of the *Italia* smacked into the rough ice and rasped along it. One side of the pilot cabin was ripped away, spilling the people and other contents on to the pack. Then the lightened airship rose and drifted away eastward into the mist.

Like a bucket of water thrown into the sea – a splash followed by a quick subsidence – it must have been much like that, with tired, strained human beings in place of water, suffering as violent a shock as one can imagine. We have Nobile's remarkably unselfconscious descriptions of his immediate reactions. Since he published them he must have wanted them to be known. Therefore he will be quoted verbatim in whatever seems pertinent.

Cast out on to the ice there were, besides the general, eight survivors: the Swedish and Czech scientists, Malmgren and Behounek; the three naval officers, Mariano, Zappi and Viglieri; the mechanics Cecioni and Trojani; and the wireless operator, Biagi. Pomella was found dead, sitting on the ice without sign of injury or expression of pain, beside the wreck of the stern engine of which he was in charge. The remaining six members of the party had been carried away in the airship.

Thrown on to an ice hummock, Nobile came to his senses soon

enough to see her drifting off, nose in the air, fabric ropes and metal-work trailing. He read with strong emotion the name *Italia* painted on her side. At first he did not feel too painfully his injuries, which he diagnosed as a broken arm and leg, wounded head and crushed chest. But he was convinced that he would die very soon. 'I was glad of this. It meant that I would not have to watch the despair and slow death-agony of my comrades. What hope was there for them? With no provisions, no tent, no wireless, no sledges – nothing but useless wreckage – they were lost, irredeemably lost, in this terrible wilderness of ice'. He had never seen 'such a terrible pack: a formless, contorted jumble of pointed ice-crags, stretching to the horizon'.

Pack ice is white; it looks like snow but is as hard as sandstone. Only small areas are flat, the rest made uneven by slabs and hummocks pushed up by the pressures of wind and current; and there are ditches or wider leads of open water owing to the movement of the floes. In winter these freeze over quickly but in late May they would scarcely do so, although with the general drift they might close up or open wider. Near where the *Italia* had struck, wreckage lay strewn about, 'a dreary note of grey against the whiteness of the snow'. This, although not at the moment realised, offered the only chance of salvation.

Close to Nobile was Dr Malmgren, nursing his left arm, Near by, Cecioni lay moaning, and Commander Zappi was flat on his back, complaining of broken ribs. Nobile turned to the young Swedish scientist who sat with ashen frowning face, his blue eyes staring fixedly in front of him. 'Nothing to be done, my dear Malmgren', he said.

'Nothing but die. My arm is broken', Malmgren answered. He got to his feet and added in English, 'General, I thank you for the trip . . . I go under the water'.

Nobile answered with religious homilies. Malmgren looked at him in surprise and then sat down again.

The uninjured men had begun wandering about. There came a cry from Biagi. 'The field-station is intact!' This was an emergency wireless set, a transmitter and receiver weighing about a hundred pounds, which had been carried in the pilot cabin. For Nobile 'a ray of light pierced the darkness'. He then called to his next in rank, Commander Mariano, said he was dying, and told him to carry on.

Mariano and the others who were on their feet also salvaged

seventy kilograms of provisions, mainly pemmican and chocolate. Nobile himself spotted near by one of the two emergency bags which had been loaded in case of a descent at the Pole. It contained a tent and a sleeping-bag, camp kit, a sextant and astronomical tables, a Very pistol and a Colt automatic. Malmgren asked to borrow the Colt but was refused.

The fit men brought the sleeping-bag to where Nobile was lying and little by little worked him into it. 'This was not easy because my right arm, leg and foot gave me excruciating pain at the least movement. Besides, I was lying on top of a hummock'.

In spite of the treasure they had found, it was a desolate scene. The only cheerful member of the party was Nobile's terrier Titina. 'The dear little thing' was scampering gaily all over the place, frisking about, wagging her tail and sniffing the air.

The tent was pitched on a level floe fifty yards square. Nobile was carried in, gritting his teeth in agony. The sleeping-bag was slit open and the fifteen-stone Cecioni was laid beside him. The salvaged provisions, enough at 300 grams per head per day for twenty-five days, were also stored in the tent.

According to a prearranged emergency schedule, Biagi was to call the *Città di Milano* at five minutes to each odd-numbered hour. He did so, but received no response from the base ship which was lying about 150 miles away. Then the set broke down. This was the final discouragement of the day. Nine men and a dog piled into a four-man tent. For a little while they talked of the six who had been swept away. Someone had seen a column of smoke to the east and it seemed likely that the airship had crashed and burned. From sheer exhaustion the survivors fell asleep – a tiny jumble of humanity in a vast jumble of 'pointed ice-crags stretching to the horizon'.

The party remained at the same site for over two months. It was utterly strange and alarming to them. Although they had flown thousands of miles over the Arctic, they had gained no useful experience; they might as well have flown over desert or open sea. Now they were stranded in the Arctic, and Malmgren alone came from a northern land. Only Biagi, because of his wireless skill, was useful; in fact he was vital. The rest, from general to mechanic, were merely men who had to keep alive on limited rations – and wait.

Wireless communication – or the lack of it – had delivered the first torture-twist. Almost miraculously the field-set had fallen with them, intact, and had been used to tap out an SOS until it broke down. On the party's first morning on the ice, the wireless was put in order again and Biagi transmitted the most urgent of all calls at the scheduled two-hour intervals – on and on throughout the day. The transmitter was in the open beside the aerial mast. For five minutes at a time he worked the key, then crawled into the tent where the receiver was and put on the earphones. The others, crowded about him, instantly read from his mobile young face that he heard nothing.

The last time they had communicated with the *Città di Milano* – by the airship's radio – and received an acknowledgement was on 24th May after leaving the Pole. Then they had said that owing to headwinds they would probably be late. It was now the 26th, far beyond the limit of any normal delay. Surely a close radio watch was being kept for them! Yet their frequent SOS calls remained unanswered. This, Nobile wrote, 'profoundly disheartened my comrades. . . . By nightfall we were in a state of utter depression'.

Biagi checked the transmitter but could find no fault, and the receiver proved that it was working perfectly. That evening they picked up the news bulletin from San Paolo, the radio station of Rome, which stated that there was serious anxiety for their safety.

During the second night the men were alarmed by the noises made by floes grinding together – a phenomenon which had frightened the earliest Arctic explorers and is scarcely less alarming even when one knows what it is. They scrambled out of the tent . . . the alarm was soon over and they crawled back into the tent. This is simply said. But they were a quart in a pint pot, and two of them were stretcher casualties – with no stretcher. Neither Zappi nor Malmgren in fact had broken bones and the Swede had recovered his balance of mind (he talked in a practical way about moving to another floe, which showed fewer signs of stress); but Nobile was in considerable pain, physical as well as mental, and Cecioni had a fractured leg which had been splinted with fragments of wood and airship fabric and he had been lugged out and in through the sleeve door of the tent. After the ice had quietened down he remained loud in his distress.

The wireless continued to mock them. A sinking ship generally received an answer to its SOS within hours at most. For nine *days* Biagi tapped out his desperate call, and received no response. Meanwhile, the stranded party heard the world talking about them. The 9 p.m. bulletin from Rome became the focus of their day, but it only accentuated their sense of helplessness. They were like disembodied spirits, able to hear the living speak but not to answer.

The talk that reached them through the ether was mainly of matters that appeared trivial; and when it concerned them it became evident that no one had a clear notion of their whereabouts.

Biagi intercepted numerous signals from the *Città di Milano* to Rome, long journalistic conjectures, and many personal messages from the crew to people in Italy. They heard the base ship call to them: 'We imagine you are near the north coast of Svalbard between the 15th and 20th meridians east of Greenwich. Trust in us. We are organising help.'

The naval officers had established by sextant that they were on the 26th meridian east of Greenwich, far from the area of search.

They heard wilder and wilder guesses at their whereabouts. It was suggested that they were near north-east Greenland . . . they were in Franz Josef Land . . . they had run into a mountain in Siberia. . . . What use was any search expedition – if any were actually mounted? They heard that the *Città di Milano* was moving from King's Bay to the north coast of Spitsbergen (she never did so). On that misty morning when the airship crashed, they had been near enough to Spitsbergen to expect to see the north coast.

Spitsbergen (now more commonly known in Norway as Svalbard) is an archipelago consisting of two large islands and many small ones. Much the biggest island is Vestspitzbergen, which has the port King's Bay on its south-west coast, the coal mines, and the sharp peaks that inspired the original name for the archipelago. It is what most Norwegians think of when they speak of Svalbard. On Svalbard's right shoulder is the quadrilateral mass of North-East Land, largely ice-capped, inhabited only by trappers who work mainly along its north coast. The other islands, numerous and for the most part very small, are uninhabited. The whole archipelago, land and a lot of sea, could be encompassed by a frame 250 miles long from north to south and rather less than 200 miles from east to west. We are concerned with King's Bay, and the north coast of North-East Land. The *Italia* should have returned to King's Bay on the main island. Instead she fell short of North-East Land, a hundred miles or more to the east.

Off this coast there are a dozen little islands. The one that the stranded party saw whenever it was clear after the first few days was Foyn, which is about fifteen miles from the main shore. The ice that the men were on was drifting from left to right as one looks at the map, from north-west to south-east. For weeks they were within twenty miles of Foyn, generally much nearer and once as close as four miles. (The drift, mainly dependent on the wind, was not consistent; it hesitated and sometimes was reversed.) The point is that the men were not lost in the midst of nowhere as they might well have been. By extraordinary luck they had instruments, could fix their position, track their drift. They could see and identify an island. They were within walking distance of it and the main shore where they should meet hunters if not rescue parties. And it would not have been an extravagant hope to reach King's Bay.

But there were two men who could not walk; and between the party and land, however short the distance, lay the 'formless, contorted jumble of pointed ice-crags'. The first Arctic artists painted pack ice as a jumble of pointed ice crags. However exaggerated in description, verbal or pictorial, this vast all-powerful inanimate thing has held man in awe from the earliest days of exploration.

It is appropriate at this stage to make a realistic assessment of the survivors. But we have only Nobile's words to go on. He had created this expedition and described its members like an indulgent, dying father. Of the foreign scientists Malmgren was his 'most valued collaborator – the only one to whom I confided my plans, my ideas, my thoughts'. Behounek, the Czech, was strong and self-contained, eminently logical, possessed of 'Olympian serenity'. The Italians were blood of his blood. Only Cecioni, because of his pain, and Trojani, because of his 'invincible pessimism', failed to respond to his exhortations that they should trust in God and let His will be done. Nobile, in spite of his airship, was as pious in phrase as a sixteenth-century explorer.

On 28th May, when they still had had no response to their SOS signals and had realised that they were drifting south-eastwards several miles each day (for the moment converging on the coast but likely to be carried past it), the idea was born that they should walk to land. The first that Nobile learned of this suggestion was when he overheard Commander Mariano discussing it with Dr Malmgren. 'With them?' the Swede asked, pointing at the General and Cecioni. 'No, that's impossible'.

Later Mariano, Zappi and Malmgren spoke with their leader and propounded a revised plan. The three or four fittest men should make a dash for North-East Land before they drifted past it. Nobile, who preferred a consensus to direct orders, suggested a general discussion in the tent. This was held, but no clear decision was reached.

The main contentions were: should the fittest make a dash to get help; or should they all move, the two casualties dragged on sledges made out of wreckage by Cecioni; or should all but the casualties and Biagi go? This last suggestion was logically discarded by Behounek: 'For my part, I willingly remain with the General. But I do insist that one of the naval officers stays with us. We must have someone who can take our bearings. Otherwise what's the use of a wireless operator?' At one stage Biagi had asked to go too, and had been told by his General that he could if he wanted to. But Malmgren, the 'Arctic expert', said that in that case he would stay with the sick, and Biagi apologised for his moment of weakness.

Nobile advocated deferring a start by any party. Their wireless calls must eventually receive an answer. Zappi said they must start at once because food was limited. Cecioni was dragged out of the tent – at his own urgent request – to hammer at fragments of metal tubing with the object of making sledges. He did not want to be left behind. But although he hammered diligently he could not make a useful sledge.

At this time an event occurred that revealed Malmgren not as a suicidal depressive but as a bold man of action. A polar bear approached the tent during the night. Malmgren went after it with the Colt pistol – something that an experienced hunter would have hesitated to do. But he knocked it over from fifteen yards. 'The poor brute', as Nobile called it, did not swipe anybody's head off. It had only a few pages of their Nautical Almanac in its stomach, and no fight at all in its heart.

Nearly 400 pounds of meat, however unappetising to conservative tastes, was thus added to their rations. This weakened Zappi's argument that the land party should leave at once because of the shortage of food. But he still wanted to be off, as did Mariano. Although the problem as to who should go remained unresolved, it was generally accepted that these two should be in the party.

Nobile did not want Mariano to go in any case. He said he wished to speak to him alone. Mariano went out of the tent without answering. Soon afterwards Nobile heard him say loudly to Zappi, 'We two should go as we are such great friends'.

'That was his answer', Nobile noted. 'Whatever I had said I could not have held back either of them. So I decided to object no longer.' He also agreed that Malmgren should go and that the start should be made that evening, 30th May. So without a single order being given

43

this important matter was finally settled.

Shortly before leaving, Malmgren talked with Nobile about the difficulties of the journey and the probable drift of the ice on which the tent party remained. He voiced his opinion quietly and in a matter of fact tone: 'Both parties will die'.

It is difficult to justify his pessimism. The men in the tent could subsist upon the food they had for a couple of months at least. The three travellers carried among them 120 pounds of provisions, chiefly pemmican and chocolate, with some malted milk and butter. They were clad in Arctic clothing. They had a blanket for the night and the necessary instruments and maps. Judging by photographs, the ice in the area of the tent was not unduly rough or broken by open leads. Apart from the first night's scare, the pack had not grumbled or shifted strongly. They were only seven miles from Foyn Island, not much more that twenty from the coast of North-East Land. There they would almost certainly meet Norwegian trappers or a rescue party and would soon be within the area where the *Città di Milano* had said they were expected to be. At the very worst they would have to walk on a couple of hundred miles to King's Bay. It was a courageous and arduous venture but, with ample rations, by no means a desperate one. The chief concern should have been the weight of the packs carried by men unused to portage. Mariano and Zappi bore sixty pounds each; Malmgren, because of his still painful arm and shoulder, twenty pounds less. There is nothing like a heavy load for upsetting balance and depressing the spirit.

The travelling-party offered to carry personal letters. Nobile described the scene that followed. Trojani, who considered writing 'perfectly useless', merely wrapped up a sum of money for his wife. The rest wrote absorbedly, lost in thoughts of home. 'Behounek was the one who struck me most. I had always seen him so self-contained that I had ended by considering him incapable of emotion. Yet now tears were running down his cheeks as he wrote.'

During the official inquiry on the expedition some significance was attached to the fact that Behounek had entrusted two letters to Malmgren, and it appeared that neither Mariano or Zappi knew of this. Since Behounek had behaved in so uncharacteristic a manner this seems surprising. There was no privacy in these circumstances.

When the three had gone to a shout of 'Viva l'Italia', the six remaining men experienced a sense of relaxation. The days of argument were over, they had more room in the tent and something

44

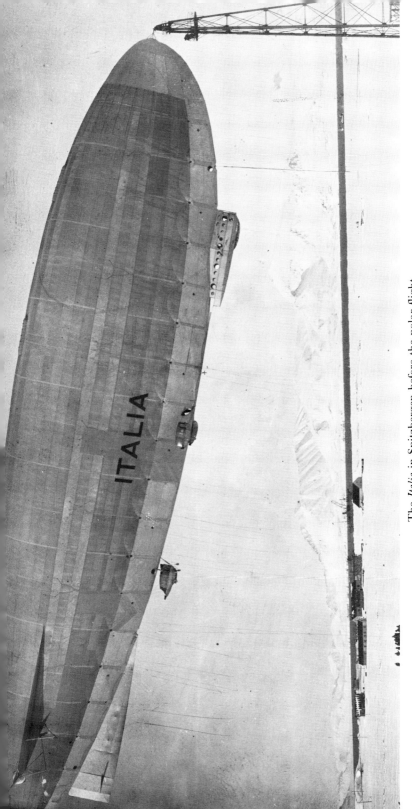

The *Italia* in Spitzbergen before the polar flight

Lundborg's Fokker makes its second rescue mission landing beside the Red Tent

The Russian ice-breaker *Krassin*, designed to run her bows on to thick ice and break it by downwards pressure. Note the look-out barrels on the masts

Nobile at the window of the command cabin of the *Italia*, 1928

Nobile at the Jubilee celebration of the polar flight, 1978. His wife, Dr
Gertrude Nobile, is on his right, his daughter, Maria, on his left. He is
being congratulated by the Chief of Staff

positive was being done for their salvation. But very soon they once again became preoccupied by their helplessness on the drifting pack and their inability to make themselves heard on the wireless. The drift carried them still nearer to Foyn Island – within four miles. Seagulls flew out from it and squawked at them. The desert island was their barometer of hope. Nobody lived on it or could subsist there, but it was *land*. For many days Viglieri was unable to take an observation because the sun remained hidden by a high layer of cloud. But if the island looked near they were happy. . . . They drifted past it. The island became a vague shape in the distance. The sea birds flew lazily back to land and the men despaired. Cape Leigh Smith, the last point of land, was not much further east. Although the packed floes hesitated or occasionally reversed direction, the general drift was easterly. The *Pilot Book* said so. Malmgren had said so. Beyond the limit of North-East Land was a 250-mile stretch of desolate ice-covered sea leading to ice-clad, inhospitable Franz Josef Land where they would certainly be out of wireless range from Spitsbergen and where no one would find them 'even by chance'.

Nobile exhorted Biagi to increase his calling-time. The sturdy operator checked that his wave length was exactly thirty-two meters and for an hour at a time tapped out the SOS. Unsure of their geographical co-ordinates, they mentioned Foyn in the signals.

No one responded. Biagi was 'nervy and thoroughly out of temper: it seemed at times that he even doubted his own competence'.

They were all gloomy. Nobile tried to cheer them up. 'After all, we can die quite tranquilly here', he said. 'We have done our duty and very nearly achieved everything on our programme.'

The response to this was less than wholehearted. Nobile, lying incapacitated in the tent beside a large and equally incapacitated companion, evidently thought too much and in a less than practical vein. He asked himself the agonising question whether two casualties had the right to condemn to death four who were fit to walk. Once they had drifted east of Cape Leigh Smith they would all be beyond hope. Therefore, those who could walk should be sent off to seek their salvation while he and Cecioni, whom he believed he could console, drifted on to die. Of the able-bodied, Viglieri and Biagi would, he believed, obey a 'peremptory order'. But he felt it necessary to ask Trojani and Behounek if they would go when they were told to.

Trojani answered, 'I will do what you command'. But Behounek said trenchantly, 'I don't know why you ask me this. I have come here with you and I am not going away without you'.

The scientist who thus scotched the heroic idea was getting on with his work as well as he could, using such instruments as he had found scattered in the snow. The rest of them were existing, subsisting, waiting for a response to the continually repeated call for help. The oft-repeated tapping – dot-dot-dot, dash-dash-dash, dot-dot-dot – and then the putting on of earphones to listen uselessly resembled a ritual of a disproved religion.

On the evening of 6th June, a week after Mariano's party had left and nearly a fortnight since the first SOS had been sent out, Biagi was sitting by the receiver in the tent wearing the earphones. He was a dark, thick-set Italian, a Bolognese, not particularly even-tempered, and the others never interrupted him at his thankless task.

He suddenly shouted, 'They've heard us!' and began to write. Nobile leaned over to read: 'The Soviet Embassy has informed the Italian Government that . . .'.

It must be one of the most extraordinary stories in radio history. The newspapers and news bulletins of the civilised world had reported that the *Italia* had disappeared on a return flight from the Pole. The lost party knew all about that! There had been international interest and sympathy. The sacred obligation to rescue castaways had caused Sweden, Norway, Finland, Germany and France to set about organising relief. But in the seemingly limitless Arctic nobody knew where to look.

During the evening of 2nd June a Russian amateur radio operator, named Schmidt, who lived near Archangel, picked up between two concert broadcasts a faint fragment of a Morse message, 'SOSFOYNCIRCA'. He reported this to his local Soviet station, who in turn reported it to Moscow. It took time to establish that this was not a bid by Schmidt for notoriety. How could he have heard what the base ship and major stations had failed to hear?

It took still longer to interpret the scant message. SOS was clear but the rest was guessed to be 'Francesco' – which was interpreted as Franz Josef Land. It would have been ironic if Nobile, who feared that he might drift to Franz Josef Land where nobody would look for him, had been searched for in Franz Josef Land when he was near Spitsbergen. He was spared this, but Fate was not to bring him home as the heroic leader he tried so earnestly to be.

After Comrade Schmidt had convinced the Russian authorities of his genuineness, there was still doubt and confusion for a day or more.

How could the airship have got so far off course as Franz Josef Land? Was there another interpretation of Foyncirca?

Professor Samoilovich, Director of the Soviet Institute of Arctic Research, studied maps and examined records of winds and currents. He announced his conclusion that the castaways were near a tiny island that no one had heard of. And so through diplomatic channels Rome radio received and broadcast the information that Biagi then picked up.

Next day the *Città di Milano* heard them clearly and spoke with them. The subsequent Commission of Inquiry – whose report is now a rare document of the Fascist era, which later we will examine – was satisfied with the explanations of the ship's former deafness (interference by the local King's Bay station or engines on the vessel); but the simple and shameful explanation obtrudes that they were not listening, too busy communicating journalistic and private messages to Rome.

At that moment in the tent nobody thought of explanations. They were in touch at last! 'We all looked radiant', Nobile recorded. 'The lines graven by the previous days had been blotted out. How splendid it was to see men laughing again'.

Men of the Mediterranean laughing on an ice floe, dirty, bearded but happy with exaggerated optimism. They gave praise to their general for trusting in the wireless, and he accepted it althouth his confidence had not gone so far as to prevent Malmgren, Mariano and Zappi from setting out for help on foot. But when Trojani asked him as a prophet if they could now hope to see their families again Nobile answered that one series of anxieties had ended and would be succeeded by another – he was right.

For four days there was a flood of messages between the tent and the *Città di Milano*. The base ship told of rescue expeditions on the way by aircraft, Russian ice-breakers and on foot. Nobile listed the many needs of his party and advised on methods of rescue by air and dog sledge. To make it more easily visible the tent was smeared with red aniline dye. (The newspapers later said it was painted with the blood of a bear, a nice Arctic Old Testament touch). The south-easterly drift was reversed by a change of wind and Foyn Island became again clear and close.

But after 12th June Commander Romagna Manoia of the *Città di Milano* severely cut the number and length of interchanges. The Red Tent faded to a dirty brown, the eastwards drift resumed and morale went down. Hope deferred made hearts sick.

The party on the ice, intercepting news bulletins, learned of the concentration of aircraft in Spitsbergen. The response had been magnificent. Unfortunately, being international, it was not co-ordinated and aircraft crossed singly the stormy Barents Sea which separates the archipelago from Scandinavia. One was the flying-boat in which were Amundsen and five other men, French and Norwegian. Amundsen, who had been in France at the time, had decided at once to join the search for the man with whom he had quarrelled so bitterly after their expedition together in the airship *Norge* two years earlier. But he did not reach Spitsbergen. More than two months later some wreckage from his flying-boat was found.

On 17th June the men of the Red Tent saw the first aeroplane. Although it came within a couple of miles, it failed to see them in spite of their smoke fire and Very-light flares. This happened several times during subsequent days. The men who for so long had been inaudible began to think themselves invisible.

Appropriately, it was an aircraft with red, white and green markings that found them, on 20th June, and pitched out parcels of provisions and stores. The following day two Italian flying-boats came with more supplies. On his final run one of the planes swooped down very low over the tent, and the pilot leaned out of the cockpit and shouted, '*Arrivederci!*' Aeroplanes were much less efficient fifty years ago, but they were also less impersonal.

In fact it was not *arrivederci* but 'good-bye', for Italy – apart from wireless communications and land patrols – took no more effective part in the rescue. Nobile later on bitterly criticised his country for doing so little, comparing its efforts unfavourably with those of other countries. He put it down to politics and personal jealousies. If Mussolini's Italy attempted something spectacular it had to succeed, and a crash was a failure, certainly not to be publicised. Commander Romagna Manoia, he suggested, had sensed the climate and hindered rather than helped. Balbo, a Quadrumvir and Under-Secretary for Air, at that time in Spain arranging details for his flight across the Mediterranean with sixty aircraft, remarked when he heard of Nobile's disaster, 'Serves him right'. This was not a Fascist venture, he said – although *Italia* carried the Fascist emblem.

Such bitterness, whether justified or not, emerged later. At the moment Nobile was stimulated. He recorded: 'The man of action had fully reasserted himself in me. Once more I was the leader: I wanted to see all my men saved, now that there was a chance'.

The flying-boats had failed to find an extensive enough open lead to come down on, but a light aeroplane could surely land on the ice. A suitable floe was located. It would probably be impossible for the rescuers to carry out more than one man at a time, so Nobile worked out the order in which they should go. He put Cecioni at the top of the list and, at first, himself at the bottom. Then he realised that the wireless operator would have to remain to the end to guide the planes in, so he put Biagi at the bottom and himself second last.

The next visitors from the skies were two Swedish seaplanes. They dropped parcels attached to red parachutes with a note in English to the effect that the parachutes should be used to mark out a landing strip for ski-planes. This was immediately done and Nobile wrote a long message of instructions to be transmitted to the *Città di Milano*. But the ship was not in the mood for reception – or transmission. So the party on the ice was taken by surprise when a seaplane accompanying a light aeroplane appeared on the evening of 24th June.

The seaplane circled like a guardian angel but the Fokker ski-plane landed on the marked floe 150 yards from the tent. The pilot, Lundborg, got out, leaving his co-pilot in the cockpit. Viglieri and Biagi conducted him to the tent, where Nobile had himself lifted up to embrace the man 'who alone of all those who had been trying during a whole month to reach us had succeeded in his purpose'.

Lundborg was polite but brief. 'General, I have come to fetch you all. The field is excellent. I shall be able to take away the lot of you during the night. You must come first.'

Nobile replied that that was impossible. Cecioni must go first. But Lundborg was emphatic: 'No, I have orders to bring you first because we need your instructions to start looking for the others.'

Nobile says he 'instinctively considered' that by 'the others' were meant the six who had been swept away in the airship. This weakened his resolve to stay, yet he pointed at Cecioni and said, 'Please take him first. That is my decision.' Lundborg became impatient. He said Cecioni was too heavy to take unless he left his co-pilot behind, which was impossible. 'Please hurry up,' he urged – a Swede speaking to an Italian in English.

Nobile followed his rule of asking the opinion of the others. He says that they all urged him to go first. 'Then whatever happens there will be somebody to look after our families', was Cecioni's argument.

'I made up my mind. I would go', Nobile recorded. 'This was not easy. It needed more courage to go than to stay, but in the circumstances I felt it my imperative duty to give way to Lundborg.'

So he allowed himself to be carried to the aeroplane and flew away, clutching his dog and notebooks containing the signals he had sent, or failed to send. Among these was one entitled, 'Data and instructions to search for the airship'.

An hour later he was in Spitsbergen. He did not then realise the significance of what he had done. But he did next day when Commander Romagna Manoia came to his cabin on the *Città di Milano* and said, 'People might criticise you for coming first, General. It would be as well to give some explanation.'

Lundborg had gone back alone as he had said he would. The Fokker had somersaulted on landing. He was unhurt, but the only aircraft suitable for rescue was a write-off.

We must leave General Nobile to suffer 'thirty-two interminable days of indescribable torment' in a small cabin. He still had his rank but had lost authority, everyone knowing that he had no one to back him up in Rome. Commander Romagna Manoia behaved with scrupulous politeness but took no notice of what Nobile said and found good reasons for not obeying his orders.

Fourteen days after Nobile's rescue, Schyberd, Lundborg's co-pilot, fetched the Swedish pilot away. After that no more landings were attempted. The thawing ice was considered too wet for skis yet there was not enough open water for floats. In spite of the earlier international fervour, rescue was tacitly left to the Russian ice-breaker *Krassin*, which was stolidly barging its way through the pack.

Nobile tried to join the *Krassin*. This was forbidden by the Ministero della Marina. He asked to fly with the Finns who were preparing a large aeroplane. He would see his companions picked up and stay behind himself . . . but the aircraft never took off. No serious attempt was made to locate the wrecked airship and the six lost men. There was no news of Mariano's party which had set out for land less than thirty miles away more than a month before. Parties of *Alpini* and hunters were searching the coast of North-East Land; so, once ashore, there was no question of the three men having to walk on to King's Bay.

There is no complete first hand account of this extraordinary journey though Mariano and Zappi – and everyone else concerned

50

before and after – gave evidence to a Commission of Inquiry. The resultant report devoted more space to this march than any other single incident of the *Italia* expedition, describing it as 'a tremendous Odyssey, one of the most tragic episodes told in polar history'.

It was certainly tragic; it was also mysterious, because so few facts or clear statements were provided by the two survivors. Using only these the story may be briefly told. The report is long because the uncertainties, plus some excited remarks by Zappi, provided meat for the macabre imaginations of news-starved journalists.

The stated facts are as follows. The party set out from the Red Tent at ten o'clock on the evening of 30th May (the thawing snow and ice would be in the best condition during the summer night). The first march, according to Mariano, was of twenty-four to thirty hours' duration with a rest after every 400 or 500 metres. Malmgren, the arctic expert, was reported to have said that he had never experienced pack ice which offered so many difficulties. The three men only covered a small fraction of the ten or twelve kilometres that had been forecast for each march. Foyn Island, which had been some eleven kilometres away when they started, was not even mentioned. The temperature was low. Malmgren suffered a frozen foot and Mariano symptoms of a frozen hand.

The second day's march was even worse. At the end of it Malmgren became hysterical. He was miserable, trembling, and spoke words that his companions did not understand. They comforted him, massaged him and gave him a hot drink. (It is not said how this was heated.) He recovered quickly and apologised for his lapse. Then they talked things over, wondering whether they should try to return to the Red Tent. But they decided that it would be extremely difficult to retrace their steps. Besides, theirs was a vital mission on which the salvation of the whole party depended. They themselves had no tent, only a blanket each which was probably wet like everything else. They must certainly have felt miserable.

Nothing is told in the report about the next ten days except that Malmgren's condition deteriorated. He did not trust his legs to jump – as he would occasionally have had to do when crossing from one floe to another. When he fell down he had to be helped up and relieved of his load of rucksack and blanket. His right big toe was frozen; the nail came off and the skin peeled. He became taciturn. He suddenly broke silence to ask his companions to hit him on the head with the hatchet they carried, first covering him with his windproof

51

jacket so that they should not see the effect of the blow.

Naturally they refused. But suddenly on the twelfth day of the march Malmgren threw himself down, crying out decisively, 'I can walk no further. Leave me here. You go'.

Mariano and Zappi begged him at least to come on a little further to a more suitable place to bivouac. Malmgren stripped his boot and sock from his right foot and displayed the frozen big toe, whitish in colour, the flesh wrinkled. He asked them to tell his compatriots why he had given up and once more asked his companions to hit him on the head. When they still refused to do this he insisted that they should not leave him any food which would only prolong his suffering. He asked Zappi to see that his mother had his compass, a cherished souvenir of former expeditions, also his doctorate ring. The latter, however, could not be taken off because the finger was too swollen and his companions declined to cut it off.

They dug a trench for him and gave him a few lumps of salt-free ice to suck. Zappi, remembering that he had said men of science had no religion, moistened a finger with snow and made the sign of the cross on Malmgren's forehead, pronouncing the words of baptism. Then the two Italians went on a hundred yards or so and bivouacked for twenty hours, hoping that Malmgren would change his mind.

But he suddenly heaved himself up from his icy grave and shouted to them that they must continue their march. Then he collapsed, disappearing so suddenly that Zappi thought he must have committed 'some desperate act'. He did not go back to check.

He and Mariano went sadly, slowly on. Zappi now becomes the major chronicler, for the spirits of Mariano, the leader, were evidently sinking. They encountered great difficulties, although these are not specified, and we are seldom given an indication of where they were.

On 17th or 18th June – they were vague about dates in the endless daylight – a seaplane passed low over their heads but did not see them. During the following days four other aircraft passed over them.

On 21st or 22nd June they were within a kilometre of Foyn. They had been held up because Mariano had twice become snow-blind. Zappi had to lead him by the hand, but even so Mariano fell and hurt his leg. He exhorted Zappi to leave him with a packet of pemmican and go on. Zappi attempted to go on but found, between him and the land, patches of open water which he could not cross without help. (What help could a crippled, snow-blind man have given him?) He returned to Mariano.

52

Between 23rd – 25th June, owing to the drift of the pack, they were six to eight kilometres, four or five miles, from the coast of North-East Land. Mariano again exhorted Zappi to leave him and press on. But Zappi decided that he could not cover the distance alone. So, in a snow shelter constructed on an ice block, they settled down to wait for rescue. They had rations for ten days. They waited for fifteen. On 10th July a scouting aircraft from *Krassin* spotted them. Two days later they were picked up by the ice-breaker.

The Commission of Inquiry, having set down the story, filled fifteen more pages of their report in considering the behaviour of Mariano and Zappi. Only after reading between a good many lines does one realise that the two Italian naval officers had been accused by the Press of the world of killing Malmgren to eat his flesh, or at least to obtain his share of the rations.

From the story as told in the report it probably never would occur to the reader that any such thing might have happened. But since the Commission dealt with the accusation, even if obliquely, it must be examined.

The Commission slightly obscured its conclusions by making philosophical observations such as 'The truth in this world has always cost something to those who spoke it' and 'The polar desert produces effects of a kind inexplicable in other regions of the earth'.

The least heinous charge they dealt with was that Malmgren had been deserted and left to die. He gave Mariano and Zappi no written statement, no receipt for his life. Nor did he entrust to them Behounek's letters to his fiancée and sister. The Czech professor said in evidence that he had handed over the letters privately, speaking German. If the Italian officers heard they might not have understood. But why did not Malmgren send a note, even an oral message, to his mother? He only handed the compass to Zappi. What course did his mother steer by that? She accepted what she was told. She presumably knew her son.

Mariano and Zappi felt it their duty to go on and get help for the whole party. The Commission accepted this as justification. But the two men did not press on. They waited for almost a day within a hundred yards of Malmgren. Only when the Swede made his brief resurrection and exhorted them to go did they obey – without going back that short distance to find out whether his sudden disappearance was owing to suicide. For this Zappi must be blamed. Of the two only he was fully mobile. Mariano was already a limping casualty.

Zappi and Mariano admitted taking Malmgren's share of the rations at his request. They had ample for survival. When they started from the tent on 30th May they had 120 pounds of rich, concentrated food. They said they finished their provisions on 30th June. So, with Malmgren dropping out half way through the month, the two officers ate on average over a pound and a half each per day. That (pemmican, chocolate, malted milk, butter) would provide over 4,000 calories, much more than people normally consume. One cannot believe that on 1st July there was suddenly nothing left. But on 12th July Zappi walked unassisted up the steep gangway of the *Krassin* (there is a photograph of this) and said that he had had nothing to eat for twelve days. His veracity must have been affected.

Mariano was carried on board on a stretcher and could only show his gratitude by reaching out to touch the leg of Professor Samoilovich, who was in charge of the rescue expedition. Mariano was all in. He had a foot amputated and died some months later.

Zappi was in a highly excited state. He talked volubly and wildly, avoiding questions about Malmgren. He told of a pact that he and Mariano had made that if one died the other would drink his blood and eat his flesh. But the nearest to a specific charge of cannibalism resulted from the first report of the pilot of the scout plane who spotted the party on 10th July. He said that he had seen three men. When the *Krassin* reached the scene on the twelfth there were only two. Mariano explained that he had spread his trousers on the ice to dry and the dark smudge looked like a prostrate third man.

With Mariano and Zappi on board, the *Krassin* barged on the short distance to the Red Tent, picked up the other six and took them to King's Bay. No search was made for the airship, partly because the *Krassin* was short of coal and partly because seaplanes were not made available for reconnaissance.

When Nobile met Zappi he was struck by his overstrung state of mind and remarkable physical fitness. He told him that he disapproved of his talkativeness since being rescued. Zappi had evidently tried to work up the drama of the situation (Nobile was quite a good psychologist). With the crippled Mariano the General could only commiserate – and politely refuse when asked to recommend him and Zappi for the gold medal for valour.

That was the nearest the two naval officers came to criticism. The Commission arrived at the conclusion that their conduct could not be censured; in fact it was worthy of praise.

The *Italia* expedition did not receive the tumultuous reception in Rome that had greeted the crew of the *Norge*. Thousands of ordinary people turned out to express the warmth of their sympathy, but welcome was officially muted. There was no speech from the balcony of the Palazzo Chigi, no patting on the shoulder in the floodlights, no bunch of roses for the Signora. This was not an international expedition which must be placated and, as Balbo had commented, it was not a Fascist enterprise. It had been a failure, bad propaganda.

But the officers and N.C.Os were of the armed forces, the sinews and glory of the State. Nothing must be done to denigrate them. So Mussolini ordered the Commission of Inquiry – admirals and generals and Roman senators.

They sat throughout the winter and came up with their verdict in the spring. At the expense of one man, if sufficiently mutilated, the whole party could be honoured. We have already quoted from the report but it deserves to be looked at as a whole, for it is a remarkable document. Every aspect and incident of the expedition is examined in detail and judgement passed on it. All the conclusions are unanimous, of course.

The inception of and preparations for the expedition, the choice of men, the flight to Spitsbergen and the first exploratory voyage eastwards are thoroughly examined. Already it has become evident that what was wrong with the expedition was its creator, organiser and leader. Everyone else behaved perfectly. This is brought out most clearly in the polar flight. One is given the impression from cross-examinations that each member of the crew knew what ought to have been done and if he did not do it unordered that was because he was well disciplined.

Giving evidence about the final sudden descent, Cecioni said, 'There was a moment of wildness and confusion. From the moment when the airship began to fall there were no more precise orders'.

And Mariano said, 'It would have been enough to head into the wind'.

Mariano, next in rank to the general, was in the pilot cabin. Nobile was at a porthole gauging the altitude by timing the drop of glass balls filled with red dye. There is a time for initiative, more valuable than later criticism. But the Commission did not see it like that. They praised everybody but General Nobile: 'In the whole conduct of the expedition until the catastrophe and after it General Nobile demonstrated that he possessed limited technical ability as a pilot and a negative capacity for command.'

When the Inquiry moved on to Lundborg's landing near the Red Tent, Nobile's men showed no inclination to back up their leader. Yet the official account based on Lundborg's evidence did not differ very much from Nobile's.

Lundborg said he told Nobile that 'in the general interest' he should come out first. The rest of the party would be rescued that same night or the next. Nobile produced his list, but Lundborg objected that Cecioni was too heavy. Nobile then turned to the others and there was a conversation in Italian that Lundborg did not understand. At the end of it Nobile turned to him and said, 'We are agreed. I will go first'.

Cecioni rendered this conversation as follows: 'The General said to us all, "Boys, what do you think? Lundborg wants me to go first". I said, "Do so. You are Commander". The others said the same. It was not for us to ask to go. I would have liked to go. No one asked anything.'

On reaching the *Città di Milano* Nobile told Commander Romagna Manoia he had come first so that he could supervise rescue of the airship party. In that case why had he not put himself first on his list, the Commission asked?

The conclusion of the Commission was: 'This action by General Nobile, contrary to every tradition and law of military honour, has no plausible justification and can be explained, not justified, only by his physical and moral depression. He had no right to behave as he did even under the pressing encouragement of Lundborg.'

Nobile was also criticised, at least by implication, over the Mariano *pattuglia*, patrol, as it was called. It is stressed at some length that since he was in command he was responsible for ordering it. We know in the general's own words how he reached a decision and gave orders. But the emphasis given to this suggests that the Commission members were slightly embarrassed – which is to their credit.

The Commission of Inquiry concluded its report with an assessment of the work of the officers of the expedition, of the *Città di Milano* and the Italian aerial unit. This provided another opportunity to praise Mariano and Zappi; the Italian navy could be proud of these two sons. Romagna Manoia who commanded the base ship 'in particularly difficult conditions' had been prompt and precise in executing the orders of the Ministero della Marina. Of the pilots, Major Maddalena and Lieutenant Cagna, it was stated: 'Theirs was a splendid example of skill, the spirit of self-sacrifice and of modesty. They threw themselves into doing the duty involved in their mission, frequently risking their lives.'

This is an example of the Commission's capacity to praise. It was not squandered on Nobile. He was very good at building airships, they said. But there the compliments ceased. Even in the organisation of the expedition he had been less than loyal, having obtained financial backing from the city of Milan by talking of a non-existent German polar expedition, thus gambling with patriotism to obtain his ends.

There is no advantage in criticising criticism. There were good and worthy men on the Commission – Admiral Cagni, General Pinedo and others. But if they did not stand up to Mussolini in more important matters, would they have done so in this? And Nobile was the almost self-chosen scapegoat, willing to be sacrificed.

In his own words he comes over as a gentle, indecisive leader. He may well have deceived others besides himself. It is only because nobody else gets any blame at all that the question of bias appears – in fact it is inescapable.

The rescue operations were ill organised. The concentration of aircraft from several countries achieved nothing in proportion to its size. The aviators proved their courage and skill in getting to Spitsbergen. That was the most difficult and dangerous part, as the loss of Amundsen's party showed. From bases in Spitsbergen they had only short distances to fly. They did quite a lot, but one feels it fell short of their potential and their will.

Nobile's criticisms obtrude. The *Città di Milano* co-ordinated rescue flights. The base ship governed radio communication with the Red Tent, once Comrade Schmidt had unlocked the door. Commander Romagna Manoia was commended for his promptness in obeying the orders of the Ministero della Marina. There is no record of these orders but Manoia seems often to have postponed action, or taken none.

Suppose Amundsen had arrived safely in Spitsbergen. He would have waited for instructions from no one. Something very definite would have been done at once.

Suppose further that he had been on the *Italia* flight, been stranded on the pack. Not for long! Those few miles of ice would soon have been crossed. Amundsen was not the only polar man available in the world. An 'Arctic expert' was not essential, just someone with a bit of experience and determination. But Nobile took only the *simpatico*, unreliable Malmgren. Nobile was a highly skilled technician, a man who could build good airships. He happened to come down in a place where his skill and experience were of absolutely no use to himself or his party.

After the publication of the report he resigned his rank – that was how it was put – and went into exile. The *Italia* expedition was then honoured and the story of the Red Tent became a patriotic tradition.

Fate, of course, had a twist up its sleeve to end the story. The Russians recognised the value of a good technician and gave Nobile a job building airships. In 1931 he went on an expedition to Franz Josef Land in the *Malygin*, sister ice-breaker of the *Krassin* and had the bitter sweet experience of being invited on board the *Graf Zeppelin* for tea with Dr Ekner and Lincoln Ellsworth of the 1926 *Norge* expedition.

In 1945, with Mussolini gone, Nobile was recalled to Italy and rehabilitated as a general. At that time I happened to meet him on an aeroplane, a composed, well-preserved and strictly reserved senior officer in uniform. But his experiences had changed him. The following year he became a Communist deputy in the Constituent Assembly.

On 24th May 1978, he attended the jubilee of the *Italia* polar flight and the Red Tent. Present at the ceremony were the Chief of the Italian General Staff and the Minister for Air, and the ambassadors of all the countries that had assisted in the rescue. But of the members of the expedition there were only Viglieri, and Nobile in a wheel chair. All the rest were dead.

After the complimentary speeches the general mildly hinted that he wished something to the same effect had been expressed fifty years earlier. However, he blamed nothing except the weather and those who forecast it.

He then returned to Lauro, his home-town, for good. He liked to sit in the square, now Piazza Nobile, and tell the story to anyone inclined to listen. He died in July of the same year, aged ninety-three. His daughter Maria, whose eyes in a photograph had appeared full of tears when he saw them during the death throes of the *Italia*, said to reporters, 'He has a whole column in the *Encyclopaedia Britannica*.' It is not precisely true, but it suggests loyalty, of which he had known little. His second wife works for the Centro Documentazione 'Umberto Nobile', in Rome.

3

Inexpressible Island

The *Terra Nova* disembarked the Northern Party at Evans'
Coves for a six-week geologising trip. They dragged their
ready-loaded sledges over the half mile of sea ice to the shore
while a ship's party transported stores for a depot on the moraine.
This was done very quickly and simply. Then the *Terra Nova* sailed on
for Captain Scott's base camp at McMurdo Sound. The date was 8th
January 1912 – full summer in the Southern Hemisphere. The
arrangement was that the ship would return to pick them up between
18th February and 15th March.

Evans' Coves sound as attractive as a seaside holiday haven. You
might be surprised to find from a map that the coves form part of
Inexpressible Island. The Northern Party gave it this name.

The six men returned from their sledge trip up the glaciers on 7th
February, eleven days before the ship could be expected. But we can
ignore the periods of expectancy and disappointment. The *Terra Nova*
did not return to pick them up. So there they were with the winter
before them – Commander V. L. A. Campbell, R.N., Surgeon G.
Murray Levick, R.N., Raymond Priestley (the only civilian) and
Petty Officers, R.N., Abbott, Browning and Dickason. They were
dressed for summer skiing and had not much other serviceable
clothing, for they had already been out for almost a year in a hut
further north on the coast. They had two pyramid tents and what was
left of their sledging-rations. In their depot on the moraine were the
skeletal rations of pemmican, sugar, cocoa, chocolate and biscuits for
four weeks.

The *Terra Nova* could, of course, have provided other stores, but
these were intended for the main party, and Campbell had not felt
justified in touching them. Inexpressible Island had not the
reputation of being inaccessible, quite the reverse. On past

experience there was no reason to doubt that the ship would be able to return. But it happened to be an exceptional year.

Campbell's strict principles were also largely responsible for another lack which came near to being fatal. When the sledgers returned to the coast, seals were basking on the ice-foot and the rocks, thick as sunbathers on Brighton Beach. But Campbell was unwilling to kill any quantity before it was certain that the slaughter was necessary. And when the last possible date for the ship's coming had gone, so had the seals – with the first storms. It was much the same with the penguins.

The island was some 200 miles in a straight line from the expedition's base. The sea was open and they had no boat. The mountainous coast was impassable. They would have had to find a way to the head of a heavily crevassed glacier and on to the ice plateau beyond, trebling the length of the journey. The six men were marooned at least until the next spring in a land which was not merely inhospitable but hostile. The first gales tore and knocked down their tents. All but a few animals had had the good sense to go elsewhere. There was no vegetation and no topographical shelter from the cold and from the heavy wind that poured down like a cataract from the icy plateau.

Survival for seven months or so depended not only upon food and keeping warm, but also on maintaining harmony and morale. What follows is Priestley's story, based on his book *Antarctic Adventure*, checked for true day-to-day feelings from his private diary (now in the archives of the Scott Polar Research Institute) and with memories of the yarn as he told it to me when he was a don at Clare. It is not a heroic tragedy like the South Pole journey – which naturally dwarfed it. There is nothing dramatic about it, no exciting end. What makes it worth telling is the proof it provides that extraordinary circumstances can be made ordinary by down-to-earth common sense and a sense of humour.

For a time the six men worked in two parties and made short exploratory journeys. Levick's party found a small penguin rookery and saw something never before witnessed: the parents were enticing the young ones into the water and teaching them to swim. (No food was collected.) But both parties spent most of their time in the tents, enduring storms. One split Levick's tent right across, and Abbott got out palm and needle and sewed it up on the spot.

Clearly they could not endure such conditions for long. So

60

Levick's party was left on the moraine to hunt and keep watch for the ship, though they no longer expected it, while Campbell, Priestley and Dickason went in search of durable quarters on Inexpressible Island.

Almost anywhere else in the world they might have overcome a total lack of wood by going underground or making bricks without straw. But the ground was bare rock. An igloo would not have endured in autumn even if there had been plenty of snow and they had known how to build one. The only possibility was to burrow into one of the old snowdrifts.

Priestley took over control of the rations. Making such stores as they had last throughout the winter was a task demanding skill in accountancy and finesse in psychology. How, for example, do you work out the length of time a seal should last six men and then persuade them to accept your calculation? Priestley admitted that it worried him all the time – which was a good thing, he said, because it prevented him from worrying about anything else.

As they had been living on much less than full rations since they landed (they cannot have been as sure as they pretended to be that the *Terra Nova* would manage to come back for them), Priestley decided that the remaining sledging-rations must last until they had settled down in their cave. And even from this he subtracted the luxuries – sugar, chocolate and raisins. Breakfast and supper consisted of half rations of pemmican and hunted meat, weak cocoa and one biscuit a day. Lunch was cut out altogether, with the result that hunger hurt from noon onwards. A civilian imposed that regimen on five ravenous sailors. Priestley comments: 'We were able to eat a fair quantity of meat because we did not realise how scarce even that was to be, but the one biscuit a day [the full ration was eight] left us with a continuous longing for carbohydrates, a desire that nagged us persistently and finally overcame our dislike of blubber'.

The blubber served a double purpose. I quote (as always unless otherwise stated) from Priestley's diary:

Both tents now have a blubber lamp made by suspending a few strands of lamp-wick from a safety-pin which is stretched as a bridge across the mouth of a small Oxo tin full of melted oil. The light is splendid, better than I should have thought possible, and the lamps will be very economical. The only drawback at present is the expenditure of paraffin oil necessary to melt the blubber. We must make the lamps melt their own oil when we get into our winter home. The lamps also give a surprising amount of heat and very little smoke. We ate the pieces of blubber after the oil had been extracted from them and found them excellent. They tasted to me equal to any ordinary variety of fat one gets at home.

The acceptance of blubber was important. All except Campbell came to be able to eat it, oil included, with some degree of pleasure. Abbott and Dickason said it tasted of melon. But the real achievement was the invention of the lamp by these same A.Bs. Priestley admitted that there had been moments of blackness in more senses than one, and it was the creation of perpetual light, or light at will, that marked the dawn of invincible optimism.

They needed that, for as March came in like a polar bear they were still in their tattered tents – with the whole winter before them. It took almost three weeks to chip out a habitable cave from the old snowdrift which had consolidated into a miniature icecap. Campbell, Priestley and Dickason camped on the site, and as soon as they had made a large enough excavation they slept inside it, bunging up the entrance with their tent canvas jammed in place with ice axes.

Levick, Abbott and Browning, who were still camping on the moraine, were less fortunate. At eight o'clock on the morning of 10th March, a hurricane gust broke three of the four stout bamboo poles as if they had been reeds and pressed the tent down on top of them. They endured in their sleeping-bags sandwiched between wind and rocks until evening. They had a lump of raw seal meat, frozen hard. They nibbled off the corners, but once it became streamlined it might as well have been a stone, and of course they could not light a stove to thaw it. They decided to make a move before dark. They could not take their precious sleeping-bags; the wind would soon have stolen them. So they left everything inside the flattened tent, which they weighted down with rocks and lumps of ice, and then crawled on hands and knees to Inexpressible Island, going flat on their bellies in the gusts. Thus they reached the barricaded cave entrance and shouted against the storm until they were let in. After supper there was a sing-song which was finally silenced by the increasing cold. The men had been in high spirits but they did not see anything funny about sleeping two to a bag – or not until the night was over.

After that night the Levick trio somehow fetched their kit and lived on the job with the others. When basically completed – there were later improvements – *Sea View* was an ice-chamber 14 ft. × 9 ft. in area and 5 ft. 6 in. high, not quite lofty enough to permit standing upright but they dared not chip out more in case the roof fell in.

That is a prosaic, civilian description of one of His Majesty's shore establishments. The first seven feet of H.M.S. *Sea View* was the galley. Beyond that was, to port, the ward room and, to starboard, the mess deck. When the party lay down in their sleeping-bags, snug and overlapping as sardines in a tin, the officers were in their quarters and the men in theirs, and either could say what they liked about the other. Though there might be a sing-song in which everybody joined, naval discipline ruled – except that there was no question of privilege over the unpleasant jobs that had to be done.

The wind blew hard for the next 180 days without lulls of more than a few hours, generally of only minutes or even seconds. Since the men's clothing was so thin and worn that even covered parts of their bodies were liable to be frostbitten, they went out of the cave only for necessities. These consisted of freshwater ice (consolidated snow) for drinking, salt-water ice for cooking (they had no salt), hunting, or bringing in portions of a seal from a cache.

Priestley had calculated that they would need at least fifteen seals to get them through the winter on half rations, and at the beginning of their durance in the cave they had only six. Weddell seals, for all their grace and agility in the water, are enormous slugs when on the ice; and as they made no attempt to flipper-run away – since killer whales cannot follow them out of the water – hunting consisted of no more than sighting them. But this meant long patrols along the rocky foreshore or on the ice. Once killed, the seals had to be chopped up into portable pieces and cached in a safe place. They were far too big to be moved whole and, in any case, there would have been no room for one in the cave. So apart from hunting there was heavy porterage of frozen meat and ice; and this had to be done over an uneven slippery surface under the buffetings of wind. The men used to argue as to whether the gusts or the lulls were worse; a gust knocked you over backwards, and in a sudden lull you went on your face.

The force of these gales was best conveyed by a diary entry from the year before. Priestley was in charge of meteorology as well as geology. A pebble thrown by a breaking wave from a 'safe' distance from their hut went through the glass of an instrument as cleanly as a bullet, not shattering the rest.

Only ice collection was a daily task; a load of seal meat stored in the passageway lasted quite a time – it had to. None of them liked seal much; it is rather tasteless. But they never had enough of it. They were always hungry, with achingly unfilled bellies. The thin hooch was thickened with a dicing of blubber; it was found that this shape released least oil into the gravy. Some of the party further thickened their own mugfuls with the dried seaweed that had been found well above the high-water mark and was used for insulating the floor; but Priestley would not allow this to be cooked as a general ingredient, for he believed it had been walked on by penguins for at least a century and what gave it flavour might be unhealthy. One or two of the men became addicted to it, however, or resorted to it from sheer hunger, and would reach out from their sleeping-bags in the night for a piece to chew.

One seal was a bonanza. It was found to contain thirty-six fish which it had swallowed so recently that two were still alive. The whole party had a fish supper and a fish breakfast. Any change was appreciated. Adélie penguin was much preferred to seal. It had a taste of its own, and when available made 'a different meal'. They soon wanted change of taste even more than additional food.

If ever men ate to live instead of living to eat, it was these six. Yet they were obsessed with thoughts of food and for them the word 'luxury' had an infinitely richer meaning than it has for people in ordinary life.

Once they were settled in the cave, Priestley opened the cases of emergency rations which had been cached on landing, before the geologising trip up the glaciers. He at once put aside sufficient to supply a month-long sledge journey on half rations to the main base in the spring, also some Oxo and a few goodies for birthdays and other celebrations. The remainder he handed out in quantities sufficient to last throughout the winter. The following constituted their luxuries: 12 lumps of sugar to each man every Sunday, 1½ oz. of chocolate every Saturday and alternate Wednesday, 25 raisins on the last day of each month, and 1 biscuit a day.

The most important daily item because the most durable (if not over-baked) was the biscuit. Here, however, there was difficulty: most were broken, some smashed into many pieces. So one whole biscuit was kept as a model and the individual rations jig-sawed together to its proportions. But no amount of care could make the six identical; there remained a choice, or an imagined choice, that had to be obviated. . . . The six fabricated biscuits were set out on the lid of a box. One man knelt in front of them while a second turned his back. The first man pointed at a biscuit and asked, "Whose is this?", and the second man answered with a name.

This excellent plan broke down over discipline. The three A.Bs could not bring themselves to name the party except in order of seniority, starting with Campbell and ending with the most junior of themselves, Dickason.

Much of their behaviour may seem childish. It is child-like. Such an existence brings out the essential qualities of childhood, the foundation of life.

Levick used to read aloud in the evenings, first a chapter a night of *David Copperfield*, then *The Life of Stevenson*, then *Simon the Jester*. That was their library, and thus rationed lasted them about half way through the winter. But every Saturday night after toasting sweethearts and wives in cocoa just strong enough to neutralise the taste of oil, they lay and sang. On Sunday nights they sang with a religious bias. From their pooled memories they 'managed to patch up a few hymns', and after a while they 'got through the Te Deum without a hitch'. The last day of a month, birthdays, every festival evoked their repertoire. The only trouble about singing was that, like exercise which they avoided as much as possible, it made them still more hungry.

Priestley had the gift of recognising blessings in disguise. He described the paucity of seals and penguins as one of these. Had there been unlimited meat and fat they would, he believed, have become liverish, quarrelsome and ill. Instead they were hungry, fit and good-tempered.

Another effect of their short rations was that they dreamed about food. After an early preoccupation with rescue and catastrophe, their subconscious minds were forever sitting down to a meal. Priestley told me that the smokers – soon reduced to raisin stalks, seaweed, secondhand tea-leaves and the dried grass used in the Finnish fur boots – also dreamed of real tobacco. But for the most part each man dreamed of his favourite food – or rather of the food he most longed for in the circumstances, which is not necessarily the same thing. Priestley dreamed of his schooldays' favourite, treacle tart with breadcrumbs. He was rash enough to mention this in his book – with the result that every hostess who had done her homework gave him treacle tart for the rest of his long life.

All but one of the party woke as the food neared their mouths. But

Murray Levick ate country-house afternoon teas and even went through the whole menu of a City banquet – which he described in detail over the real-life breakfast.

One food dream was common to them all – except Levick, I suppose. A man woke (in his dream), felt hungry and suddenly remembered that there was a confectioner-tobacconist shop just over the hill. So he got out of his sleeping-bag and crawled out of the cave, experiencing all the real inconveniences of this action. He hurried to the shop, and found that it was afternoon and early-closing day. The day was always the early-closing day of his home-town.

The dreams of rescue or disaster which varied the food dreams concerned themselves and the *Terra Nova*. They often thought and sometimes talked in the evenings about the Polar sledge party. But they never dreamed that it suffered disaster.

The actual diet did not suit them all. Browning was upset by the salt water used for cooking and had diarrhoea for seven months. The cook and messman spent a good deal of time cutting up the meat, melting ice, tending the fire, obstructing the passage of anyone going out or coming in. The door measured 2 ft 6 in. by 18 in. Fortunately Browning was the smallest of the party.

During their brief-as-possible sorties the six men watched with practical interest – for their chances of survival would be affected by the result – the continual battle of ever-changing fortune between the wind and the cold.

A full gale swept out all the sea ice and left a turmoil of breaking waves. Then, with a decrease of wind or increase of cold, ice crystals formed. They calmed the waves much more effectively than oil, binding and forcing them down. The crystals coagulated into a complete covering like a tarpaulin. The next scene was of undulations moving snake-like with the swell.

As the ice thickened, it lost its elasticity and was shattered by the heaving into fragments a foot or two across. These ground together and formed pancakes of ice. (Note the food metaphor. The round pieces look more like large water-lily flowers.) If there was little wind, the cold bound the fragments together. The scene was then again one of continuous ice stretching to the horizon. If this was consolidated it would be possible to walk on water to the base in McMurdo Sound.

But, because of currents or tides, a crack appeared between stranded icebergs or two points of land. A reinforced wind exploited this, widened it, whipped up new waves which smashed the ice before it was thick enough to resist and soon swept the whole seascape clear except for a narrow margin where the ice was bound to the rocks, or where a cove or headland sheltered it.

One day when Campbell and Priestley were watching this drama – the rapidity with which the changes came was dramatic – they thought they saw a rescue party approaching. The winter light was bad but the four figures were too big for penguins and they advanced in extended order as if drawing a sledge. Campbell went back to the cave for his binoculars.

The figures were too big for Adélies – they were Emperors. These ninety pound birds indeed proved to be a rescue party, for the cavemen were particularly short of food just then. Priestley remarked on how quickly their hard life destroyed sentiment. They killed without emotion, as do animals.

But the Emperors took their revenge. Though the meat was preferable to seal, the blubber was not. It was all oil, and this instead of gravy was more than their long-suffering stomachs could take. The men drank as much as they could and poured the rest of their mugfuls into the reading-lamps where it burned beautifully.

It was by this time May, full winter yet more than a month to Midwinter's Day, so any change there might be could still only be for the worse. This was the darkest hour of the year. But for the invention of the blubber lamps (invention because none of them had Arctic experience), they would literally have been in darkness in the cave, not only at night. They were short even of matches. When Campbell, having awakened, guessed it was about seven o'clock in the morning, he wound his chronometer watch. If it took eight turns he had guessed right; it was twenty-four hours since he had last wound it. If it took only seven turns he was three hours too early. He had to judge the interval, then ask Levick to wind his watch as a check.

At seven, as near as might be, Abbott was told to strike the one match of the day and light a lamp. From this other lamps and the stove were lit with spills. The cook and messman started their laborious chores.

The rota was one day on and two days off domestic duties. Barring outside tasks, the two days were spent idling. However energetic they might be by nature they were all by this time sailing at half stream or less, content to laze. They did not even talk much, having run out of conversation. They were fairly comfortable. The floor was well insulated with pebbles and seaweed, the ice walls with snowblocks to a height of three feet. This was high enough and left a convenient shelf. They did not want it too warm, not above freezing, or the place dripped or icicles dropped into their sleeping-bags.

But the cook and messman felt the cold and had a busy time, fetching in ice and meat and chipping a joint up for the hooch with the geological hammer and chisel. The fire needed constant attention although it had been highly developed from the early days. There was an ingenious method of drip feed from suspended strips of blubber. And Levick had hit on the idea of using old bones as firebricks. The bones came from a seals' cemetery on the mainland and being dry as blotting paper sucked up the hot oil, so that if the fire went out in a fit of temperament it could be relit quite simply with a spill. But it smoked. At risk to the roof they had chipped out a chimney, but orange wreaths of blubber gas belched upwards from the flames and wandered up and down under the low ceiling. Apart from the inconvenience the gas caused to breathing, it attacked the eyes. The cook quite often had to lie down temporarily blinded and sometimes was incapacitated for quite a long time. 'Smoke' was inadequate to describe this caustic gas. Browning from his West Country background brought out 'smitch'. Thereafter smitch-blindness was a term in frequent use.

Although they were always hungry, they grew deadly tired of their unvarying diet. Kidneys, livers, hearts and brains were put into cold storage for Midwinter's Day, so it was just plain boiled meat with such flavour as sea water gave it – and of course blubber. They developed a longing for 'clean-tasting food'. And the biscuits from the current tin were overbaked. Being crisp they cracked and vanished in the mouth instead of providing half an hour of gnawing. Priestley's diary for the month is spattered with references to the privation thus caused. This may sound trivial but it was not; it definitely lowered morale.

I do not think Murray Levick (the only one of the sailors I knew) rose more than he felt he had to but he always did to an occasion. He opened the medical chest and got out tabloids of ginger, of citric acid, and lime juice. 'It was an exquisite pleasure to eat anything we knew to be clean and which had no taste of meat about it,' Priestley noted.

Spurred by praise and gratitude, the doctor offered a mustard plaster for the hooch. This caused great anticipatory excitement. But the result was disappointing. They could not taste it. The recipe should have been '. . . add *three* mustard plasters'.

Captain Scott's Northern Party
(*Back row*: Abbott, Dickason, Browning; *front row*: Priestley, Campbell, Levick)

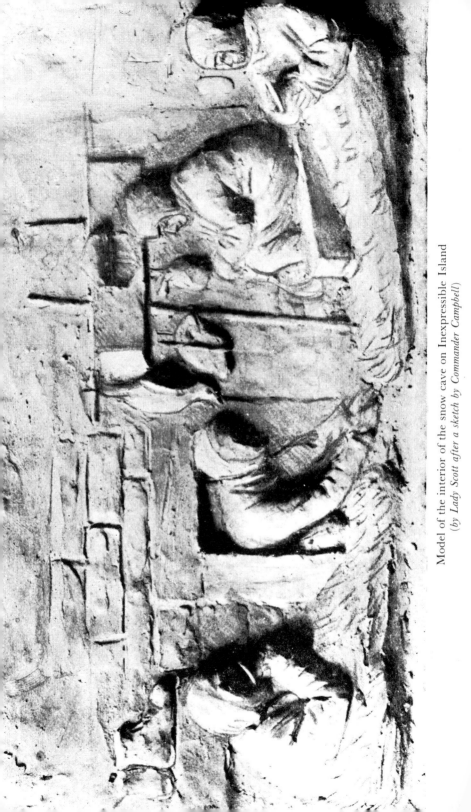

Model of the interior of the snow cave on Inexpressible Island
(*by Lady Scott after a sketch by Commander Campbell*)

So the watches were wound, and ran down, throughout the long dark days to midwinter. But less than a month before this festival all six men were nearly snuffed out. This is the diary entry for 25th May:

Westerly wind with heavy drift continues, and we have been drifted up all day. This afternoon we had to do away with the blubber fires because of the smitch, for the drift kept on filling the chimney and preventing the draught from flowing. Afterwards Dickason started the hooch over the primus, and this rapidly used up our limited supply of oxygen. First of all the reading lamps went out and refused to be lighted with a flaring spill, and then the spill went out and could not be relighted at the primus. Next the primus went out and could not be relighted because the matches would not burn. By this time we were opening up the chimney and the drift at the entrance to the shaft, and Campbell drove his ice axe through the latter with immediate relief to everybody. Since then things have gone pretty well, but we all have had headaches, which we had put down to the smitch, but which were more probably directly due to lack of oxygen. It is a great nuisance this new danger having arisen after we thought we had avoided the utmost malice of the weather, but it is lucky we were not caught at night and asphyxiated in our beds.

Thereafter a bamboo pole was kept in the chimney to clear it. But snow-bearing gales gave them a lot more trouble. They had cut a shaft outside the entrance, a sort of communication trench, and roofed it over. Blizzards filled this up in no time, and the messman could not fetch the necessities for the day. He was faced with the seemingly impossible task of having to dig away the snow before he had anywhere to throw it. When he did get outside he was blinded, half suffocated and almost certainly knocked over by the wild white eddies. Under such conditions it is by no means impossible for a man to become lost when only a yard from home.

But they all survived to see Midwinter's Day. The Commissariat Officer – as the housekeeper was properly described – had some time previously worked out what he could spare for the feast and noted it in his diary:

I am serving out four biscuits, four sticks of chocolate, twenty raisins, and fourteen lumps of sugar per man, increasing both hooches to three-quarters ration and we are having full ration of cocoa as in the hut [the year before] with four lumps of sugar per man in the cocoa. Our bottle of

Wincarnis [from the medical chest] will give us a good tot each, and we ought to turn in well satisfied with the world.

On the great day they all had a wash. They could not afford to use blubber to heat water for so non-nutritive a purpose, but they had what was called a Browning Wash. Browning had crawled in from outside, his balaclava helmet white with snow. When this was remarked on he took the helmet off and rubbed it on his face. This had an appreciable effect, for they were all 'like well-kippered herrings' from the smitch. They dressed for the occasion in that they did not take off any clothes, and all except the messmen had the meal in bed. By custom there was a pause for notes and diaries, and this evening Priestley wrote:

> Levick and I have just finished an excellent day as messmen. The hooch, flavoured with seal's brain and penguin's liver, was sublime, the Wincarnis tasted strongly of muscatel grape, and the sweet cocoa was the best drink I have had for nine months. The only accident of the day was when I upset my Wincarnis, but we had so much else that I did not miss it much. The smokers are having a cigar and the sixth of a plug each, and we are looking forward to a long and cheerful evening. Since we started to serve out the hooch the igloo has resounded with chorus after chorus and they have all gone splendidly. . . . We really have had a much more enjoyable day even than last Midwinter Day, and it is comforting to think that every day now the sun will come nearer and nearer to us until on August 10th he will be above the theoretical horizon, though owing to the foothills to the north of us we shall not see him until the 15th or later.

Hopes for the future were high. They hoped to be able to leave on their journey of salvation in August – in not much more than a month from that 22nd June. They began to repair the sledges, to mend the tents, to try to patch their clothes; and Priestley put away slices of undercut for sledging-rations. But the battle between wind and cold remained unresolved and the sea was never covered with ice for long. To the south of them the Drygalski Glacier stuck out a tongue thirty miles long into the sea. They needed stable ice conditions to round that. The steep and crevassed inland levels of the glacier would be slow and difficult to cross; they would need longer days than August would bring. Therefore they could not start until September.

That meant that there would be not even one biscuit a day during the intervening period, for the sacred sledging-ration could not be touched. They had suffered psychologically from a month of overbaked biscuits. They now suffered physically on none at all. And something began to poison them.

Browning, as has been said, had been ill throughout the winter. The sea water was thought to be the cause. He was given special hooches boiled in fresh water, and steaks fried on the primus using the precious paraffin. His condition improved for a while, but not for long. Dr Levick feared for his life and watched over him unceasingly, but admitted later that it was the patient's indestructible cheerfulness that kept him going.

Then they all became ill. The hooch the day before had tasted strangely. But they were used to that. The wrong things often got into food and drink. Priestley had managed to keep the secret that when cook he had fished out a lump of raw liver from the boiling cocoa. Feathers and unidentified objects often got into the pot; they drank with their teeth clenched. The cave was dim from shortage of light and black from smitch. Paradoxically, as it may seem, the only clean part of the walls was near the stove – because the thawing ice washed itself there. When frozen meat was cut up with hammer and chisel, fragments flew all over the place and a collection had to be made. It was never quite certain that a piece picked up from the seaweed floor had not been there for days. And the cooks found that the only time their hands were clean was after preparing the meat. The conditions were not hygienic. But there was not much to be done about it except to try to be more careful.

Soon after the first attack they all, except Campbell, who had been strong-minded enough to refuse a strange-tasting hooch, became quite seriously incapacitated. Levick diagnosed ptomaine poisoning. The disease was virulent and lasting, a bad preparation for a sledge journey by men already weakened by months of short rations and little exercise. In desperation they changed the old oven (in which the meat was thawed) for the last emptied biscuit tin. This was an improvement but did not effect a complete cure.

On top of all that the roof began to fall in.

They finally got away on 1st October. That cured most of them. The clean conditions, the sledging luxuries so long kept in store and, most of all, the exhilaration of at last being on the move towards comfort and companionship worked a miracle. To crown their happiness the day was fine and calm. But they managed to cover only a couple of miles before the two tents were pitched for the first night.

Browning was 'wholly incapacitated with diarrhoea and general weakness and Dickason half crippled by the former'.

Although the midwinter feast was the only occasion when they had not gone to bed hungry, they had got through the winter without suffering from malnutrition. This was a great achievement by the male housekeeper. Would they have been better off with a woman – ignoring any complications of sex, of course, thinking only of the profession of housewifery? She might have been more sophisticated but scarcely as calm.

Yet, at the period of poisoning, the cave beginning to fall in and preparations for a journey of some doubtfulness, Priestley shows in his diary symptoms of serious mental stress. He could not find the rock specimens he had cached the autumn before on the moraine. He induced invalids to help him and finally searched with unconcealed desperation. Then Campbell strolled over and found the box of rocks at once, eighteen inches outside the area Priestley had marked out as the maximum worth excavation in the winter snow.

The journey down the coast was hard. It was considerably longer than the 200 mile straight-line distance, for they had to travel inland until they had crossed the Drygalski Glacier, the wind having been victorious over this extent of the battlefield. And the rest of the way was nearly all rough ice. It took them two months instead of the estimated four weeks. But, compared with the winter they had come through, the sledging can be considered as little more than routine. The party had another scare of ptomaine poisoning when the meat they were carrying in bags became tainted in the warmth of the sun. They were able to replace it when they met a seal, but Browning would certainly have died if the rest of the party had not contributed to his biscuit ration. For a while they were all reduced to minimum working-rations. They progressed slowly, often having to relay their load and sometimes covering only a very few miles in a day. But privation was over when they came on a depot left in April when an attempt to reach them had been stopped by open water. They lay up for two days and stuffed themselves like schoolboys. Even after this, when they reached the base at McMurdo Sound, Priestley weighed under 10 stone. Within six days he went up to 12 stone 5, which must be a record for de-slimming.

So their longing for food was reduced before they reached the base, but not their longing for news. And they arrived to find the hut empty.

Soon Debenham and Archer, who had been left in charge, came back from a short trip. Most of the officers and men had returned the autumn before to New Zealand on the *Terra Nova*, which (they heard later) had been prevented by storms and ice from coming back to Evans' Coves. The rest, ten men led by Atkinson, had gone south along the Polar trail as soon as the weather made travel possible. It had for some months been realised, of course, that Captain Scott and his four companions must be dead. But whether the bodies and the priceless records could be found after the terrible winter was more than doubtful.

They were found, and the diaries told the sad, heroic story. This was the greeting of the Northern Party who had survived their own trial for life and returned in a mood of dreams come true. But they had had an education that no other school provides. Priestley summed up what he had learned. 'Pleasure can be as acute as pain and may be derived from things as small and simple as an unexpected lump of sugar.'

This discovery brought him a contentment more valuable to the science of living than his rock specimens. He lived to be ninety-two.

4

The Million Dollar Ticket

I f you were likely to inherit a million what would be your ambition? Lincoln Ellsworth never had any doubt, nor any practical choice. He was, he admitted, a hero worshipper and a sentimentalist. He could not follow in the footsteps of the frontier marshal, Wyatt Earp, 'the bravest man I ever heard of', because the Wild West had been tamed. But there were still vast areas in the polar regions to explore. He prepared to do so, in a sentimental way, by dreaming.

His father, who was a millionaire, might have helped to make these dreams come true. But he did the opposite. James W. Ellsworth had made his fortune by single-minded determination and was absorbed in investing it as a collector. He had acquired the Schloss Lenzburg in Switzerland, the Villa Palmieri in Florence and so many works of art that he had to build a new residence to house them. He did not mind his son working off his energy as an axeman on a railway survey, but he would not have the heir to his business and his treasures risking his life on some hairbrained Arctic project. Thus Lincoln's early schemes were stillborn, and so things remained until he was forty-four.

The clash of wills between father and son developed to crisis point when Roald Amundsen arrived in New York in the autumn of 1924. The explorer who had been at the South Pole and had navigated both the north-west and north-east passages wanted to fly to the North Pole, but was bankrupt. A sour and grizzled man of fifty-two, he had come to the United States on the slim chance of being able to make enough money for his purpose by lecturing.

Lincoln Ellsworth sought him out at his hotel on the first night and offered – father permitting – to pay for the expedition if he was flown to the Pole. Amundsen naturally was delighted at this stroke of fortune. But father did not permit; he would not even lend the money

74

to his son. Yet Lincoln persisted and at last the old man who had never before done anything against his better judgment agreed, first to meet Amundsen, then to put up $85,000 to buy two long-range aircraft. The price seems modest but the dollar was then worth twenty times more than it is now.

A contract was at once drawn up and signed before witnesses – at the extra cost of family goodwill. James Ellsworth never forgave his son for persuading him to change his mind.

Amundsen went back to Norway to set the preparations in motion. For pilots he chose Hjalmar Riier-Larsen and Leif Dietrichsen and sent them off to select suitable aircraft. They settled on Dornier-Wal flying boats with twin 450 h.p. Rolls-Royce engines and duralumin hulls. After these had been purchased, still more money was needed – the fees for the two pilots and two mechanics, food, winter travel equipment, transport to King's Bay, Spitsbergen, from which the flight was to be made. But money breeds money. All this was covered by the Aero Club of Norway which thereafter came to rule the character of the expedition. It was to be purely Norwegian, carrying the Norwegian flag to be planted at the Pole, and with Amundsen as commander. Ellsworth's money bought him only a place as 'observer' on one of the two aircraft.

He crossed the Atlantic from New York by liner in March 1925 and was dined by Amundsen in Oslo, Norwegian fashion, until the whole expedition sailed for Spitsbergen from Tromsø in two overladen little ships. At King's Bay there was another hospitable pause while the flying boats, N24 and N25, were made ready. On 25th May they flew north, taking off from ice which provided a better surface for heavily laden planes than water.

Ellsworth wrote in *Beyond Horizons*:

> I don't know how any of the other five felt at that moment, but in me there was not the slightest trace of fear. I know that in that silent throng there were men who never expected to see us again. In New York and Oslo were plenty of people who regarded our flight as stark suicide. . . . Yet if my own pulse quickened then, it was only with elation that at last I had accomplished the ambition of my life.

He may have accomplished his ambition yet the flight was only just beginning. The official plan, approved by the Norwegian Aero Club, was to fly to the Pole over 500 miles away, land there for observations and then fly back – daring enough in those pioneer days. But Ellsworth says that their secret intention was, at the Pole, to transfer men and fuel from one plane to the other and then fly on to Alaska, six men in the refuelled machine. We need not bother about the practicability of this for it was not attempted. But it shows the boldness of the party.

They flew above fog for two hours. 'It was unreal, mystic, fraught with prophecy.' It was also cold, for the cockpits were open and the big machines were trundling along at 75 m.p.h. They flew abreast but without communication because N24, Ellsworth's machine, had no wireless set. He, sitting in the nose, saw Amundsen in the other nose, stooped and apparently writing. There was nothing else for an observer to observe except the twin haloes below the aeroplane and its shadow loping over the undulations of the fog-roof.

Then the fog dissolved. They were above ice floes, open leads of water between, with a view of sixty or seventy miles in every direction. Ellsworth felt that he had never seen anything so beautiful, and he was impressed by the thought that 'Every hour we were putting behind us a journey that would take a sledge party a week to accomplish. Every hour we added to known geography more than 9,000 square miles of the earth's surface. . . . But it grew monotonous, the endless white expanse'.

Thus they continued for seven hours. The midnight sun shone straight ahead. Ellsworth's 'shaky observations' with his sextant told him that they had reached 'a very high latitude'. They must soon land – but where? There was far more ice than water, not the smooth bay ice from which they had taken off but tilted, tangled floes. Even if they had ski undercarriages they could not safely have come down.

In these conditions Ellsworth appears to have felt nothing stronger than surprise when he saw N25 dip and begin to spiral down, Amundsen waving for N24 to follow, which Dietrichsen did. The crew of N24 saw the commander's plane drop between hummocks and ridges, where it disappeared. Dietrichsen sought for a possible landing place, came down with a bump and put his machine out of action.

There followed twenty-five days of strain and frustration. For five of these days the two crews were separated. For the remaining twenty they worked with a hand axe, knives, ice anchors and wooden shovels to make a runway for N25. Amundsen calculated that they moved 300 tons of ice and snow. If they should fail to get their remaining machine into the air – with six men on board – the alternative to static starvation was a 400-mile walk over rough pack ice to the almost uninhabited East Greenland coast. In fact their position seemed about as hopeless as it could be.

Ellsworth described his mental state as 'a sort of blessed apathy'. Besides that lack of sensation he recorded pride. They had come down not actually at the North Pole but in Latitude 87° 44', 136 nautical miles short of it. But while airborne their view had extended to within ninety miles of the Pole.

N25 did manage to take off, and with the petrol from the wrecked N24 managed to get close enough to Spitsbergen to be picked up by a sealer. Thus the 'scientific results, from an expedition that cost 150,000 dollars, consisted in the exploration of 120,000 square miles of hitherto unknown regions and the taking of two [echo] soundings which showed the depth of the Polar Sea at that latitude to be 12,000 feet'.

Leave aside the exploration, if absence of fear is courage, Ellsworth was the bravest man I ever knew. It was not inappropriate that he received from the King of Norway the Gold Medal for saving life. (He had pulled to safety two of his companions who fell through the ice.) His courage fully deserved recognition.

He came to England and visited the Royal Geographical Society where I was doing a minor job. The secretary, Arthur Hinks, deputed me to take him about London. I wondered what one did with a millionaire – by then he had inherited from his father who had died of pneumonia while Ellsworth was marooned in the Arctic. He was twice my age, active and upright, with a parchment face and hair just long enough to be nearly brushed. He told me that all he wanted was exercise. He liked to walk eighteen miles a day. But not in town, fortunately. He was as modest and unassuming a man as I have ever met. He neither patronised nor snubbed my eagerness, yet confided nothing. He said nothing about his recent experience or his plans for the future. We parted as good friends with a recognised but unmentioned common interest. He was a polite oyster, essentially modest and gently spoken – when he spoke.

It is evident that he opened his heart to Amundsen. He was dominated by that old bachelor Viking. 'His long head and hooked nose gave him the look of an eagle, an effect which the imperial white moustache accentuated. Yet his eyes were the most arresting feature. Years spent on the decks of vessels and amid limitless sweeps of ice and snow had given them a chronic squint. Through narrowed lids peered those grey eyes, boring through one as their gaze passed on into infinite distances.' This corkscrew effect held Ellsworth. Not only would they reach the Pole but fly right across the Arctic basin. There were still a million square miles of unseen ocean.

After his experience with flying boats, Amundsen's inclination was towards airships, which had a far greater range. A zeppelin was prohibitively expensive even for a millionaire but the comparatively small semi-rigid dirigibles that Colonel Umberto Nobile was building in Italy appeared entirely suitable – if Mussolini would sell. He proved ready to sell at a very reasonable price. No doubt he saw a flight from Spitsbergen via the North Pole to Alaska as excellent publicity for N1, the available airship. Amundsen and Ellsworth could have her for $75,000, and Mussolini would take her back for $46,000 if still in good condition. His main stipulation was that five of the airship's Italian crew should travel on the flight along with the Norwegians who would make up the number to sixteen. Nobile, being approached to act as pilot, accepted $11,000. It was further agreed that the enterprise should be known as the Amundsen-Ellsworth-Nobile expedition, a three-nation affair, with the airship being named *Norge*. The Norwegian Aero Club had stepped in, accepting all expenses above Ellsworth's $90,000 plus (at the last moment) $25,000 for insurance. The Aero Club's contribution, covering the construction of a hangar at King's Bay and the provision of sea transport, brought the gross cost up to something approaching half a million dollars. However, on the credit side there were press, book and film rights. Amundsen was no businessman but his name was worth a lot.

In April *Norge* flew up from Rome, 5,000 miles in 103 hours, and reached King's Bay where Amundsen and Ellsworth were waiting for her. She had already covered more than twice the distance she would have to in the Arctic. If the weather proved fair – and a wide network of reporting stations had been arranged – the flight should encounter no difficulties.

They had a rival at least as far as the North Pole. Commander Richard Byrd and his pilot Floyd Bennett had arrived at the end of April with their Fokker monoplane on board the *Chantier*. Byrd's official purpose, says Ellsworth, was to search for Crocker Land, the mirage of mountains seen by Peary on a polar journey. But in fact he flew straight to the Pole and back on 7th May. His flight made no claim to scientific value; it was merely an achievement. Crocker Land had been forgotten – if it had been seriously considered. Any anxiety for the *Norge* team came from fear that they might have to go to Byrd's assistance at the expense of their own flight to Alaska.

The *Norge* flew on 10th May, and in almost perfect weather followed the same route to the Pole. There they stood with bared heads while the three national flags were dropped, and circled low for an hour. 'There was really nothing to see', said Ellsworth. To back this up he quoted Conrad, 'There is no more evanescent quality in an accomplished fact than its wonderfulness. Solicited incessantly by the considerations affecting its fears and desires, the human mind turns naturally away from the marvellous side of events'.

So far so disillusioning, but their 1,500-mile course on to Nome, their destination in Alaska, had never been travelled. The Canadian archipelago, the scene of the north-west passage and the Franklin search, lay to the east of it. They were about to penetrate an area blank on the map.

The first land they saw after two days and nights was the Alaskan coast. It must have been very cold and uncomfortable in the cabin, which was a structure of basket work and canvas only thirty feet long by six broad and with no more than folding camp stools to sit on. Although it was continuously light they saw the land only briefly and dimly, for by then they were in fog. The weather had steadily deteriorated since passing the Pole and now they did not know their location. They glimpsed an Eskimo village and thought of going down to ask the way to Nome. One wonders what response they would have received if they had. Every wireless station within range was listening for them, but they had lost contact because their trailing aerial was iced over. The whole airship was covered by a ton of ice. Pieces flew off and made punctures in the envelope which had to be mended quickly.

For another twenty-four hours they zigzagged about until they caught a few words of a message from Nome. After three days and nights of sleeplessness and strain they were exhausted, and landed without danger at the village of Teller, ninety miles from Nome. This was a creditable feat by the pilot and crew without a trained land gang to help them. But unfortunately on the financial side the *Norge* could not be returned to Mussolini in good condition for her fabric was torn to pieces by souvenir hunters.

As for scientific results they could, the observer says, 'conservatively claim to have looked down on a hundred thousand square miles of unexplored territory. . . . We had established the scientific fact that the North Polar Region is a vast, deep ice-covered sea. The white patch on top of the globe could now be tinted blue.'

For a while thereafter Ellsworth felt that his life's ambition was accomplished, that he was done with the Polar Regions. He began hunting fossil algae from the Grand Canyon to Labrador. But the algae didn't hold him long, they lacked something. Riier-Larsen, Sir Douglas Mauson, Wilkins and Byrd were flying about in Antarctica. At the Schloss Lensburg in the spring of 1930 Hubert Wilkins (not yet knighted) came and talked to him about crossing the North Pole in a submarine. Ellsworth became enthusiastic and was ready to put up money as 'scientific adviser', but not actually to go on the expedition. (This was just as well for the ancient *Nautilus* never got under the ice.) They talked of flying in the Antarctic and Wilkins offered to act as an adviser if his host ever went there. Their talks were long and on a bold scale in Barbarossa's castle.

When Wilkins went off on his submarine attempt Ellsworth answered a cabled invitation from Dr Eckener and boarded the Graf Zeppelin at Friedrichshafen as 'Arctic navigation expert', and also 'explorer for the American Geographical Society'. Fifteen scientists did a cruise of Franz Josef Land, Nova Zembla, Nicholas II Land and the Taimur Peninsula – Arctic de Luxe, Ellsworth called it – 8,000 miles in six days. Goodness knows what it cost. Then he was back in New York waiting for Wilkins to re-emerge and talk about Antarctica. He was determined to go on one more expedition, and to be its leader. He was over fifty and there was no time to lose. This last venture had to be something really big.

When Wilkins appeared they pored over the map of Antarctica. The Southern Continent, almost as large as North America, has something the shape of a tadpole. The tail – Graham Land, South Shetlands, South Orkneys, South Georgia – curls up towards South America. The great mass of the body is roughly spherical with two large indentations – the Weddell Sea to the east of the tail which faces the Atlantic, and the Ross Sea facing New Zealand and the Pacific.

How best to do something big in this vast area? Ellsworth's first idea was to cruise round the Pacific Quadrant and make deep penetrations of the continent in an aeroplane catapulted from the ship. This had to be abandoned because his pilot considered catapulting too risky. So he changed to another plan which was surely no less hazardous – to fly from the Ross Sea over the continent to the Weddell Sea, and back. This double journey would be 3,400 miles. 'But dependable aeroplanes were being turned out with that range and more,' he says.

He had resolved to allow himself the best of men and materials for this expedition. He hired the most experienced pilot, Bernt Balchen, who had flown to the South Pole with Byrd. He sent him to California to watch over the building of a special plane by the Northrup Company. His personal assistant was Sir Hubert Wilkins, 'a most thoughtful and sanely courageous man'. He retained him for over three years. Wilkins advised that the best type of base ship would be a Norwegian trawler. Ellsworth sent him to Norway to buy him one. He named her *Wyatt Earp*.

'On this, my own expedition, I could indulge every whim and fancy that did not interfere with efficiency,' he says, 'and one of my whims was to imbue the whole enterprise with the spirit of Wyatt Earp.' He stocked the ship with books about the frontier marshal and those lawless days. The Norwegian crewmen who understood English translated the books to the non-English speakers, he says. (Can one picture them doing it?) He hung Wyatt Earp's cartridge belt in his cabin, and determined to carry it on his trans-antarctic flight. Thus, in a sense, his two lifelong dreams were combined. If he could not follow in the footsteps of Wyatt Earp, the frontier marshal would accompany him to the polar regions.

His flight would be recorded by camera. Still in search of perfection he went for lessons to 'the best photographer of mountains in the world', Walter Mittelholzer who operated from Zurich. Here he met 'a slender, long limbed, dark haired, brown eyed young woman. . . . I protracted my camera instruction for two weeks, greatly to my technical and domestic advantage. . . . At the end of my two weeks in Zurich I, a lone eagle of fifty-two and almost a creature of the womanless parts of the earth, was engaged to marry Mary Louise Ulmer'.

The wedding trip was a voyage to New Zealand. There Ellsworth joined the *Wyatt Earp* and, sending his wife home, sailed to the Ross Sea. The ship was anchored to the bay ice not far from Little America, Byrd's large deserted base from which he and Bernt Balchen had flown to the South Pole. The Northrup ski plane, *Polar Star*, was unloaded on to the ice and Balchen and Ellsworth made a short successful trial flight. Everything was set for the double crossing.

During the night the thick ice unaccountably broke up. There was no storm. Ellsworth thought the cause must be seismic. The result was that the 37,000 dollar *Polar Star* had to be shipped back to California for extensive repairs and the whole expedition, costing $5,000 a month in running expenses alone, was off for a year at least.

This disaster possibly saved Ellsworth's life for his plans had been hazardous. His only havens were the *Wyatt Earp* and Little America, both in the Ross Sea. By starting from the Ross Sea he would be flying away from these for 1,700 miles. On the Weddell Sea there was nothing and no one to help him, so in the event of mechanical failure he might well have had an impossibly long walk.

Before the next season he realised this and altered his plans. He would take the *Wyatt Earp* to the Weddell Sea side and make a single crossing to the Ross Sea. There he could exist in Little America until the *Wyatt Earp* sailed round to pick him up.

He did not know whether Byrd had left any food at Little America, so he would have to carry rations for a wait there of perhaps two months, and his diet must of course be the best possible. Therefore he engaged Dr Dana C. Coman, a dietician of John Hopkins University, to sail with him on the *Wyatt Earp*. Dr Coman might, perhaps, have worked out the ration in the United States. But Ellsworth felt that it would be better to have his dietician, who was also a doctor, in Antarctica.

On this second Antarctic expedition (1934-35) the *Wyatt Earp* sailed from New Zealand to Deception Island which is in the archipelago we have called the tail. This involved 4,000 miles of stormy seas, and the dietician was sick all the way. A base was made in the deserted whaling station, with a good stretch of snow for take-off nearby. The *Polar Star*, better than new after returning to her factory in California, was warmed up for a test before starting on the trans-continental flight.

After half a turn of the propeller a connecting rod broke, and they had none spare. 'It went to show what attention must be given to detail in the preparation of a polar expedition', was all that Ellsworth said.

Fortunately it was still only October – early in the season. Arrangements were made by radio to fly a connecting rod from California to Magellanes near Cape Horn and the faithful *Wyatt Earp* went bucking off a thousand miles through the stormiest seas in the world to fetch it. She brought it back on 16th November and the reassembled engine worked perfectly. What else could go wrong? The weather turned muggy and the snow runway on Deception Island disappeared. It was necessary to find another, which they did on Snowhill Island, further south in the Weddell Sea. There was still plenty of time to make the flight. And Byrd had reoccupied Little America. He would be there to welcome them and his met. man was daily sending weather reports to the *Wyatt Earp*.

But now Balchen began to raise objections. For one reason or another he would not fly. On record, he was the best pilot in the world for such a flight, but since the fiasco of the connecting rod he had become moody and unpredictable. Everything depended upon him.

Finally, on a fine evening, Ellsworth jolted him with an impulsive, 'Let's make a try!' Balchen agreed at once.

While preparations were being made Ellsworth wrote a press report: 'Flash – Balchen and I took off at seven this evening, heading for the unknown. The great adventure so long awaited is at hand. The motor is warming up and soon its roar will be breaking the silence that veils the earth's last great unknown as Balchen and I wing our way across Antarctica with the opportunity of all that pertains to the opening up of a continent for the last time in human history.'

This written, they took off. They had scarcely reached the mainland when Balchen turned back. Ellsworth shouted a question. 'Bad weather,' Balchen answered.

They landed again on Snowhill Island two and a half hours after take-off. Ellsworth walked down to the shore in silence. Wilkins asked Balchen what had happened. 'Ellsworth can commit suicide if he likes but he can't take me with him,' Balchen said.

Thus ended the second expedition.

Back in New York everyone tried to dissuade Ellsworth from another attempt. He had spent a fortune – or quite a large part of it – risked his life. Why not try something easier?

But this second failure – not his fault any more than the first had been – was like a second drink, stimulating him to further effort against all odds. He had already filed that press report about the great flight. He was going to make it true. Only, another name must be substituted for Balchen's.

He advertised for a pilot. Of those who replied two were outstanding – Herbert Hollick-Kenyon, an Englishman, and J. H. Lymburder of Canadian Airways. He could not decide between them so he hired both. Wilkins, of course, remained with him. So did most of the crew of the *Wyatt Earp*, which waited in Montevideo.

For Ellsworth nothing was changed except the pilot. His dream would be made to come true at whatever cost.

He and his wife flew to Rio in the Graf Zeppelin. Arriving early, they had time for two weeks jaguar hunting in the Matto Grosso. Then Mary Louise went back to the United States and he joined his ship. This time he sailed to Dundee Island, avoiding nearby Snowhill Island, and found a magnificent sweep of snow for a flying field. But Byrd had left Little America, so there could be no more weather reports from the Ross Sea end. However, Ellsworth had decided to take the weather as he found it – fly when it was fine and land and dig in when it threatened to be bad, and Hollick-Kenyon approved of this.

There were two false starts, one due to a mechanical fault, the other to weather, but 22nd November was the day of no return. They were called at one o'clock. Ellsworth dressed in layers of camel hair, wool and fur and breakfasted on bacon and five fried eggs. Hollick-Kenyon, whom he found shaving with an electric razor, wore tailored trousers – which retained their crease to the end of the adventure – and ate more sparingly.

They were at the flying field by three o'clock when the snow was still well frozen. Lymburner, the spare pilot and expert mechanic, had been tuning the engine for a couple of hours and Wilkins had been about still longer, overseeing every detail. Ellsworth had surrounded himself with the best possible men.

A handshake all round and they were off, exactly to schedule. For 600 miles they followed the tail of islands. Then they were over the body of the continent, obliquely crossing a great mountain range.

'We were indeed the first intruding mortals in this age-old region, and looking down on the mighty peaks I thought of eternity and man's insignificance,' Ellsworth wrote. 'So these first new mountains we saw will, I hope, bear the name of Eternity Range.'

He had already named three mountains, Faith, Hope and Charity, and was shortly to call another Mt Mary Louise Ulmer. He was an excited and happy man, very busy with his camera.

The mountains were gradually swallowed up by ice. The intruding mortals flew on over a white plateau. Here they began to be uncertain of their position, being unable to estimate land speed or drift, and the *Wyatt Earp* complained of difficulty in hearing them.

Hollick-Kenyon was silent and self-contained. He did not

Three very different explorers: seated, from left – Amundsen, Ellsworth, Nobile (holding Titina)

Ellsworth and Hollick-Kenyon aboard the *Wyatt Earp* after their Antarctic flight. The spare aeroplane rushed from California is above them

Ellsworth and Mary Louise Ulmer on the drawbridge of the Schloss
Lensberg

shout – the only possible form of conversation – but he handed two laconic notes to Ellsworth. The first was, 'Transmitter out of action. What shall we do?' Ellsworth answered, 'Keep on to eighty'. From this longitude to that of 120° was a sector of unclaimed territory that he would have risked anything to reach. The second note read, 'I really have no idea where we are. . . .'

Nor had Ellsworth, but when he estimated that they must have passed out of the Falkland Islands sector at the eighteenth meridian he decided to land. He had to put his feet on this new world. He noted, 'I felt a very meek and reverent person. To think that I, of all those who have dreamed this dream, should be permitted its realisation! For the moment I lost all sense of the troubled beginning, had no thought for the journey ahead. I was content, grateful. So here I raised the American flag. The area extending from 80° W. to 120° W. I named James W. Ellsworth Land after my father. That part of the plateau above 6,000 feet I called Hollick-Kenyon Plateau.'

His notes are like those of a man intoxicated. 'What a thrill!!!' He and his pilot spent most of their nineteen hours on the snow taking observations – with a faulty sextant as it proved. Roughly, they were 650 miles north of the Pole, 450 miles inland of the coast, 670 from their destination at Little America, out of range of a return to Dundee Island – at the most inaccessible point they could be, and without wireless contact. Yet Ellsworth's dominant thought was, 'We stood in the heart of the only unclaimed land in the Antarctic – in the whole world.'

These landings en route were bold indeed. Any damage on touch down or failure to take off and they would have been done for. They would never have been found.

They made four safe landings before their final one – a tribute to the skill of the pilot. At Camp III they were held up for a week by blizzards. They sank there to a low ebb of morale, but at least discovered the fault in their sextant – nothing worse than a loose screw. They were short of petrol and could not risk deviating from the true course. So they lay in the tent, eating frugally but with an evening aperitif from a bottle of grain alcohol given them at parting by Wilkins.

When they flew on they reached the Ross Sea but could not locate the snow-buried village of Little America. They were still looking for it when they ran out of petrol. They were in fact only sixteen miles away but trudged a hundred weary miles before finding it.

There, in a radio hut which they entered by the skylight, they subsisted for a month – over Christmas and New Year – living on the ample food they unearthed and two bottles of Napoleon brandy which Ellsworth had carried in his rucksack for three years – a present from his wife to be drunk on crossing the Antarctic.

They were rescued – Ellsworth calls it 'aided' – by *Discovery II* which the Australian Government, backed by that of Britain, had sent to look for them. The alarm had been sparked by the failure of their radio. The newspapers had shouted that they were 'Lost in the Antarctic'.

The trouble had proved to be no more than a bad connection but it must have been the most expensive technical fault in history. Besides the voyage of *Discovery II* from Australia, Wilkins had an aeroplane flown down from the United States. He picked it up in Chile and sailed round in the *Wyatt Earp* to the Ross Sea and Little America, arriving soon after *Discovery II*.

Heaven knows what these three years of expeditions cost. In modern terms it would certainly top a million. The result was a flight from the Weddell Sea to the Ross Sea and a lot of good photographs of mountains.

Was it worth it? It was Ellsworth's own money so he was the best judge. No life was lost on the expeditions with which he was concerned between 1925 and 1936 – it was his own life he risked, almost exclusively. He was not a scientific explorer. He was a pioneer, recklessly appreciative of the romantic. He found his Eternity Range which is more than most millionaires do.

5

Eismitte

When the last group of the British Arctic Air-Route Expedition arrived in Copenhagen in November 1931 some of those who had got home earlier went to meet them. In the throng after the first greetings we were approached by two men with close-cropped hair. The first clicked his heels, bowed from the waist and said, 'Georgi'. Then the second clicked his heels, bowed from the waist and said, 'Sorge'.

In the exhiliration of the moment we called them Georgy and Porgy. But we were impressed. This unlikely looking pair had manned a station on the middle line of the icecap 300 miles north of ours. Georgi had been there for a year, alone at first and at the end. He, Sorge, and some of their companions had had remarkable adventures and achieved ten times more sheer scientific work than was dreamed of in our philosophy. Professor Wegener's Greenland Expedition was the most ambitious of the century. But how many people even then in Britain heard of it, less remember it now? That needs to be rectified. They faced among other things the classic situation of having to perform amputation for frostbite while in the field. That aspect of polar private life, though often referred to in a romantic way, has never been described with such Teutonic precision as it was Wegener's men.

Alfred Wegener had made a crossing of the icecap with the Dane, J. P. Koch, in 1913. This achievement posed numerous questions to Wegener's scientific mind. But first the war, then the economic difficulties of Germany made it impossible for him to return and seek the answers. Not until 1928 when he was, at forty-eight, Professor of geophysics and meteorology at the University of Graz, did an opportunity arrive. He seized it at once.

His ambition was to study the icecap in detail – its altitude, the thickness of the ice which would be ascertained by echo sounding, the consistency and temperature of the snow at various depths, and icecap meteorology by ground level observation and pilot balloons. Gravity determinations would be made to discover whether the whole massif was rising or not. The geophysical work would be concerned with Wegener's theory of continental drift – that the great land-masses float on the heavy plastic foundations of the earth somewhat like drift ice on the sea – if the sea was viscous as treacle. There would be three stations – on the west and east coasts and on the central line. The necessary party was large, finally of twenty-two Europeans, most of them doctors of science and considerably older than we were. Iceland ponies would be the means of transportation across the rocky coastal fringe; a varying number of dogs were to be hired with their Eskimo owners in addition to other teams driven by members of the party. Wegener took considerable risk depending on Eskimos. There was also an untried mechanical factor – a couple of motor sledges, propellor driven, with 110 h.p. aero engines.

From late spring until autumn in 1929 Professor Wegener, Dr Loewe, Dr Georgi and Dr Sorge made a reconnaissance of the west coast – which is accessible for most of the year – in about Latitude 71° to find a site for the main base and a way on to the icecap. They returned to Europe for the winter, and the whole expedition sailed the following spring, the east coast party going to Scoresby Sound independently. Wegener was full of optimism, having proved to his companions and himself on this strenuous journey that at forty-nine he was still in excellent condition.

The two coastal stations were comparatively easy to establish, Eismitte extraordinarily difficult. Yet this central station was the most important for offering an opportunity to get at the heart of the problem. Greenland is 500 miles wide in Latitude 71°, so this heart lay 250 miles inland from the sea and some 9,000 feet above it. To this point sections for a triple-walled hut were to be carried – the scientists would need space and comfort for their work – as well as food and fuel for a year and instruments too numerous to be listed. Wegener believed in a varied diet – something far better than sledging rations – and a paraffin allowance of over a gallon a day. (We considered a gallon a week luxurious.) This represented many tons, far more than hundreds of dog sledges could manage in even the best conditions. That was where the motor sledges were to prove their worth. They were Swedish built and in that lakeland country had proved invaluable for winter travel between the islands. There, 20 m.p.h. was a normal speed. But they had not been tried out on the icecap.

After they had been landed on the sea ice it took many weeks before they could be hauled up an improvised track and the first steep ice slopes to the point of travelling by their own power. By then dogs had run the first laps of the tortoise and hare race. But we may anticipate – as Wegener had keenly done in imagination – their trial-run in late August. The engines were started up, and the crowd of watching Eskimos had their caps blown off. The lean, serious professor took his seat in one of the two driving cabs and they were off. He smiled like an excited boy. To sit on a cushion and be able to smoke his big curved pipe, this was 'travel first class!'

The first dog-sledge party had set out on 15th July with three and a half tons of food, fuel and equipment loaded on twelve sledges. Three of the party were Germans – Doctors Georgi, Loewe and Weiken – the rest were Eskimos. From the first the Greenlanders were half-hearted. They had not objected to the coastal transport but they disliked penetrating this lifeless, featureless desert. Officially they were Christians but the icecap was more ancient than any religion, and seemed to represent evil. Although they were earning the good wage of four shillings a day, were fed and provided with extra clothing by the Germans, they hated this incomprehensible, frightening journey more and more.

The arrangement was that at half way – 125 miles – the sledges of Georgi, Weiken and three Eskimos were to be fully loaded with essentials for establishing Eismitte, while the rest of the party were to turn back with Loewe. But at half way *all* the Greenlanders stated that they were going home.

This would mean failure of the most important part of the expedition plan. It was a bad moment – far more than a moment for the argument went on for hours with a minimum of language in common. Georgi, a direct and purposeful individual, revealed some impatience with the native mentality in his diary account. None the less he went so far as to dump some of his precious meteorological equipment. But that was not enough. Extra pay was not enough. They would be unable to breathe further on, they said. (They were already at 8,200 feet.) Their dogs would die. They had to go home before being forced to eat their boots.

Loewe finally settled the matter, quite simply. He told them that they could go home – but without his guidance. If they turned back he would go on with his two compatriots.

The route they had followed was marked with black flags every 500 yards and a black pillar made of bamboos and bunting every three miles. But the Eskimos dared not travel it alone. They decided that not only three, but four of them, would go on so long as Loewe relented and guided the rest back. This was agreed.

The four who went on became tremendously pleased with themselves – the first Eskimos ever to penetrate the centre of their country – and as helpful as they could be. So the position chosen for the station, Eismitte, was reached with part of the intended stores.

Dr Loewe, though he diplomatically turned back on this occasion, reappears in the story in an important role so I will introduce him personally. I had met him earlier that summer when I was buying dogs in West Greenland. He, being similarly employed, might not have had much sympathy for me. But he was perfectly polite. I, aged twenty-two, was at once impressed both by his physical appearance – he was a fine strong man – and his air of intellectual superiority. He spoke fluent English but suddenly broke off to ask what language he was speaking. When I told him he said, 'Pardon, it is confusing. Danish and English are so similar'. I did not tell him that on the boat I had laboriously been studying Hugo's *Danish in Three Months*. I doubt if he would have seen the joke.

But to return to Eismitte – Georgi remained there alone from 1st-18th August, Weiken and the four Eskimos having returned to the coast. From his diary-style account, and judging from what he achieved, he did not waste a moment. He was a well-built man with a prominent nose and large, intent, observing eyes. In character he was purposeful and meticulous, by temperament always busy. During the first eighteen days of solitude he slept in a tent '7¾ feet square' until 7.30 a.m. Central Greenland time when he rose for his first observation. He immediately set in order as many automatically recording instruments as possible – intricate work with bare hands. Then he dug shelters for the barometer and barograph and a hole for his captive met. balloons with hydrogen (the gas was made from a solid hydrate with a lot of water, which had to be melted from snow – five hours' work or more). He started digging out the winter quarters – with interruptions for more readings; on one occasion he fitted in a ski-run back along the trail to the first pillar where as a joke he put up a signpost, EISMITTE 3 MILES, SCORESBY SOUND 250 MILES.

But he got quite enough exercise in digging. He felt the exertion at a 9,000-feet altitude but continued to exert himself. He wanted something to show to Wegener if he came up with the motor sledges, as was intended.

He wrote to his wife, heading the letter: 'Eismitte, 10 August: Dear Frieda, I am sitting in my sleeping bag at 10 p.m. and trying to give you a picture of my life here quickly, before my fingers are quite cold . . .'. Five hundred words later, having recorded all he had done, detailed what he had eaten at every meal, told her the temperature inside and outside the tent, thanked her for parcels sent up on the party of which he was a member, he concluded, 'Well, my fingers are cold enough for today; good night!'

On 18th August he saw through the telescope of the theodolite that black spots were approaching over the snow. But they were not the motor sledges with all the scientific and hut equipment as expected. They were the indefatigable Loewe with five Eskimos and a cargo of 1,800 lb, chiefly food and fuel, but including 'several boxes of instruments and tools'. The party remained with him only for the night and were off for the coast the following day.

Georgi was alone again for another twenty-five days. He was as busy as ever, digging, digging, keeping the recording instruments in order, changing their paper strips every Monday, reading the rest at fixed intervals. There is no hint in his diary of boredom or loneliness. He was too well occupied in body and mind for that.

On 13th September Sorge, Wölcken, Julg and seven Eskimos arrived by dog-sledge with a ton and a half of provisions, paraffin and equipment. Sorge was to be Georgi's companion for the winter so together they checked through the inventory of Eismitte. They were lacking some essentials. Although they had enough food, they were short of fuel. Of scientific equipment, Georgi particularly needed wire cable for his balloons (he had been using silk thread which was not strong enough) and Sorge required explosives for his seismic experiments.

After long consideration they wrote Wegener a letter to be carried by the returning party. It was in part as follows:

The food supplies here would last two men for 10-11 months. . . . The fuel supply is not nearly sufficient. . . . We two agree to winter here together, even if the hut cannot be brought here in consequence of the failure of the motor sledges, but only on the following assumption: By 20 October (the latest date for returning) we must have 17 large cans of paraffin, drilling tools, snow bucket and rucksack with contents. Sufficient quantity of explosives and cables. . . . Gear for aerological work (see Georgi's letter), 2 seismic tents. . . .

If these necessities are not here, or their arrival definitely announced, by 20 October we shall start on that day with hand sledges. But we hope that you will arrive any day with motor sledges, and all difficulties will thus be removed.

With best regards to all,
Georgi
Sorge.

Wölcken and Julg carried this letter when they and their Eskimos left the next day. They were greatly relieved when they met the motor sledges at the half-way point three days later. They no longer feared that Georgi and Sorge might have to evacuate Eismitte. The two parties spent a cheerful night together. The dog sledges drove on towards the coast early the next morning, while the mechanics were warming up their motors to make the run to Eismitte which should not take them more than two days.

Meanwhile Wegener, although of course he knew nothing of these events, had decided that one more dog-sledge party must go in to make Eismitte absolutely secure for the winter. He organised a very large party, no less than fifteen sledges. This involved hiring at least twelve Eskimos and over 150 dogs. Partly to encourage the Eskimos – for his prestige was great – partly that he should be at hand to take any decision, but no doubt largely because he wanted to see the station, he decided to lead the party himself, with the well-trusted Loewe as his second.

Most of the loads were dragged over the rough coastal strip by Iceland ponies. Ten miles inland the dog sledges took over, and the big convoy set off eastwards.

They had covered scarcely two miles when they met Wölcken, Julg and their seven Eskimos returning from Eismitte. Wegener was given Georgi's and Sorge's letter. It was unlikely that his heavily laden caravan could reach Eismitte before 20th October (it was then 21st September). But the crisis probably no longer existed, for the motor sledges should have got there within a day or two of the half-way meeting on 17th September.

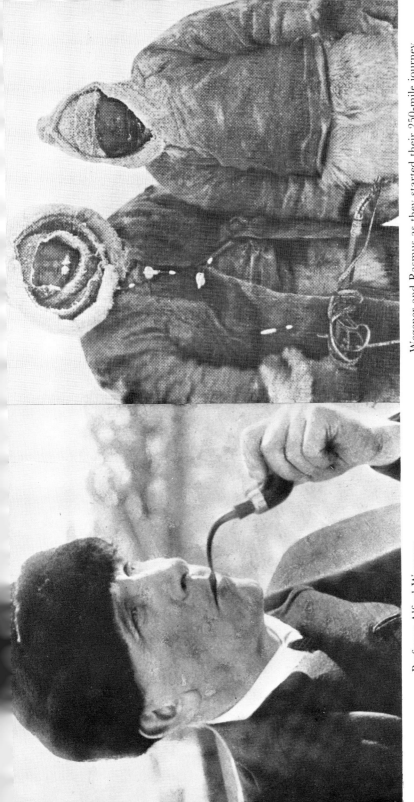

Wegener and Rasmus as they started their 250-mile journey from Eismitte for the coast, already tired and frosted

Professor Alfred Wegener

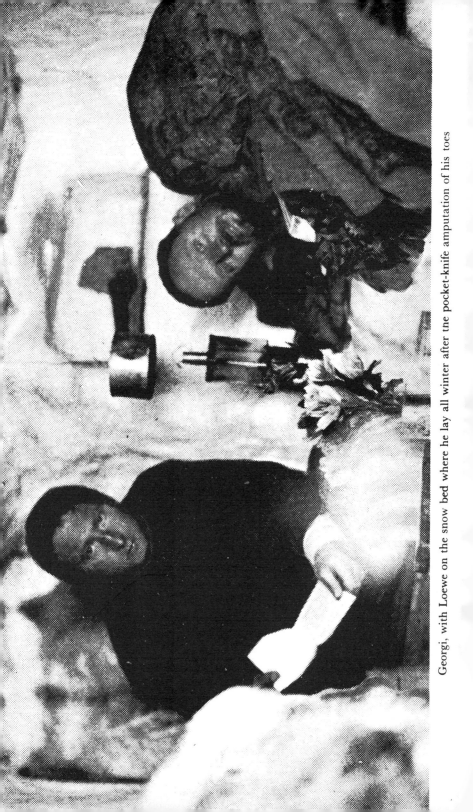

Georgi, with Loewe on the snow bed where he lay all winter after the pocket-knife amputation of his toes

Ice flowers decorated the ceiling for Christmas

A motor sledge among the coast crevasses of the ice cap. The propeller
mounting is on the right

Wegener decided to press on none the less. Thirty miles inland he came on the four men of the motor-sledge party. They were short of food, out of tobacco and very sorry for themselves.

Wegener passed his pouch round while they told their story. When Wölcken and Julg left them at the half-way point the morning was misty. It was all right for dogs, but in motor sledges it was more difficult to follow the line of flags. They could not risk losing the way and wasting precious fuel. Therefore they decided to wait for the weather to improve.

Instead of improving it snowed them in. When they had dug themselves out the engines were very slow to start. When at last they started they could not shift the heavy loads in the deep snow. It was futile going to Eismitte without loads. So they dumped the cargo and turned back – and met all sorts of trouble on the way. One machine had broken down some miles back, they said, and now the other had also failed. It was lucky they had turned back when they did, for otherwise they would probably have been stranded much further inland, and you cannot eat motor sledges.

Wegener listened quietly, smoking his big Austrian pipe and making no comment. But he was determined more than ever to press on himself. There was now urgent need to do so.

The weather was warm but the snow was soft and deep. The big Eskimo dog teams floundered and hampered each other's way. Two teams with each dog on a long trace, tangled and fighting, makes a giant's dish of animated spaghetti. Yet the drivers ignored each other's troubles because that is native etiquette. Still worse was their superstitious dislike of this journey through an accursed desert. The trail was marked with black flags and pillars, and at one point also by a ferociously snarling dead dog. It must somehow have been placed in a sitting position, for all the later parties saw it, and it gave a grisly greeting.

On the morning of 28th September the Eskimos did not break camp but crowded into the tent that Wegener and Loewe shared. They sat there smoking their pipes and looking at the floor.

At last it was spoken. Although it was still warm the cold would come and they had too little clothing to face it. The loads were too heavy. They wanted to go home.

For hours the argument went on, slowly and awkwardly. Loewe had to do the persuading for Wegener spoke no Eskimo at all. This time there could be no bargaining factor of a white man going back with some, for there was no third European. Yet Loewe eventually won something. Four Greenlanders would go on at increased pay while the rest turned back unguided.

Wegener, Loewe and the four struggled on through deep snow. Time was vital – at that season the weather could only deteriorate. But they could not travel fast. The load for Eismitte had already been cut to the bone. They had nothing more to give away if it came to another argument.

The uneasy partnership lasted until 5th October when Detlev, the senior hunter who acted as spokesman, said that all four Eskimos wanted to go home. Again the slow argument began. It continued on and off for two precious days. Finally Detlev and two others turned back, whereas the fourth Eskimo, Rasmus Villumsen, agreed to go on with Wegener and Loewe for the whole distance.

Rasmus was a good man. He was only twenty-two and had no doubt been influenced by the older Eskimos. Once he was alone with the white men he could not have been more loyal or worked harder. He went in front, breaking the trail through the deep powder snow and with his wonderfully quick eyes picked out the flags in the dim light.

Try as they might they could not cover more than three or four miles a day. It became evident that they would not reach Eismitte by 20th October. Wegener, however, hoped that they might meet Georgi and Sorge before they had dragged their hand-sledge far from Eismitte and persuade them to go back. If need be he and Loewe were prepared to take over the station from them. Eismitte had to be maintained.

That was a brave intention. But after passing the 143-mile mark it became apparent that the party which had set out with a cargo measured in tons was going to have to depend on reaching Eismitte for its own survival. All the scientific equipment had been dumped and the food and fuel intended for the station was being consumed.

On 20th October they had reached the 181-mile mark. After that they daily expected to meet Georgi and Sorge. Had they done so one wonders who would have turned back with whom. But they did not meet them, so had to press on for their lives. Loewe describes their progress as 'retreating forwards'.

The temperature so far had remained comparatively high. When men and dogs were at their weakest it suddenly dropped to −40 or −50°F. Loewe lost all feeling in his toes but continued to march. On

30th October all the dog food and the last of the paraffin were finished. Wegener, Loewe and Rasmus warmed a small meal over some tablets of meta fuel and covered the last miles to Eismitte.

Georgi and Sorge greeted them. They had decided that after all they could last the winter and therefore had not started out on 20th October. So Wegener's journey had not been necessary; in fact it was now a liability for his party was dependent on Eismitte's stores.

Architecturally the station had been very much developed. Soon after Sorge's arrival he and Georgi had gone under the snow and had excavated a complex of caves – living room, barometer room, balloon-filling room, gas production room, store room. The snow was of the consistency that is called *firn* or *névé*, of granular structure like damp rice grains frozen together. It proved to be excellent for building or excavation, very strong yet easy to work with a knife, spade or saw. Much care had been expended on the living and sleeping room. The effect was at first somewhat overpowering – white bed platforms like marble sarcophagi in a white crypt where bluish light just penetrated. But it was most practical. With a roof five-feet thick of splendid insulating material and infinitely thick walls the temperature could with a minimum of heating be kept up almost to freezing point when outside it was −60°F. And there were many minor advantages. Snow for boiling water could be chipped out of the wall, leaving the makings of a cupboard. Waste liquid could be poured down a hole and never seen again. And if a hook or peg was needed a piece of wire or a stick could be pushed into the wall. The entrance was a long passageway protected by sacks and skins, and rising outside was a tower of snow blocks visible for ten miles on a clear day.

Wegener who was in excellent fettle was impressed and delighted. He kept repeating, 'How comfortable you are!' He was also excited to learn how low the temperature had recently fallen; their forty days' journey had been a record of endurance! Rasmus was physically overcome by the suddenness of the change. He developed a headache and sat bemused, eating chocolate. Loewe got into his sleeping bag. He had walked for four days on feet with frozen toes and now that they were thawing they began to hurt.

Clearly he had to remain at Eismitte, but Wegener and Rasmus would have to set off for the coast as soon as possible. They left after only one full day of rest, equipped with all the paraffin and food that could be spared. It was 1st November, Wegener's fiftieth birthday.

Those left behind naturally felt anxiety for them on their long, cold journey – and could not hope to hear anything until late April or May when the first spring relief party should arrive. There had been talk of adding a signaller with a wireless set to the garrison at Eismitte but this plan had dropped back in priority. Now the third man was a casualty whose feet showed 'many signs of incipient blood poisoning'. The right foot was particularly bad. Georgi and Sorge tried massage in an attempt to restore the circulation, as Wegener had done on the march. They delayed more drastic action for ten days, and one can well understand it. Neither Georgi nor Sorge had any medical experience (there was no doctor of medicine on the expedition), they had only the simplest of first aid requirements – no medical books, anaesthetics, scalpels. All such things lay dumped somewhere along the 250-mile trail.

Georgi's diary which has previously been jovial suddenly becomes peevish. He complains of small things. He goes for walks alone at −62 °F. He says little about Loewe except that his pessimism is a strain. He does not say specifically that he fears having to add surgery to his skills and scholarship as a meteorologist, but it is evident.

'In a few days the fate of Loewe's toes was sealed', wrote Sorge, referring to those of the right foot. 'By 9 November they looked quite shapeless and wasted away; the sinews were sticking up like ridges among the decomposing flesh. Georgi whetted his pocket-knife until it was as thin and sharp as a safety razor blade.' He did this – which must have taken a long time – within a few feet of Loewe as he lay on his snow slab bed.

The operation was fixed for 11 o'clock the next morning. That being Monday, Georgi's first duty was to change the recording strips of the met. instruments. Nobody slept that night except possibly Sorge who had a reputation for that capacity. Loewe, although he possessed the Iron Cross, first class, and had been nagging for an amputation from the first, must have been afraid. Georgi constantly fingered the toes of his own right foot, a contortionist act in a sleeping bag.

No operating theatre could have looked more clinically clean yet been so bare of equipment. The stove was lighted because the patient could not bare his leg for as long as was necessary in fourteen degrees of frost. The foot was placed for a while in powdered snow at 25°F as a local anaesthetic. The first cut proved that this was inadequate, but

96

they dared not freeze the toes completely – which they could have done by moving outside for a minute or two – so Sorge gripped the ankle tightly.

Later he recorded: 'Georgi cut away the flesh round the roots of the toes with his sharp knife, nipped off the bones of the second to fifth toes with a metal-cutting shears, and cut through the very sensitive big toe at the softest part'.

The operation took an hour. Sorge must have immobilised the leg by kneeling on it for he held the electric torch and passed the instruments. He must have been asked to pass the shears. The bleeding stumps were washed with chinosol and water warmed over the stove, and dressed with cotton wool and bandages. 'After the operation Loewe was talkative and in good spirits – his pain and nervous excitement were lessened.'

Five days later the same operation had to be performed on the left foot. Bits of bone worked their way out thereafter – the disarticulations had not been exact – and there were minor crises. They were very short of bandages and had to cut out the stains with scissors. But to conclude this incident, after six months in his sleeping bag Loewe was again able to walk normally. The operation was more successful than could be expected.

But meanwhile they had the winter to get through. Georgi and Sorge were busy with their work, respectively meteorology and glaciology. Georgi had an exacting programme of observations, and his self-recording instruments needed constant maintenance to keep them in order at the low temperatures. One reads such diary statements as, 'On Sunday I made an electric thermometer with which yesterday and today I have been measuring the difference in temperature between the surface of the snow and the air just above it'. He was evidently clever with his hands – that is why he made a good surgeon.

Sorge's main task was the digging of a shaft which was finally more than fifty feet in depth. With a battery of thermometers he took the temperature of the snow at different levels and brought up samples for intimate examination.

As Loewe recovered – though he had many setbacks – he began to read, and when in the mood proved himself an excellent conversationalist. He was exceptionally well informed on a wide variety of subjects. The favourite reading of the trio seems to have been Schopenhauer and Thomas Mann. Their conversations were generally philosophical and sociological. At one stage Georgi noted, 'It is curious: Sorge is such a splendid mathematician, physicist, geographer and climber that I am always astonished at his almost credulous optimism regarding social questions and their solution. He really believes that men and women are good.' He added that it would be unfair not to make allowance for his being a young man of thirty. He himself was forty-two, Loewe thirty-seven.

Another favourite subject was marriage. On this Sorge knew next to nothing, having come on the expedition straight from his honeymoon, whereas Georgi and Loewe were old hands.

To have been a fly on the wall would have been fascinating. There were no flies on those icy walls. But lice, a legacy from Eskimo dog drivers, thrived wherever it was warm enough. They were easily, though inconveniently, killed by putting garments or sleeping bag out of doors. But a new generation invariably rose Phoenix-like from the frozen eggs. They found the atmosphere of Loewe's bandages particularly agreeable. He took this humorously and made 'quite a sport' of hunting them with forceps.

So they existed – more than existed, for they *worked* at their sciences and lived harmoniously, with a comparatively extravagant Christmas and occasional readings aloud of Schiller and Goethe.

The end of their vigil came suddenly. On 8th May Georgi noted: 'The motor sledges and a party with dog sledges arrived yesterday. They asked where Wegener was . . .'.

We can make a little more of it. Johan Villumsen, Rasmus's brother, was a passenger with the motor sledges. He did not understand the exchanges but he understood the absence of his brother. The Germans in the relief party knew that Wegener, Loewe and Rasmus had pressed on for Eismitte with essential stores. When they did not return, it was assumed at the western base (optimistically, for they cannot have had a rosy account from the Eskimos) that the three had wintered with Georgi and Sorge at Eismitte, in which case they would be short of food. Dr Weiken who assumed command contacted the British Arctic Air-Route Expedition in February through the Danish wireless stations at Disco and Angmagssalik asking 'Professor Watkins' (Gino had not found time to take his B.A.) if he could help with supplies. They knew we had aeroplanes and were planning to fly to Canada, so presumed our aircraft had considerable range – more than 500 miles which was the distance of the western base from us. We had our own troubles at that time with our icecap station having to be relieved and Gipsy moths to be repaired. Iliffe Cozens doubts if we would have got across the icecap. None the less Gino Watkins answered with a bold offer to fly over and supply dog-sledge parties by air. Fortunately this was declined or some of rescuers would almost certainly have been killed.

From the German western base a relief party had set out in November. They managed to travel about fifty miles eastwards and left a depot of food. It was all they could do in that latitude. The party remained on the icecap until 7th December. This was the day after Chapman, Wager, Bingham and D'Aeth began their return journey, having left Courtauld alone at our station.

In May the German relief party – dog and motor sledges – brought out Loewe and Sorge, leaving Giorgi alone for another couple of months. Sorge, who was with the dog sledges, searched for Wegener and Rasmus. At the 158-mile mark, less than half way to the coast, Wegener's sledge was found. From there he and Rasmus had gone on with one sledge between them, presumably because the mortality among their seventeen dogs had been high.

Near the 118-mile mark, 132 miles from Eismitte, Wegener's skis stood upright in the snow, about three yards apart. They had been seen on the inward journey but nothing significant had been found. This time the men dug deeper – through that winter's fallen snow and two and a half feet below the surface of the previous November. They found Wegener. He had been sewn into two sleeping-bag covers and was lying on his sleeping-bag and a reindeer skin. His clothing had been carefully brushed clean of snow, just as one used to do before coming into the tent. Everything was in perfect order. He was wearing blue cloth trousers with dog-skin trousers over them, a shirt, blue waistcoat, blue skiing tunic, a thick sweater, helmet and peaked cap. His fur boots – which need daily attention on a journey – were in excellent condition.

His face seemed younger than when Sorge had seen it last. His eyes were open and his expression was absolutely peaceful, almost smiling. He was rather pale though, and there were small frostbites on his cheeks such as often show in the evening during winter travel. He must have come into the tent as usual, lain down and died, perhaps having strained his heart by trying to keep up on skis with the dog sledge. Rasmus had cared for him, taken his diary and personal papers and gone on.

Wegener was reburied as before. Continuing westwards the

search party found near the 105-mile mark signs that Rasmus had camped there for several days. There was a hatchet that he carried and the remains of several meals. Between there and the coast none of the food depots had been touched.

Sorge searched for Rasmus with meticulous care, remaining on the icecap until his food was finished. But no further trace of him was ever found.

Thus the icecap took its toll of those who tried to find its secrets – the professor leader, the faithful Eskimo and many of their dogs. It kept them, and will continue to keep them, exactly as they were when it claimed their lives.

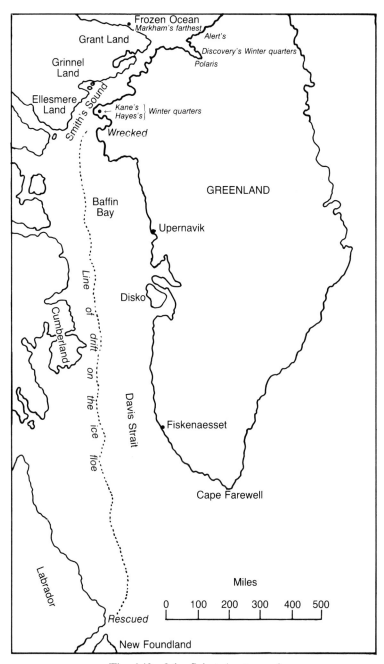

The drift of the *Polaris* (castaways)

The funeral of Charles Francis Hall

'Good-bye, *Polaris*!' the ship is suddenly swept away

6

Hall's Unquiet Rest

In 1968 Dr Chauncey Loomis and Dr Franklin Paddock made an expedition to North Greenland with a definite but unusual motive. They wanted to establish whether an explorer who died in his bed there in 1871 had been murdered.

The explorer was Charles Francis Hall who had been attempting to reach the North Pole. His ship had reached within eight degrees of the Pole, and in October he had been making a reconnaissance journey by dog sledge when he was taken ill. He became partly paralysed, as if from a stroke, and died on 8th November shouting that he had been poisoned. A naval court of inquiry in the United States concluded, mainly on the evidence of the expedition's doctor, that death had been due to natural causes. Diary entries by crew members, which were not studied until later, did not bear out this verdict, and had perpetuated a rumour which persisted for ninety-seven years. The two doctors went north to quash or confirm the rumour.

Dr Loomis was a professor of English who was collecting data for a biography of Hall (*Weird and Tragic Shores*); Dr Paddock was a pathologist. They found the burial place, Hall's Rest, without difficulty – a cairn and a crowbar in a cold and empty landscape. Sixteen inches below the surface and resting on the ever-frozen subsoil was a plain pinewood coffin. They prised this open and were sickened by the stench, for in spite of the cold, decomposition had set in. The pathologist realised that the internal organs would no longer be useful for analysis. They took samples of hair and finger-nails. These were examined at the Centre of Forensic Science in Toronto. As stated in the succinct account in *Newsweek*: 'Neutron-activation analysis was used. In this process a specimen is placed in a nuclear reactor and irradiated so that the chemical elements present will be transformed into radio-active isotopes. Each element treated this way produces its own radio-active signature.'

Hall's finger-nails showed that he had ingested large doses of arsenic, and since nails grow at a precise rate of a tenth of a millimetre a day it could be fixed that this had occurred during the last fortnight of his life.

Dr Loomis and Dr Paddock went to a lot of trouble to prove that Hall died from arsenic but not that he had been murdered. Arsenic would have been included in the medical chest. It was, for instance, an ingredient of a tonic tranquiliser. Prescriptions at that time were often made up as required, not previously prepared. They might be made up by the doctor or an assistant. A medicine containing a poison can kill or cure. The choice, apart from chance or error, lies in motive, which cannot produce a signature even in a nuclear reactor.

So we cannot hope to identify the murderer, if there was one. Never mind. An expedition that loses its leader in unexplained circumstances when far from civilisation suggests an intriguing theme. Anyone with a spark of the researcher in him would have to dig. What came out of the hole in the library was of interest regarding subsequent events and the reactions of individuals.

Hall's early life does not explain his dedication to Arctic travel. He was born in 1821 and is listed as a citizen of Cincinnati. He had a grammar-school education; he did not study any science. He tried his hand at a variety of jobs – blacksmith, seal engraver, publisher of a local newspaper. In 1859, aged thirty-eight and married, he wrote an article, 'Is Franklin Still Alive?' and a sentimental poem as if by Lady Jane complaining of the loss of her husband.

This suggests that he was romantic and read Arctic books. His subsequent behaviour shows that he was also violently impulsive. He sold his newspaper, left his wife and family and launched 'The New Franklin Research Expedition'. He was its only member. A whaler dropped him off in Baffin Island which he hoped to cross through 'Frobisher Straits', the non-existent waterway (now called Frobisher Bay) marked on sixteenth-century maps. These 'straits' would have taken him across to the known route of Franklin's *Erebus* and *Terror*.

Hall remained in Baffin Island for two years, travelling long distances by dog sledge, with no company except Eskimos and the occasional whaler. He became enchanted with the Arctic and its people. He took back with him to the United States an Eskimo couple whom he called Hannah and Joe and kept them with him almost without interruption for the rest of his life. He disliked and mistrusted his own race; he was a lone wolf, and capable of ferocity if hindered. He shot a man who refused to go on when he ordered him to do so. But this incident cannot be connected with his own subsequent death and merely shows that in the Arctic a sudden urge to kill someone might be acted upon.

The published story of his first expedition was widely read for its ebullient descriptions of primitive life. With the money he made he was very soon off again with Hannah and Joe, this time directly to King William Island, the scene of the Franklin tragedy. He spent five consecutive winters there, and found many posthumous records of the English explorers, which effectively answered his original question about Franklin. But his passion for the North remained. He set his sights on 'the northern axis of the great globe'.

The North Pole could be attained only by a full-scale expedition, which entailed management of a ship and crew and the inclusion of science in the programme. The Navy gave him a ship, an old river steamer which he adapted by naming her *Polaris*. He signed on an experienced whaling skipper, Captain Sydney Buddington, as sailing master; an exceptional first mate, Captain Tyson; a very sound second mate named Chester; and a crew mostly of American nationality but including some Germans. The Smithsonian Institute enabled him to enlist a scientific team led by Dr Emil Bessels, also German. In addition, since Eskimos dislike travelling without their kin, there were Eskimo families – those of Joe and those of a Greenlander named Hans Hendrick. In overall command of this very mixed company was Charles Francis Hall – stocky, heavily bearded and with, at least when photographed, a fiercely concentrated expression in the eyes.

Trouble erupted as soon as the *Polaris* began working her way up the west coast of Greenland. Hall managed to discipline his tongue at least, but Captain Buddington, a hard drinker and therefore unguarded in what he said, objected loudly to his professional caution being overruled. Dr Bessels who was an ambitious man felt, and showed it silently, that he was not given sufficient opportunity for scientific work. The German crew members were not in harmony with their fellow sailors. The Eskimo children and the dogs got in everybody's way. We know this from the diaries – which expressed the different points of view of men taking sides. But they all argumentatively agreed that the real difficulty lay ahead.

103

Baffin Bay, which washes Greenland, narrows to a gut that drains into the polar ocean. The drift ice is so constricted in the gut that former expeditions had not travelled far up it. The *Polaris* found a way virtually to the shores of the ocean, within 500 miles of the Pole. This was a magnificent achievement in the eyes of Hall which did not focus on the possibilities of getting back. He even tried to work further along the north Greenland coast, to a better jumping off place for the Pole, but a change in the weather began to drive the *Polaris* back.

The ship's southward drift was finally halted when she steered into an open bay protected only by an enormous grounded iceberg. Hall named the bay Thank God Harbour and the iceberg Providence Berg. From this anchorage he would still be within sledging distance of the Pole next season. But Captain Buddington, Dr Bessels and others of the ship's company, did not share his enthusiasm for wintering so far north when they might have continued to drift towards safer waters.

Hall cared nothing for their opinions. The reconnaissance trip he made lasted nineteen days. His companions were the two Eskimo men and the second mate, Chester, who was too well disciplined to have taken sides. Hall had told Tyson that he would have liked to have him on the journey but dared not leave Captain Buddington in charge of the ship without someone whom he could trust to supervise. The official expedition account states that he was in poor health during the journey, feeling compelled to ride on the sledge instead of running in front of the dogs as usual. He was fifty years old. Tyson says that he returned in an exultant mood and that it was only after drinking a cup of coffee that he was taken ill. We do not know who gave him the coffee.

Dr Bessels diagnosed apoplexy and treated him with mustard baths and quinine. During the short period when he rallied he was up and about and ate normally. Latterly, Hall was often unconscious and his cries that he was being poisoned may have been uttered in delirium. He died ten days after returning to the ship.

He was buried near Thank God Harbour at a spot that was called Hall's Rest. It was surely an emotional occasion for, like him or not, Hall was a strong personality. One of the crew sketched the long line of well-muffled sailors drawing the funeral sledge over the snowy ground, not a tree or bush in sight. The grave had to be shallow because even with a crowbar the frozen soil could not be penetrated beyond the limit of the summer's semi-thaw. It must have been difficult enough to loosen stones to make a cairn. The shivering mourners knew the scene, the situation, knew each other to the point of irritation. It is on record that they talked of murder by poison, not by accident. On motive – if the wish to turn back can be considered motive for murder – we can narrow the choice of prime suspects to two men. But we have no means of getting further than that.

So, most unsatisfactorily, we are finished with detection as a theme. What follows is survival. Hall's last expedition would be much more of a mystery than it is if his men had not reached home to tell their story, and they very nearly failed to do so.

Survival depends to a large extent on state of mind. Morale on the *Polaris* was deplorabe during the winter of 1871-72. The carpenter, whose name was Coffin and who must have made the coffin, became convinced that he was going to be murdered. Someone was going to bore through to his bed and spray him with carbonic acid. He tried to change his sleeping place every night but had little choice on a crowded ship banked up with snow and tented with canvas. His crewmates worsened their natural fear of wintering in an open bay protected only by an iceberg by discussing what had been overheard from Hall's cabin. The Eskimos, who could not have understood the words, were keenly receptive to atmosphere. Eskimos believe that an unquiet ghost (the spirit of a dead man) can cause much harm to the living until it finds a home that suits it.

Captain Buddington did nothing to calm or divert such anxieties – except open up the wine and spirit store for himself and his cronies. There were no depot-laying journeys, no concert parties, theatricals or ship's magazine. And Dr Bessels, who might have found plenty of medical work to do particularly in the psychological field, was chiefly interested in the observatory he had built on shore.

In the spring and early summer a few journeys were made, but with little purpose or determination. No one was thinking of the North Pole any more.

In August the *Polaris* was freed from the ice by a storm which bumped her against Providence Berg. Captain Buddington, a man of action at least, saved her from serious danger and set a course for home. The first stage was the gut which begins in the north as Robeson Channel and finally opens through Smith Sound into Baffin Bay. In spite of the captain's skill they were caught and held by the pack in Robeson Channel. But the ice was drifting southwards. The *Polaris* was anchored to a large floe and with it moved slowly down the waterway between Greenland and Ellesmere Land.

On 15th October, when she was almost out of Smith Sound and into Baffin Bay, a gale lashed the pack to madness. The huge fragments of ice which had been quiescent, ground against each other with an appalling noise. The old river steamer was helpless. The ice, infinitely heavier and thicker than she, was tilting and barging, smashing itself to pieces by its own violence. But the ship made a temporary windbreak, anchored as she was to the ice itself. To leeward of her the near floes were still intact. To windward they were piling up.

The *Polaris* was squeezed. The log records that she shook and trembled. She was raised up bodily and thrown on her port side. Her timbers cracked with a loud report, especially about the stern. A fireman rushed on deck shouting that a piece of ice had been thrust through the sides. Water was pouring in.

To conserve coal the engine room fires had not been lighted during the drift, so there was no steam to work the main pump. The hand pumps were manned, the fires were lit and since the ship seemed to be sinking, essential stores and equipment were thrown onto the ice with hectic speed. 'Men performed gigantic feats of strength, tossing out with apparent ease in the excitement of the moment, boxes which at other times they would not have essayed to lift.' Pemmican, coal, clothing, bedding, ammunition, musk ox skins, tobacco, boxes of records were hurled over the side.

But as the ship continued to heave with the pressure it became evident that if she sank – as she might do at any moment – all these stores would be carried down with her. So Tyson, with some of the crew and the two Eskimo men, began to make heaps in safer parts of the floe. They laboured for an hour and a half in the dusk and the howling wind.

They had scarcely finished when the floe rapidly began to break up. Dark cracks ran across its white surface separating the piles of food and stores, and the people. The sailors and the Eskimo families tried to get back to the ship they had been glad to leave. But they could not. Two boats were lowered. They failed to pick up anybody and were left on the ice.

In the middle of this feverish activity the *Polaris* was swept away before the wind. Her anchors had fallen through the ice in which they had been embedded. She did not yet have steam and so was uncontrollable. Those on board paused for a moment, staring in

106

silent horror at the people on the ice, the scattered stores. They saw Hans Hendrick rush to pick up his child as another crack formed. They heard a voice cry, 'Good-bye *Polaris*'. Then they turned back to their own struggle for survival.

On board with Captain Buddington were thirteen men. Since the ship had been nipped these men had been labouring continuously at the hand pumps and at stoking the fires with coal and blubber. Water was coming in fast and if it rose sufficiently to extinguish the fires there would be nothing more to be done. The only hope lay in reaching land quickly. So they worked for their lives through that 'dark and tempestuous night'.

By dawn they had the steam pump working and so could master the incoming water. And they found that in spite of the damage to the stern both the rudder and propeller were in order. So they might in daylight have gone in search of the people on the floe. But it was recorded that they could not see them. The people on the floe saw them clearly making for the Greenland shore with sail and steam. This story of stress and danger contains very few examples of selfless courage.

The *Polaris* reached the shore and sat on the bottom. A hut was built of her spars and roped with canvas. But long before it was completed – within a day of the ship's arrival – Eskimos appeared on sledges out of the seemingly empty land. They had smelt the smoke of the *Polaris* and they are an inquisitive race, with plenty of time on their hands during the winter. They squatted down to look at the strangers and to drink coffee. Captain Buddington, being an old whaler, had learned a few words of their language, and asked if they had seen the people on the floe. But neither the first visitors nor the many who came later knew anything about them. The Eskimos did not offer to help the ship's party to travel south. Presumably they preferred things as they were.

By the end of winter 102 Eskimos had visited Polaris Hut, generally for a long stay. They slept on the floor until there was no floor left and a guest tent had to be erected. The coffee was soon finished and boiled rye substituted. The white men were short of supplies. Although they had brought their ship to land they had in the emergency thrown on to the ice everything that had seemed valuable. They were left with just enough for subsistence and, having nothing to hold onto except convention, stuck to fixed meal times. Observance of the habits of civilisation no doubt helped to keep them normal.

107

They hunted with the ammunition they had but shot little except foxes which inquisitively scouted round the hut. The Eskimos occasionally brought walrus liver which upset their stomachs but was preferable to the taste of fox. The Eskimo women sewed clothing and cobbled sealskin boots. The younger Americans, who had not previously displayed much initiative, improvised equipment and played baseball. Dr Bessels bought a dog team and made a couple of sledge journeys to study a glacier. So the winter passed.

In the spring, Chester, the second mate, who stands out as the most useful member of the party, made two twenty-five foot boats. The *Polaris* had been broken up for fire wood, there being none in that barren land. But he had conserved all the best timber, all the screws and nails.

By the beginning of May the boats were ready, sails and all. They were provisioned for two and a half months and the crews were allowed eight pounds of personal luggage per man – not much change of clothing for a wet voyage. They crept down the coast, camping ashore, hoping to meet a Dutch or Scottish whaler. They were fortunate. After only three weeks, Chester shouted 'Ship ahoy!' Three masts and the smoke of a barque were in sight only about ten miles away. The men set off for them on foot over the ice.

The crew of the Dundee whaler, *Ravenscraig*, met them on the way. They were soon on board, all safe and sound. There had been only one casualty, the ship's cat. Throughout the winter in the hut it had lived contentedly enough on the captain's bunk. But it disapproved of the boat journey, and, one evening had disappeared among the icy rocks.

The crew of the *Polaris* were not only welcomed but expected. They were given news of their marooned companions. That dark and tempestuous October night when the ship was swept away Tyson had displayed the gift of leadership. He had gathered everybody on a floe which was about a 150 yards square. The tally was eighteen – himself, the steward, the cook and six sailors, Joe and Hannah and their children, Hans Hendrick with his wife and family. With the two boats they salvaged all the stores they could – some bread and pemmican, a tent, a compass and a chronometer. They waited for the light.

This revealed a jumble of floes and bergs and the *Polaris* sailing rapidly towards the Greenland shore. There could be no advantage in trying to reach land themselves, for the boats were to light to force a way through the floes yet too heavy to be dragged over them. Besides, the two Eskimo kayaks could not transport eighteen people, and there were small children in the party. Their fate lay with the floe on which they gathered – cold, wet and exhausted.

Tyson had nothing at all except the clothes he was wearing. The others had left *Polaris* equipped for reaching the shore. But he had vaulted from the ship at a moment's notice to save the stores on the ice.

Joe and Hans built three snow houses, a remarkable achievement for the snow can scarcely have been suitable. Possibly the igloos were made of ice blocks. Certainly the party were extremely lucky in their Eskimos. Hans Hendrick was one of the best known in exploration history, having served Kane and Hayes as well as Hall. Joe was a skilful hunter while Hannah was invaluable for keeping up morale. They kept the party supplied with food. But it was not a case of regular civilised meals, rather of barbaric feast or famine, chiefly famine. The skills of the cook and steward were not called upon. Tyson's diary tells of the ravenous excitement when the first seal was killed. It was eaten raw, hair, skin and all. On Christmas Day they feasted on extra bread and the few comparative luxuries they had. But at New Year, Tyson stated, 'I have dined today on two feet of frozen entrail and a little blubber. I only wish we had plenty even of that.'

They were drifting down the middle of Baffin Bay. In February they saw land for the first time. It was to the westward and only about thirty miles distant. Hannah and Joe recognised the mountains of Cumberland Sound where they had lived. They were tempted to try to reach shore, working from floe to floe. Now that father Hall was dead they felt no allegiance to white men. In fact they did not trust them. The white men could not catch seals, and if they became really desperate might they not feed on Eskimos? There was good reason for this anxiety. All the sailors were armed – except Tyson who could only try to maintain discipline through strength of personality. The mixed crewmen behaved like a pack of famished dogs. They grabbed and gobbled anything that was killed. But Hannah told her husband that the Eskimos owed it to the memory of Hall to look after his compatriots who would die if deserted. This was undoubtedly true; the kayak hunters were essential.

Cold was almost as serious a trial as hunger. One of the boats was broken up for fuel. The only alternative was blubber which was food, and scarce.

They came through the winter without sickness except for one Eskimo child who became so ill that she could only eat seal (the stomach is conservative). She was kept supplied with seal meat and recovered. By the spring they were out of Baffin Bay and into Davis Strait, over 200 miles from Greenland on one side and Labrador on the other. Tyson estimated that they were drifting some twenty miles further south every day. The sun's return cheered them, but it and the slightly warmer water eroded their floe. Tyson wrote, 'The cracking of the floe was so alarming that the people remained up and dressed, and kept themselves and all their necessities of life ready in case of sudden disaster. . . . Fortunately the place originally selected for the snow houses proved to be the thickest and most solid part.'

They were heading out into the Atlantic and were rocked by waves. 'The 31 March was a day of great anxiety and peril. Although the floe was constantly diminishing, the appearance of heavy weather made it unsafe to venture in the open boat. The party could only suffer and hope for the best.'

But the following day they were compelled to make the break. The eighteen men, women and children crowded into a boat built for a maximum of eight. To have any free board they had to jettison 100 pounds of meat and all spare clothing.

Now began the most anxious period of the voyage. When there was wind they steered among the small floes; men stood on the ice holding the gunwhale to keep the boat off and steady it. The boat began to leak and had to be hauled out to be repaired. Once it drifted away from them but was recaptured by kayak. They had little food and no time for hunting. The one seal they found was gobbled raw and they they were back in innumerable difficulties. They were exhausted, almost without shelter. They could not go on struggling for long.

On 28th April, four weeks after the big floe had melted under them, they saw a ship. They raised a flag and lit a smoky fire from precious blubber. The ship turned towards them. They were wild with exaltation. By then they were off the southern tip of Labrador, having drifted 1,200 miles in six and a half months. The ice was finished, their boat was finished, they were finished. It was miraculous to be picked up at the last moment.

In the evening the ship turned away. Next morning it was nowhere to be seen.

They continued to struggle, by habit or will. They baled and patched their boat, kept going, fed the children. A sailor or guard stole pemmican during the night. There was nothing to be done about that. The thief had a rifle and Tyson had not.

Next day another ship appeared. They raised a flag, lit a blubber fire, the smoke curling about them with an intoxicatingly appetising smell. But again the ship turned blindly away.

The last day of April was foggy. No hope. . . . A ship loomed up close beside them, the barquentine *Tigress* from Newfoundland. Swift as a dream they were on board being cosseted. The crew of *Tigress* having grasped the essentials of their story were as amazed as they were. These people from the far north whom they had blundered upon in home waters had not only lost no single life, but they had increased their number by one. Hannah had had a baby.

Thus they all got home to tell their harrowing story, softened by a nice touch of Eskimo lore – an unquiet spirit rests peacefully in a new child.

7

A Scurvy Tale

In 1619 Captain John Monck made a voyage in search of the North-West Passage on the orders of King Christian of Denmark and Norway. With two little ships, the *Unicorn* and *Lamprey*, and sixty-four men he sailed to Hudson Bay; after fruitless wandering in that inland sea he wintered at the site of present-day Churchill. This is his story as it first appeared in English.

On the 27th of November there appeared three Suns to them, and on the next following 24th of January two. On the 10th of December Old Stile, there happened an Eclipse of the Moon, which they saw about Eight a Clock at Night; after which they saw the same Night the Moon surrounded with a very bright Circle, through the middle of which was a Cross, which divided the Moon in two. This seem'd to be the fore-runner of those Evils which those poor Wretches were to suffer hereafter, as will appear out of the following Account.

The Cold began to encrease with the Winter-season, to such a degree, that they saw Ice of 300, nay 360 foot thick; no Beer, no Wine, or Brandy was strong enough to be proof against it, but froze to the bottom, and the Vessels split in pieces; so that they cut the frozen Liquor with Hatchets, and melted it before the fire, before they could drink it. If they happened to leave any quantity of Water in their Copper or Tin Vessels, they found them all in pieces the next morning; Neither were the poor Danes able to resist so excessive a Frost, which mastered the Metals, for they all fell sick, and their Sicknesses encreased with the Cold; they were generally seized with a Griping Looseness, which did not leave them till it put an end to their days. Thus they dropt away one after another, so that about the beginning of March the Captain was fain to do Duty as a Sentry, for want of others. The worst was, that the Spring did augment their Distemper, for their Teeth were ready to fall out, and their Gums swell'd to that

112

degree, that they could not take any other nourishment but Bread soak'd in Water. The poor remnants of these unfortunate Wretches were in the next following May seized with another Looseness, with such violent pricking pains in their Limbs, as made them look like meer Shadows; their Arms and Legs being quite lame, and full of Blew spots, as if they had been beaten; being a Distemper not unknown to Seamen, by whom it is commonly call'd the Scurvy. So many of them died, that there were not enough left to bury them, the rest being likewise sick and very weak: and to compleat their misery they began to want Bread, instead of which they made use of Rasberrys which they dig'd out from under the Snow, which supply'd the defect of Bread; but they were fain to eat them as soon as they were taken from under the Snow, where they kept fresh, but soon grew useless afterwards.

On the twelfth day of April it rain'd the first time after seven Months; and toward the end of May there appear'd again all sorts of Fowl, such as wild Geese and Ducks, Swans, Swallows, Partridges, Ravens, Snipes, Faulcons, and Eagles, but they were too weak to catch them.

On the 4th day of June Captain Monck himself fell so dangerously ill, that he did take no food for four days together; and expecting nothing else but present death, he made his last Will, in which he desired those that might by chance come to this place to bury his Corps, and to send the Diary of his Voyage to the King of Denmark. After four days were past he began however to recover a little, and with much ado got out of his Hut, to see whether there were any of his Ship's Crew left alive, of whom he found no more than two of Sixty four Persons he brought along with him. These two being over joyed to see their Captain in a condition to stir abroad, took him in their Arms, and carried him to a Fire, to refresh his Spirits. They now began to encourage one another, promising to stand by one another to the last gasp. They dig'd every where among the Snow, till at last they met with a certain Root, which being both Restorative and Food to them, they were restored in few days. The Ice began now to melt apace, so that on the 18th of June they catch'd some Salmons, and other Fish, which with what exercise they used in Hunting, so strengthened them in a little time, that they resolved to return to Denmark.

They did. Sixty-two men had died, but the three who ate some plants were within a few days restored to such health that they could sail across the Atlantic a ship normally manned by about thirty. A mysterious, terrifying sickness and a seemingly miraculous cure.

Captain Monck's strange story was not the first recorded example of scurvy. The disease was known in the thirteenth century. It occurred during sieges and long sea passages. Because people were crowded together in these circumstances, it was thought to be contagious. The dark, damp and often cold conditions aboard ship were also believed to be a cause.

Ten years after Monck, Captain Thomas James wintered most miserably in Hudson Bay. In the following June, the ship still icebound, his men gathered 'vetches' with strikingly beneficial results. 'For now our feeble sick men who could not for their lives stirre these two or three months can indure the ayre and walke about the house; our other sicke men gather strength also and it is wonderful to see how soone they are recovered.'

Other explorers of the period ate 'scurvy grass' and sorrel. On a diet of salted meat and bread they would naturally find any green food attractive. They ate whatever herbs were available during a short season. If they had fruit or fruit juice it was also welcomed. What they fancied did them good.

The true cause, treatment and prevention of scurvy was demonstrated as early as 1753 by a naval surgeon named James Lind. He took twelve men with scurvy, divided them into couples and treated each with one of the various remedies popular at the time. The lemon-juice pair were cured very quickly whereas the others showed little change in their condition. As a result a daily dose of lemon juice became compulsory in the navy within fifty years (1803), and scurvy was virtually eradicated from the fleet.

But not for long. Limes tasted much the same as lemons so were considered the same. (The two juices were indifferently called 'lime juice'.) Limes were easily and cheaply available in the British possessions in the West Indies whereas lemons were expensively bought in the Mediterranean countries. The same dose of lime juice was substituted for the lemon juice. Lime juice is much less effective, so scurvy reappeared in the fleet. In consequence 'lime juice' (meaning both juices) lost its reputation. The Australians who had begun calling us Limeys may not have realised quite how disparaging the term was.

'By the end of the nineteenth century,' writes Dr E. J. C. Kendall, 'ideas on scurvy were again chaotic. Infection, toxic substances contained in improperly canned food, intestinal toxaemia and changes in the blood caused by varying diets were all brought forward to explain the disease.' So we are back to the days before Dr Lind.

Scurvy is a deficiency disease. The requirement for health is featherweight small – a matter of milligrams of vitamin C. This has to be put in to the human machine to make it work. Men, guinea-pigs and monkeys cannot synthesis their own vitamin C however much of anything else is pushed into their stomachs. And there is another awkward symptom. Men cannot store a large quantity of antiscorbutic. Four grams of vitamin C saturates them – any excess is excreted. With this they can live on a scorbutic diet for twenty-five to thirty weeks. Then trouble starts.

Citric fruit juices are by no means the only antiscorbutics. Vitamin C is present in all fresh foods, animal and vegetable, so long as it is not cooked out of existence. Preserving food – except by refrigeration – involves a certain amount of cooking. Polar expeditions depended almost entirely on preserved food at bases apart from anything gained by hunting. But they could have variety – canned vegetables, bottled fruit, jam – because weight did not matter. Sledging rations on the other hand were entirely scorbutic, for lime or lemon juice was never carried until quite recently. Therefore the length of time that sledging parties could be in the field without suffering scurvy symptoms depended on how near they were to vitamin C saturation when they set out from base. In other words it was the base ration that supplied the vitamin C for the journeys. They lived on capital with no possibility of increment.

When members of a sledge party had exhausted the vitamin C in their bodies they suffered loss of energy and muscular inefficiency, then softness of gums and loose teeth, never-healing wounds, stiffness of the legs, swelling of the joints, rigidity of the hamstring, shortness of breath because everything was much more effort, bruising (Monck's 'Blew spots'), then disorders of the heart which might be fatal – all from lack of a featherweight of vitamin C.

The sailors of the many Franklin relief voyages of the 1850 decade did not suffer seriously from scurvy – though Franklin's men may well have died from starvation because of the physical inefficiency it induced. The next major British expedition was that of Captain Nares, R.N. – still in the naval tradition. He thrust up between Greenland and Ellesmere Land for the North Pole in 1875-76 with H.M.S. *Alert* and *Discovery*. It was one of the least successful and most courageous expeditions in history. It was devastated by scurvy. One cannot be certain of the exact reason for the journeys were no longer in time and distance than some made during the Franklin search.

It seems that Nares's men did not get enough vitamin C at base. Those of the *Alert*, beset on the shores of the Arctic Sea, had little fresh food in the form of game during the winter. And the cooks, often well meaning villains, were certainly at fault. The 'fresh' ship's food consisted principally of tinned carrots and onions. To quote Dr Kendall again:

> At this period canned carrots and onions were simply boiled in cans and sealed. Little damage was suffered by the vegetable before canning, and most of the air was excluded from the can early in processing. It is therefore probable that the cans contained as much Vitamin C as cans packed today. However, these vegetables were generally recooked in soup or served mixed with meat. . . . The lime juice [available only on the ship and possibly in depots] was extracted from West Indian fruit, shipped to the United Kingdom in casks and bottled with 10 per cent rum. The initial low content of Vitamin C (as compared with that of lemon juice) would be further reduced in storage and during clarification.

So the men set out on their journeys in the spring seriously unfortified with the vital ingredient. They dragged cumbersome sledges loaded with equipment that might have been designed by a blacksmith, *and boats*. They did not have dogs. Each man dragged several times his own weight over the outrageous inequalities of pack ice. Their stories are told most vividly – in the first person – in dispatches, diaries, letters preserved in *Parliamentary Papers*, 'Blue Books'. 'It was a gradual run right from the beginning to the end, from the time we were first taken. . . .' 'Craig and Dobin almost dragged themselves along, their breath failing entirely at every ten yards. Paul and Jenkins gasped for breath at the slightest exertion. It was painful to watch them. . . .' 'Our travelling has been over rough sastrugi [snow drifts] and as I have to be blindfolded on account of my eyes I have been tumbling about in the most absurd manner.'

Their teeth fell out of their pulpy gums. They could not fit their footwear by themselves because they were so stiff. They walked like dummies, with constricted hamstrings. As their loads of food decreased they were replaced by men lashed onto the sledge because they could not walk at all. Sometimes there were as many men on the sledge as hauling it. A mile a day was good progress towards the end. They were unsung heroes who reached no Pole. Forty of the sixty-two men of the *Alert* and twenty of the sixty on *Discovery* had scurvy. There

116

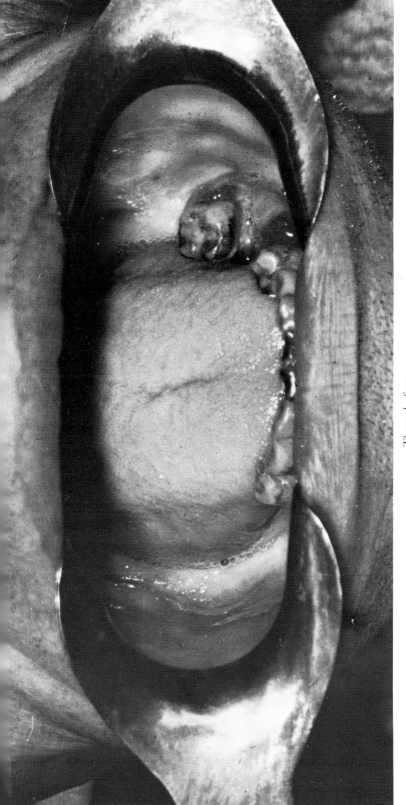

The ugly face . . . .

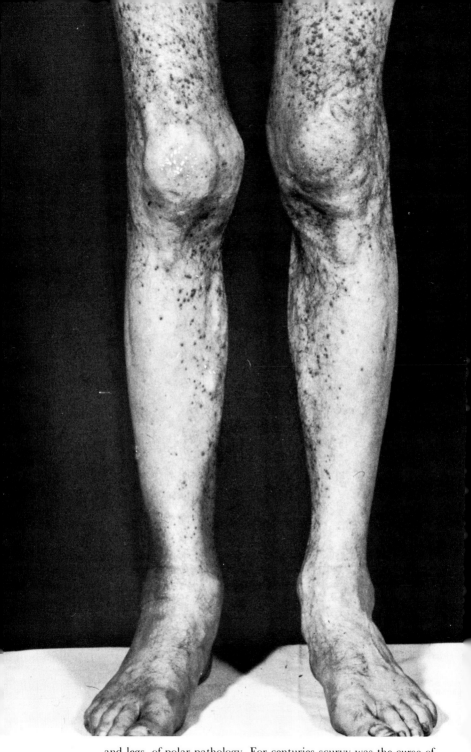

... and legs, of polar pathology. For centuries scurvy was the curse of explorers and mariners, until it was finally accepted that the answer is a lemon

were deaths on the march or soon after. Captain Nares, initially commended for a splendid effort, was blamed by a court of inquiry for not including lime juice in the sledging ration. Lime juice was then still the darling of the naval establishment. Certainly it had value, but if dragged along in effective quantity it would have been a considerable extra burden.

The National Antarctic (*Discovery*) Expedition, 1901-04, was led by Lieutenant R. F. Scott, and had a number of naval officers on its planning committees. So its diet had many hereditary qualities – except that lime juice had fallen out of favour with the Admiralty. (Scurvy was caused by ptomaines in tinned meat.) Lime juice was however available on the ship, and on the insistence of Dr Armitage was served at each meal at the base. Again, the cook, aided and abetted by personal tastes, did his best to reduce the vitamin C intake. He used the jam and bottled fruit for tarts, thus cooking it a second time. Ordered to use fresh seal rather than preserved meat he served seal steaks at every meal until nobody could stand the sight of them. Virtually no seal was eaten at the base except for a liver hash at Sunday breakfast. The sledge parties must have been well below saturation with vitamin C when they set out.

Some seal meat was added to the otherwise wholly scorbutic sledging ration. At base it was fried in margarine and dried in the oven. Thus its weight was reduced by half – and the vitamin C content more than halved.

(One realises how easy it is to be wise in retrospect. But, in the longer view, one cannot escape the impression that Homo Sapiens did not show much 'sapientia' throughout the scurvy story. He threw knowledge away as often as he cooked vitamins, and entrenched opinions too often won a battle.)

The main southern journey was made by Scott, Wilson and Shackleton, man-hauling. They were out for ninety-two days, just over thirteen weeks. Dr Wilson found no trace of scurvy after thirty days. After fifty, Shackleton's gums were abnormal and those of the other two were soon affected. After eighty days all three had swollen legs and Wilson a stiff knee. They believed that an increase in the seal meat allowance helped them, but they were all deteriorating fairly rapidly by the end of the journey and probably could not have gone on much longer.

On Shackleton's own expedition in 1907-09 he aimed at a more varied base diet. There was two or three times as much bottled fruit as on the *Discovery* expedition and five times more dried milk, well prepared in New Zealand. Although the cook managed to use much of the milk for baking there was enough over to do considerable antiscorbutic good. Shackleton's southern journey lasted for 122 days with no fresh food expect pony meat at long intervals. The South Magnetic Pole journey lasted 111 days, the rations having been supplemented with seal. Neither party suffered scurvy. The base ration must be given credit for that. Things were improving although the ideal of antiscorbutic for the march had not yet been found.

Captain Scott reached the South Pole on his last expedition without any dietetic advantage. And his party was not killed by scurvy. That they were almost certainly suffering the early debilitating effects of scurvy only adds to their achievement of dragging a sledge for twenty-one weeks.

With the knowledge of the time no antiscorbutic could be concentrated to sledge ration proportions without such damage by heat or air as would make it useless. Only with the end of the heroic antarctic era came scientific break-through. When Shackleton sailed in the *Endurance* in 1914 with the intention of crossing the antarctic continent from the Weddell Sea to the Ross Sea – an intended sledge journey longer than any previously attempted – he had on board lime juice concentrated *in vacua*. It went down with the *Endurance* when she was crushed by ice. Ironically his supporting – or welcoming – party which was laying out depots at the Ross Sea end of his route needed it. They made journeys of outrageous duration and suffered badly from scurvy. But there was no opportunity for anyone to try out a concentrate in the Polar field until much later. The war and post-war convalescence intervened.

When at last concentrated *lemon* juice, a last-minute logical advance, was thoroughly tested in the right environment, it was invariably used thereafter, with complete success. Capsule form is no doubt convenient yet seems a waste of the astringent taste most welcome with fatty foods. Our lemon juice was in bottles, with the old-fashioned ginger beer bottle type of levered stopper. We acutely enjoyed it – a clean sharp drink after hot hard work in dry cold. Take it with all the water that can be spared, otherwise it would screw your head off.

So the long human struggle against scurvy has ended both simply and pleasurably after seven recorded centuries. Why did it take so long? There were several contributory factors. Scurvy was a result of

118

catastrophic crop failure – something that recurs in distant parts of the world. It was 'contagious', due to overcrowding in ships and besieged castles – not much different from conditions in fall-out shelters; it was a thing of superstition – Monck's three suns and the cross over the moon; and it turned to folklore – an apple a day; it became a subject of tradition – Dr Lind and the Limeys. At long last science achieved something definite, recognised it as a deficiency disease and supplied the requirement. All that cost time, money and lives.

But Eskimos have never suffered from scurvy.

8

Records of Travel

The reasons why men go exploring are various. But all those who discover something have a point in common. They earnestly desire that the knowledge they have gained be passed on – it must not be lost even if they are themselves. They care for their records as ardently as a mother for her child.

By the turn of the century the outline of Greenland had been charted except for the north-east corner. There, at Navy Cliffe, Peary had looked down upon a channel of sea-water cutting through from coast to coast. Any land beyond the Peary Channel was therefore assumed to be off-shore islands. He drew on his map an almost straight dotted line indicating the 'probably coast line' to the south. He also marked Independence Bay opening eastward from Peary Channel.

Peary was a pioneer, less interested in detailed surveying than in reaching the Pole. In 1906 the Danmark Expedition led by Mylius Erichsen set out from Copenhagen to confirm the outline he had dotted in.

The unmapped coast extended from Cape Bridgman, which Peary had reached from the northern sea, to Cape Bismarck, 700 miles to the south. Mylius Erichsen wanted to make his base in the middle of this stretch. But the sealer *Danmark* managed only to lay down a depot about a quarter of the way up it, then had to retreat to Cape Bismarck before the advent of drift ice. Thus the sledge parties were faced with journeys of well over 1,000 miles. They could not carry sufficient provisions and would have to depend on finding game in the unknown country, mainland or islands, which lay to the north.

In March 1907 four parties set out. The long-distance men were Erichsen with Lieut. Hoeg Hagen and the Eskimo Bronlund, and Lieut. J. P. Koch with Bertalsen and the Eskimo Tobias. Alfred

Wegener led one supporting party and Thostrup, the ship's mate, the other.

In late April the supporting parties made up the loads of the long-distance men, laid down a depot and turned back. Erichsen, Koch and their companions went on, following the shore in very difficult conditions. Glaciers rising steeply to the icecap were on their left, the rough sea ice on their right. There were no inhabitants in this part of Greenland. To their dismay the coast curved more and more to the east – dismay because this greatly increased the estimated distance to their objectives – Peary Channel and Cape Bridgman respectively.

Then the coast swung abruptly round to the west, evidently leading into a deep bay or fjord. Here, on what was called Northeast Foreland, the most easterly point of pear-shaped Greenland, the two parties separated. Koch went north for Cape Bridgman while Erichsen turned west in search of Peary Channel.

Koch, travelling at first over the sea, passed the mouth of another fjord which formed a V with the one up which Erichsen was going. Being unable to make headway over the hummocky sea ice he turned in to the shore beyond the two fjords and followed the coast to Cape Bridgman, thus completing the outline from Cape Bismarck to the most northerly point.

He paused to hunt musk oxen and then turned back. At the point where the mouths of the two fjords joined on the open sea coast, his party met that of Erichsen. Erichsen, Hagen and Bronlund had been to the head of the more southerly fjord, which they named Danmarks. It did not lead to the Peary Channel but ran between steep mountains to end 150 miles inland against the icecap.

Erichsen was delighted that Koch had finished his task but did not feel that he had fulfilled his own. He had merely proved that Danmarks Fjord was *not* Peary's 'Independence Bay' seen by him from Navy Cliff at the same time as he saw the channel cutting through to the north coast.

Koch said that he had had a view right up the other fjord which did not appear to lead to Peary Channel either. But Erichsen felt that it was worth a few more days exploration to make quite sure.

This was typical of the spirit of the expedition. They had been travelling for two arduous months and were already depending on hunting for their food. Yet Erichsen was ready to add another 300 miles or so to the long distance already covered from his base.

Koch and Erichsen parted again at the end of May. Koch returned to Cape Bismarck, checking the depots as he went. His party reached the ship four weeks later, tired out by a journey of 1,400 miles. They waited for Erichsen's party. But July with no snow on the rocky coast led to a stormy autumn, and they had to wait until the coastal ice formed in October before a search party led by Thostrup could leave Danmark Havn. Failing to meet the missing men, Thostrup laid down depots to supplement those already established.

Koch led out another search party in the atrocious weather of early spring, fierce storms and bitter cold. They got as far as Lambert's Land, two thirds of the way to Northeast Foreland. Here was a depot that they all knew well, a small cave. The entrance was packed with snow. Shovelling this away they found the body of a man. It was the Eskimo Bronlund. Beside him was his diary and a bottle which contained the maps drawn by Hoeg Hagen, the surveyor of the party.

The diary was in Eskimo which they could not read but the last entry was in Danish:

> Perished 79 Fjord after attempt to return over inland ice in November. I arrive here in waning moonlight and could go no further for frozen feet and darkness. Bodies of others are in middle of fjord off glacier (about 2½ leagues). Hagen died 15 November, Mylius about ten days later.
>
> *Jorgen Bronlund.*

Koch could not find the bodies of Mylius Erichsen and Hagen or anything they might have written. They were lost in the middle of the fjord. It was due to the heroic Eskimo that a vital record had been saved. He must have been in as bad a state as the others – starving, exhausted and with frozen feet. Yet he had taken the maps and struggled on to a place that would certainly be visited.

The Danmark Expedition returned to Copenhagen in the autumn of 1908. They brought back answers to most of the questions about the unknown corner of Greenland. Koch's map showed that the coast was nothing like a straight line. It projected as a huge triangle. But what was the base of this triangle? Where exactly was Peary Channel? Erichsen had gone on to find this out, and had not returned. The information had not been contained in the maps that Bronlund had saved. But, following the unwritten law of explorers, Erichsen would certainly have left a record about so important a fact. Somewhere under a cairn of stones must lie the answer.

Ejnar Mikkelsen volunteered to go out and look for it. Mikkelsen was less than thirty when he sailed for northeast Greenland in 1909. Twenty years later I spent six weeks with him on a Faroe island. He spoke of having searched for a needle in a bundle of hay. There was still the same reckless yet determined spirit.

Mikkelsen had taken with him only six men on the forty-ton sloop *Alabama*. He carried, of course, a translation of Bronlund's diary, which told of how they had explored Independence Fjord after Danmarks Fjord. The second expedition was even longer than the first. They had been much harassed and delayed by bad ice and deep thawing snow, and by scant hunting which made both them and their dogs hungry and weak. There was no mention of Peary Channel, only that they had started homewards at the end of August. They had found the coastal route blocked by open water, so climbed onto the icecap. By that time all their dogs were dead. The next entry was the final one written in the cave. That was all Mikkelsen had to go on.

The little *Alabama* took a hammering from the pack ice but reached Shannon Island near Cape Bismarck where in due course she was frozen in. There was not much travelling weather left but Mikkelsen at once went north to Lambert's Land with Lieut. Jorgensen and Iver Iversen. Their outward journey was made dangerous by thin new ice which the necessity of haste made them take risks in crossing. Approaching the position of the depot, Mikkelsen went ahead and was guided by converging fox tracks to the exact spot.

Bronlund had again been buried by snow. They made a tomb of rocks for him and searched unsuccessfully for any other records. But Mikkelsen found only unopened tins of pemmican, peas and corned beef. Bronlund had not eaten the food in the depot. He could go no further, so why prolong life? Such was the Eskimo mentality.

The return journey was hard and cold. The three men reached the *Alabama* after an absence of ninety-five days, Jorgensen with badly frozen feet which incapacitated him for the much longer and more important journey the following season.

Mikkelsen planned to cut the corner made by the triangle of projecting coast, and aim straight for the head of Danmarks Fjord over the ice cap. This would save him 200-300 miles, allowing more time to search for records. Having done his work he would, instead of returning to his base, go on through Peary Channel to the first Eskimo settlement on the west coast.

The journey started inauspiciously – a joke that Mikkelsen enjoyed twenty years later. Carl Unger, the carpenter, felt that the occasion called for some display and hoisted a flag. Unfortunately he failed to get it right up and flew it from half-mast.

Mikkelsen and Iversen, with three others of the party supporting them for the climb, found a way up onto the icecap and then set a course for the head of Danmarks Fjord. They had their full share of the obstacles of such travel. But their most acute danger was when, with already depleted dog teams, they descended the precipitous slopes to sea level.

Mikkelsen mused on the fate of those who had been down there before him at the end of long explorations yet still far from their ship.

> Poor fellows what must they have felt when, after sledging all those toilsome miles out of their way, they reached the inland ice at last only to find instead of the easy ascent they had expected a sheer wall of ice a hundred feet in height. But their lives were at stake and under such conditions the impossible often becomes possible. Up they must and up no doubt they came however improbable it may seem, but where and how we shall never know.

That was imagination. At this stage his only knowledge of events came from Bronlund's brief diary.

A few days later he and Iversen found something positive, and puzzling, While still near the head of Danmarks Fjord they found under a pile of stones a spent cartridge which contained a tightly rolled up message signed by Mylius Erichsen. They smoothed it out and read it without difficulty. What was at once surprising was that it was dated 12th September 1907, over three months after Erichsen's chance meeting with Koch, and after already exploring Danmarks Fjord having decided to spend 'a few days' making sure about Independence Fjord. The long interval was puzzling, being only partly described.

> Since leaving our summer camp about eleven miles [forty-four English miles] from here on 8 August we have had to kill seven dogs for food for ourselves and the remaining dogs, and lay sixteen dogs on the sea ice about half a mile from land stopped by the water from the melting ice. At last on 25 August we reached land and shot four hares. Have since moved our camp about eight miles in all, in to Danmarks Fjord, moving by short stages and continually hindered in our progress towards good hunting

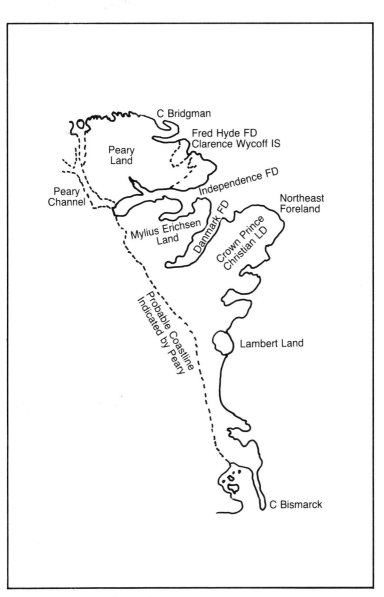

C Bridgman

Fred Hyde FD
Clarence Wycoff IS

Peary
Land

Independence FD

Peary
Channel

Northeast
Foreland

Mylius Erichsen
Land

Danmark FD

Crown Prince
Christian LD

Probable Coastline
Indicated by Peary

Lambert Land

C Bismarck

The north-east coast of Greenland

Ejnar Mikkelsen, a studio portrait

Mikkelsen, after two years and four months alone with Iver Iversen (see overleaf)

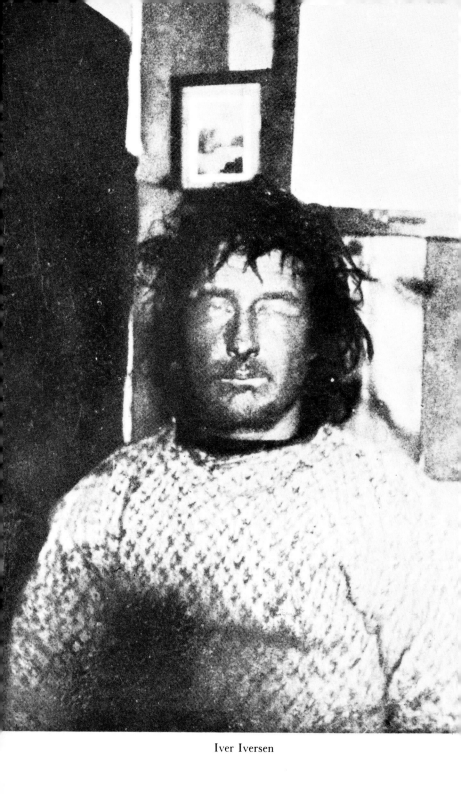

Iver Iversen

grounds by mild weather and impassable young ice, and at last by *open* waters from coast to coast . . . .

They had wandered over the hills on foot, obtained game and carried meat to the sledges but could not progress further up the fjord. 'Otherwise had thought of possibly returning via the inland ice from the head of Danmarks Fjord to the fjord 79° N. . . . Shall follow the bay for the thirty-six miles or thereabouts eastward to the outer coast, and with the aid of the depots laid down there last spring and by shooting bears we hope to reach the ship safe and sound in about five or six weeks.'

This was an expansion, and in detail a correction, of Bronlund's diary. But what had happened between the end of May, when Erichsen parted with Koch, and 12th September, the date of this record? The vital question was what had been found in Independence Fjord. Bronlund had mentioned only bad hunting and travelling conditions. Details of geography in a barren district had been of no interest to an Eskimo. But Erichsen would certainly have left an account. That was the record which must be found.

Mikkelsen and Iversen continued their search until near the junction of the two fjords they found the summer camp that Erichsen had referred to. Mikkelsen described it as a starvation camp. Pieces of rope, wood and canvas were lying about, everything gnawed by dogs. But sealed into a thermometer case they found another message. It was dated 8th August, thirty-three days earlier than the other. A glance showed that it led up to the message of 12th September for it explained why Erichsen's party had returned to Danmarks Fjord where they knew from experience that there were musk oxen.

'Being without further means of subsistence for ourselves and the dogs, not having got big game since 16 July, we must today – after having ferried ourselves across to the solid ice on a berg – leave here with fourteen dogs, two sledges and all our belongings in search of some stretch of coast more rich in game, away from this region where absolutely no game is to be found.'

There was more vital information, for the account went back to the parting with Koch in May and the subsequent exploration of the whole of Independence Fjord: 'We drove westward with twenty-three dogs until the 1st June reaching Peary's Cape Glacier, and discovered that Peary Channel *does not exist*, Navy Cliff being connected by land with Heilprin Land' – part of what on Peary's map was called Peary

Land, separated from Greenland proper by the supposed channel. This discovery was both totally unexpected and inexplicable. In the strange light of the Arctic, with mirages and refraction, land has not infrequently been reported where in fact there was only sea and clouds. But land has never been mistaken for the sea.

Erichsen, Hagen and Bronlund had lost their lives in making this correction. For their sakes it must be passed on. But it had an immediate significance for Mikkelsen and Iversen, for their plan had been to go on to West Greenland through the Peary Channel. Were they justified in persisting via a channel which did not exist or should they return to their ship by the longer but known east coast route where, if they perished, the records might still be found?

Asked for his opinion, Iversen answered that he would go wherever he was led, then curled up and went to sleep.

Mikkelsen did not reach his decision until morning. Iversen was still peacefully sleeping. Mikkelsen shook him.

'Hi, Iversen, wake up – we're going home!'

Iversen sat up, wide awake. 'Back home – did you say home – or was I dreaming?'

'Yes – I mean it – I think it is the only thing to do.'

Iversen beamed with joy. They discarded all they could possibly spare and packed up the rest, stowing the precious records carefully, and started on the east coast route which had already killed three men. From where they were, with Northeast Foreland still to be rounded, it was well over 500 miles to the Danmarks Hut, the first shelter. The depots on the first half would have been used and those on the second liable to have been destroyed by bears or weather during the last two years. But they were going south towards their old ship, *Alabama*, and their companions. That meant home.

The journey that started so cheerfully was a long-distance race against starvation. They were soon facing what had caused the destruction of Erichsen's party – warm weather and lack of game. The dogs floundered in deep rotting snow and lakes formed in their path. At one stage they had to make their sledge into a boat by wrapping round it the canvas inner cover of their tent. There were two months of such struggling, with a minimum of food. Mikkelsen developed what he believed to be scurvy. His joints swelled and he could not walk. They had to lie up when their only hope was to reach at least Danmarks Hut before winter – the *Alabama* lay a hundred miles further south.

126

One by one their dogs died. Before half way they were hauling the sledge themselves. Mikkelsen's description of this journey in 'Lost in the Arctic' is not easy to follow. It was written from memory. One forms the impression only of a long series of capes and fjord mouths, of depots searched for and too often never found, or found empty of food so that the only reward was the brief comfort of a fire of broken ration boxes. They travelled in 'the semi-delirium of starvation'. There is nothing much to tell about a race except the end.

When within twenty miles of Danmarks Hut they could drag their sledge no further. They cached everything. They even left their records, well wrapped up and carefully stored. They made a dash for it – a dash interrupted by furious storms.

At last they saw the hut. 'We move forward towards it, full of a great content, but staggering still at every step, dragging our feet like old men and halting now and again to rest. By eleven o'clock on the morning of the 18 September we have reached it – the journey is at an end!'

That journey was at an end but not their trials and anxieties, for the hut, though stocked with food, was deserted. There was no sign of their companions, no message.

As soon as they had recovered from their utter exhaustion Mikkelsen and Iversen made a sledge and started back to get their records. But they were beaten by the constant storms of October. It seemed to them that their companions who must have had a comparatively easy time might do the job for them when they appeared. But they did not appear.

Next season they went on southward to look for them. They had become anxious. After a hard journey they found the *Alabama* wrecked, dismantled and deserted. A hut had been built from her timbers. It was chock full of snow. They shovelled this out and found ample stores. But they never found the note that had been left for them. The *Alabama* had been crushed by the ice. The crew believed that Mikkelsen and Iversen had gone on as intended to the west coast, and felt that, even if they did return, stores would be of more use to them than five more mouths to feed. So when a relief ship came, the *Alabama* crew decided to go off in her. But the two castaways did not learn this until they were picked up by a Norwegian sealer two years later.

Surely the most striking achievement of the expedition of 1909-12 was not the exacting journey which lasted seven months but that two men who had not previously been particular friends could live together in harmony for so long under the conditions of anticlimax, discomfort, disappointment and the uncertainty which followed and which as far as they knew might have continued for the rest of their lives.

Iver Iversen must have been a good companion. Unfortunately Mikkelsen, though a fascinating talker in his highly individual English, lacked the gift of sketching character. He only mentioned a few incidents. Iversen – he never seems to have been called Iver – was always eager to do whatever had to be done. He was boundlessly energetic yet waited solicitously by his leader when he was incapacitated in mid-journey. He was unquenchably cheerful. He sang a Danish marriage song about travelling life's road together at the worst stage of the long slog (admirable, but it might have jarred). During the long anticlimax he was the cook – an exacting, important task, with limited ingredients. He was a tireless though not very successful hunter. He never managed to kill a bear which would have dramatically improved their fortunes during the starvation march. The two men found latterly that they had to talk all the time – it did not matter about what, just talk. They never quarrelled.

Their one major task while waiting to be rescued was to get back to the cache they had made before their desperate dash to Danmarks Hut, and recover their records. After much tribulation they reached the place. They found everything except Mikkelsen's diary which had been eaten by a bear.

9

An Explorer's Wife

On his last voyage Captain Sir John Franklin had in his cabin the portraits of two women, the Queen and his wife. One symbolised his duty, the other what he had left because of it. It might, therefore, be deduced that duty – or good name, which for a serving officer is in effect almost synonymous – was the stronger magnet. But, for Lady Jane, love and duty were one. She steered by that compass, and although it may be felt that she proved a still better widow than a wife it is largely due to her that Franklin holds his high place as a discoverer.

Franklin was knighted in 1829 – the year following his marriage – for his two recent expeditions to chart the Canadian Arctic coast. But thereafter it was seventeen years before he returned to the north, and if his other work had gone better he might never have explored again. So this other work must be briefly covered.

When he married Jane Griffin he was a widower of forty-two. From his portraits he was big, short-necked, wide-bodied, his face fitting Jane's description – 'open and mild, full of benignity and candour'. He might have been a sporting country parson, but from the age when boys start reading of adventures he was living them – hotly engaged as a midshipman at the Battle of Copenhagen, shipwrecked off Australia, slightly deafened at Trafalgar, wounded in the Orleans affair, then off on an attempt to sail over the North Pole, and finally, in this phase of his life, making the coastal surveys of Arctic Canada.

She was seven years his junior, small, *piquante*, lively, highly cultured, and came from a well-to-do family who spent their time in Continental travel and the activities of London society. She was too shy to be a good talker but was a fluent correspondent and compulsive diarist. She left some 2,000 letters and 200 journal volumes which are

129

now at the Scott Polar Research Institute and add much of human interest to the official records.

He waited two years for a command, then was given the frigate *Rainbow* on the Mediterranean station – the 'Celestial Rainbow' as his happy ship came to be called. His duties were diplomatic rather than naval, which was not quite to his liking. But he evidently did well, for his four years' service was rewarded with the Order of the Redeemer of Greece and the Hanoverian Guelphic Order.

Lady Jane followed him to the Mediterranean but could seldom be with him. She had written, 'Should there be war . . . I had much rather be in the midst of it than sit brooding over disaster and bloodshed at home. I shall not be in your or anybody's way, and I am sure you will never find me any hindrance to the most strenuous and energetic exertions you can make in your country's cause.' She kept out of the way by travelling as an adventurous tourist in Egypt, the Holy Land, Turkey and Greece – 'bugs, cockroaches, ants, flies and spiders and rats for much of the long way', meeting him wherever and whenever he had leave until they were reunited in Portsmouth in October 1834.

Again there was a break in employment – until August 1836, when he sailed for Tasmania as Lieutenant-Governor of that part of the Australian colony. With him was his wife and a considerable party – Eleanor (his daughter by his first marriage, now twelve years old), his niece Sophia Cracroft, and his personal staff. The voyage took three months. Sophy was seasick all the way but everyone else enjoyed themselves.

Tasmania at that time is excellently described by Frances Woodward on whose scholarly and perceptive *Portrait of Jane* I have heavily relied, using her transcriptions of letters and diary entries as a source. 'Nature,' she writes, 'had made of Van Dieman's Land a paradise which men had done their best to mar. Noble hills, watered valleys, majestic trees; sunshine and colour: and against them a dying race of natives, an exiled body of criminals, and a fevered community of settlers divided by fate from the other inhabitants and by faction from one another.'

The British Government's policy of the transportation of convicts was turning the island into the Empire's gaol. This suited the 'gaolers', who were landed proprietors, for the convicts were assigned to work on the land for no more than their keep. It did not suit the more liberal-minded, or the unlanded settlers, who could scarcely compete against unpaid labour. It certainly did not conform with the ideals of Sir John and Lady Franklin. But though on the island he was compared to a king, he was the servant of the British Government.

His seven years' labour are well summed up in the *Australian Encyclopaedia*: 'For the world at large Franklin's work was mainly connected with Arctic exploration. For Australians he is especially the man who tried to make convictism compatible with humanity; and his failure – or, rather the decision of the British Government that he failed – was the final proof that the two were incompatible, and so the essential factor in procuring the abolition of the system.'

This does not mention Jane's part, which was important. Franklin worked against the system, tactfully, diplomatically. He was nobody's fool and his principles were as high as heaven, but his methods were gentle and gradual. Jane's hatred of injustice scorned anything less than frontal attack. She behaved as she felt the wife of a governor ought to behave – which was very far from the behaviour of the conventional governor's lady. The Establishment saw her as their principal enemy – and she could not be got rid of without her husband. So machinations were set afoot and he was recalled, without warning or explanation.

Franklin was stung by the slight – neither recognition nor blame, just a casual brushing aside. Back in England, he went to see Lord Stanley at the Colonial Office, and was fobbed off with smooth phrases. He tried at least to obtain assurance that no blame was attached to his wife (he could not defend her if she was not attacked), but his Lordship did not wish the name of a lady to be brought into the discussion.

Franklin, the calmest of men, went away and fumed.

Then Fate stepped in. The Admiralty's interest in discovering a North-West Passage had revived and a commander was needed for an expedition planned for 1845.

In what Jane had once described as his own 'peculiar department' he might wipe out the snub administered to him by the Colonial Office. He put his name forward to command the *Erebus* and the *Terror*. He was backed by all his Arctic friends, Parry going so far as to tell the Admiralty that if he did not get the command it would kill him.

The First Lord was sympathetic but dubious. He said to Franklin, 'I might find a good excuse for not letting you go, Sir John, in the rumour that tells me you are sixty years of age'. 'No, no, my lord, only fifty-nine', Franklin said earnestly. His eagerness prevailed.

And Jane wrote what is perhaps her most pregnant sentence: 'I dread exceedingly the effect on his mind of being without honourable and immediate employment and it is this which enables me to support the idea of parting with him on a service of difficulty and danger better than I otherwise should – and yet not well.'

Evidently and naturally she was deeply unhappy. With her clear brain, she must have seen the situation in its true light. During the Mediterranean period she had kept out of the way, encouraging him and exhorting him only by letters – and he had been honoured. In Tasmania, a civil appointment, she had felt justified in sharing his work – and he had been dishonoured. What could she be but disillusioned with public life? She must have longed, after seventeen years of homeless wandering, to return with her man, make a home, share their friendships, relaxations, their comfortable little fortune. Instead he was spurred into 'a service of difficulty and danger' and her part was to stay behind. She recovered her spirit only gradually.

The key scene of the drama of Franklin's last voyage was the departure from Greenhithe of the *Erebus* and *Terror* on 18th May 1845. A crowd of thousands watched the ships sail and the mass mood was jubilant. It must have been a splendid sight, of course – those noble, three-masted hearts-of-oak drawing away, 134 of the best officers and sailormen in Britain waving and cheering from decks and rigging. They were confident, and proud to have been selected. This was the climax of three centuries of exploratory endeavour and they were going to succeed. They had a loved and trusted commander, two well-proven ships, three years' provisions and the very latest equipment, even 20 h.p. auxiliary steam engines (modified railway engines) which would give them a knot or two and some manœuvrability in dead calm or open pack ice. Also, the beginning and end of the route were known – only the middle third was uncertain. There was not a faint heart or a doubting mind on board.

The Admiralty was confident; it must have been, for although money had been lavished on the fitting-out there were no provisions for rescue, or even support by land or sea for a cruise which in its critical phase would be close to land – uninhabited land.

The great crowd waving from the shore was enthusiastic and confident. The North-West Passage had been the Royal Navy's challenge since the Napoleonic wars. Britannia ruled the waves and it could not make all that much difference if they were frozen waves.

Some people were prepared to bet that the ships would get through in a single season.

The mind's eye pictures from old prints the women in the crowd, doll-like in their bonnets and long tight-waisted dresses. Franklin's daughter was among them. She was now a young lady affianced to the Rev. John Gell, a protégé of Dr Arnold of Rugby, who was headmaster of the public school which Franklin had launched in Tasmania. Eleanor wrote of the departure to an aunt: 'Dear papa left in the best of spirits – he puts his trust in God. . . . Papa has been looking so much better since he left off snuff.'

Sophia Cracroft was there. She had stayed with the family throughout the Tasmanian governorship, braving the long voyages, sharing everything. She had on this occasion three reasons to be troubled in spirit. She had recently refused a proposal of marriage by Francis Crozier, captain of the *Terror*; she did not entirely trust Eleanor to help her stepmother; and neither apparently did Franklin, for Uncle John had urgently begged Sophy to comfort and look after his wife. She took this to heart as a sacred trust. For thirty years she was Jane's friend rather than niece, amenuensis and constant companion. If this story had not already a heroine she would have been Sophy Cracroft.

Lady Jane was with Eleanor and Sophy. In a letter sent ashore to Harwich, Franklin wrote to her that he saw her in the crowd and frequently waved his handkerchief, 'which I hope you saw'. Her feelings were too strong to express in any letter or in her private diary.

From Disco Bay in Greenland there came in due course a letter from James Fitzjames, captain of the *Erebus*: 'There is an incessant laugh from morning to night.' Morale was high. Prospects were good. The two ships sailed on towards Lancaster Sound, the known beginning of the North-West Passage – and disappeared.

There was no prospect of news for more than a year, until after the next open season. Jane could not merely sit at home and wait. Travel was her antidote to anxiety. With her stepdaughter she went to France and Madeira, then on to the West Indies and the United States, a long and arduous voyage by sailing-ship. She was greeted everywhere with honour as the wife of Sir John Franklin. Explorers were lions in those days. She remained anxious and unhappy, but these travels paid a dividend later from the friendships she made.

She returned to England in the autumn carrying with her hope of news. There was none – and no hope of any for another year.

She wrote to Franklin's great friend and fellow-explorer, Sir John Ross:

> I sometimes think it is better perhaps that we should thus be in happy ignorance of any disaster that may have happened to them, or any dreadful difficulty they may have yet to overcome than to be viewing as in a magic mirror in a fairy tale, their daily vicissitudes. I dare not be sanguine as to their success – indeed the very thought seems to me presumptuous, so entirely absorbed is my soul in aspirations for their safety only.

In 1847 she kept no diary. Throughout the spring and summer – a vital period for the expedition as it proved – she was in Italy. She returned in time to receive a letter, if there were one. There was nothing.

The Admiralty was by this time considering sending out search expeditions. James Ross and John Richardson had volunteered to lead them. But they could not set out until the following year and there was much discussion as to which routes they should take – or attempt to take. The *Erebus* and *Terror*, or the men if they had been forced to abandon them, might be anywhere within an area of a million square miles, a maze of islands and straits or culs-de-sac. The sailing-season was of about two months, meaning that during that period new ice was unlikely to form. But the old ice, the fragmented floes of former winters, was on the move, more or less filling the waterways and varying the pattern of its construction from year to year. Franklin had entered this maze by Lancaster Sound, near its north-eastern corner and had been instructed to sail west as far as Cape Walker (about 300 miles), then 'to endeavour to penetrate to the southward and westward, in a course as direct as possible towards Bering Strait as the position and extent of the ice, or the existence of land at present unknown, may permit'. But he was also to consider turning north to reach 'the open sea' beyond the archipelago we have called 'the maze'.

Twenty years earlier Parry had charted Lancaster Sound, following an east to west line across the top of the maze to well beyond Cape Walker, but found it finally impossible to break free of the islands to the Beaufort Sea, then believed to be open. Franklin knew (from personal experience and the surveys of others) the continental coast – *except* the eastern corner where the Boothia Peninsula sprouts north from the generally straight line of the coast. He had said that if he could get down to this coast, where there was always open water in summer, it would be plain sailing to Bering Strait and the Pacific. But the only eastern entrance to the archipelago was by Lancaster Sound and no one knew how to get by ship from the north to the south of the maze. In 1829 John Ross and his nephew James had taken the first turn to the left off Lancaster Sound (Regent's Inlet) and found themselves in a cul-de-sac. No one had attempted any other southward-leading waterway.

Since Jane kept her deepest thoughts to herself in 1847 we cannot know whether it was by reasoning or instinct that she believed the ships to be somewhere near the uncharted corner of the continental coast. But that she so believed was proved by her instructions to those who later served her, and she more than hinted at it in a letter to James Ross. She did not, however, feel justified in asking that this corner should be searched. Her desperation was not yet strong enough to overcome her diffidence.

In 1848 action was at least begun, and Jane resumed her diary. In January H.M.S. *Plover* sailed for Bering Strait via Cape Horn to meet the *Erebus* and *Terror*. Jane wrote to her husband, and asked others who wrote to say nothing that might distress him. 'Who can tell whether they will be in a state of body or mind to bear it.'

In March, Richardson set off for his coastal journey. She felt sure that he would do 'all that experience and energy and public spirit and devoted friendship can compass'. James Ross sailed for Lancaster Sound with H.M.S. *Enterprise* and *Investigator* in May. Jane sent by his hand a long letter to her husband, of which this is part:

My dearest love, – May it be the will of God if you are not restored to us earlier that you should open this letter and that it may give you comfort in all your trials. . . . I try to prepare myself for every trial which may be in store for me, but dearest, if you ever open this, it will be I trust because I have been spared the greatest of all. . . .

It would have been a less trial to me to come after you, as I was at one time tempted to do, but I thought it my duty and my interest to remain, for might I not have missed you, and would it have been right to leave Eleanor – yet if I thought you to be ill, nothing should have stopped me. God bless you again. You will be welcomed back with joy and honour by your friends and family and country – *most* of all by your affect and devoted wife. . . .

135

With 1849 there arose to plague her that nastiest of domestic ills, a family quarrel about money. John Gell was back from Tasmania, and Eleanor and he wanted to get married – and wanted money to live on. They had become engaged before Franklin sailed but he had expected to be home in plenty of time to arrange everything and had only left his wife a power of attorney for the use of what had been her own money. (She had made it all over to him and refused to have a marriage settlement.) Now, for the first time, she felt the need of this money, for it had become her dream to launch her own expedition under her own instructions. She would do that as soon as possible. Meanwhile, she would persuade others to act.

The Admiralty offered a reward of £20,000 to anyone of any nation who found the expedition. That should induce whalers to hunt for the ships – in whaling waters. But Jane wanted governments to become involved. She wrote to Zachary Taylor, President of the United States. 'I am not without hope that you will deem it not unworthy of a great and kindred nation to take up the cause of humanity which I plead, in a national spirit, and thus generously make it your own. . . .' It was a long letter, every sentence polished and rounded and charged with emotional appeal. And it contained the hint that America might incidentally win the North-West Passage! It worked. In co-operation with the wealthy merchant Henry Grinnell, the brigs *Advance* and *Rescue* were provided. (This was the spark that lit the fire of American Arctic exploration, to blaze half a century later in the race for the North Pole.)

Still Jane was far from satisfied. The whole possible area was so vast. She wrote to the Board of Admiralty:

> I have been informed that two such vessels as Dockyard Lighters with some alteration to the rigging, would be well adapted to my purpose, and being very strong they could soon be made ready for sea. . . . I cannot attempt to conceal from the Board, that it is only by the sacrifice of all my private property (though I am not able to carry this to the full extent of what I desire) and by the additional aid of borrowed capital, that I shall be able to effect my object, if unassisted by them; but I will still by the blessing of God carry it through, certain that I shall never repent of my resolution let what will happen, and feeling that it will be a real consolation to me, in the depth of my own bereavement, if by my means, the humblest individual of that gallant band are saved from perishing.

The most striking points in this letter are the nautical knowledge she displayed, that she laid her financial cards on the table, and that she already spoke of her bereavement.

But the Admiralty was not as easily moved as the President of the United States. It would send only the store-ship *North Star* to back up James Ross, and they would not allow Jane to sail on her. But she made the best of this: 'I am of use to you, to all of you, at home – I do not let the Admiralty rest about you,' she wrote to her husband – in a letter to be carried by an American ship.

She had taken rooms in Spring Gardens, off Cockspur Street, in close range of Their Lordships. 'The Battery' was manned. But it is a measure of Jane's desperation that this strictly religious person sought help also from the Occult. What she was told proved false so the incident deserves no more than mention.

Ross and Richardson were not expected in England for some months yet. But the Arctic whalers would be back in Orkney and Shetland before that, and if there was news they might know it. So up to the Northern Isles went Jane and Sophy, even travelling to Edinburgh by sea to save money. Poor Sophy! She described in a letter a stormy passage in a fishing-boat from Hillswick to Busta and of how they were complimented for their calmness. Sophy did not utter a word – perhaps she did not trust herself. Jane read a book, and a sailor said of her, 'If the woman be such a man, what must the husband be?'

They received news. A bottle with a message had been picked up in Greenland waters. . . . But it was only a standard Admiralty form, with date and position where thrown overboard to provide, if found and returned, information on ocean currents.

Then a man was dropped off at Kirkwall from the whaler *Truelove*. He brought an account of Eskimos who had seen the *Erebus* and *Terror*, with Franklin on board, in Regent's Inlet in March of that year. The Eskimos had drawn a map showing the position of the two ships, and Ross's ships also. The *Truelove* had tried to reach them but had been stopped by ice, so had left a depot of food and coal – provided by Jane's forethought. Jane found the sailor and questioned him, and afterwards – said Sophy – looked fifteen years younger. The two women hurried to Edinburgh, where the church bells were ringing, to get further details. . . . The story proved unfounded.

In November came a message from London. Ross and Richardson had returned to England, independently but within days of each other, and neither had found any trace of the *Erebus* and *Terror*.

It was then, it seems probable, that she accepted in her heart that her husband was dead. She put on black. But simultaneously another task opened before her. She had to find out what had happened to him. She wrote: 'May a merciful God bless our efforts. May He if it is ordained otherwise vouchsafe us the *knowledge* which will better enable us to submit to His dispensations.'

She took up her quarters again in Spring Gardens and, living frugally – for she had no money to spare – began her quest for knowledge.

The clarity of her thinking at this time was remarkable. She had got out of the Admiralty all she could for the moment. (They were in fact very active as the account of the next season will show.) She had got what she could out of Washington. What else could she do? She wrote to Silas Burrows in New York. 'Do you think I could procure a few thousand pounds in America to add to my own, so as to enable me to send a small vessel or 2 small vessels of not above 100 tons each, with boats, to those especial parts where I am persuaded the lost ships and crews are most likely to be found?'

She wrote to Dr John Rae of the Hudson's Bay Company – she had met his mother in Stromness. He had been with Richardson and was to make further explorations to Victoria Island just off the continental shore. 'I do not know whether you consider that the mouth of the Great Fish River should be examined,' she said.

Sophy wrote to Franklin: 'You may wonder at my saying that even you do not know your own wife, but inasmuch as her devotedness, courage, fortitude, and extraordinary mental endowments have been tested as of late, so you have never known the full extent of her rare qualities. I cannot express to you how entirely I honour as well as love her. . . . Throughout the length and breadth of the land she is honoured and respected . . . and this, notwithstanding the most shrinking anxiety to avoid notice. . . . Pray remember me very kindly to Captain Crozier.'

And Jane wrote, 'I desire nothing but to cherish the remainder of your days, however injured and broken your health may be – but in every case I will strive to bow to the Almighty Will, and trust through His mercy for a blessed reunion in a better world!'

These letters were carried north by one of the eleven ships that sailed for Lancaster Sound in 1850. Four were of the Royal Navy – *Resolute, Assistance, Pioneer* and *Intrepid* under the command of

Captain Austin. He was a short-tempered but competent and popular commander. William Penny, a tough, blunt-spoken whaling captain (Jane liked him very much), commanded the *Lady Franklin* and *Sophia*, which carried their figureheads. Sir John Ross, now seventy-four, took the little ships *Felix* and *Mary*. There were the two American vessels, *Advance* and *Rescue*, led by Lieutenant de Haven, U.S.N. And there was Lady Jane's own ninety-tonner, *Prince Albert* (she had won the sponsorship of the Prince Regent), skippered by Commander Charles Forsyth, R.N. In addition, the *Enterprise* and *Investigator* (James Ross's ships) had been swiftly refitted and sent off under Captain Collinson and Commander McClure to sail round the Horn and enter the maze by Bering Strait where the *Herald* and the *Plover* were already on watch.

Fifteen ships! There had never been such an armada in the Arctic. Yet Jane was troubled as to whether they would search in what she considered the right areas. She was grateful to the Admiralty, to the Americans, to all the eager men who were taking part and those who were putting up the money; but for that reason, apart from others, she could not seek to dictate their plans. Nor could she very well ask for more – although in fact she did. She wanted a search of the Great Fish River mouth, of Boothia Felix and the ill-mapped lands adjoining.

As it happened, the eleven ships that entered the maze by Lancaster Sound followed very much the same course whatever the plans of their commanders. The ice shepherded them down the Sound to small, inconspicuous Beechey Island at the beginning of Barrow Strait. Here was a water cross-roads. Wellington Channel led north, Barrow Strait westward, Regent Inlet and Peel Sound south. And on Beechey Island a cairn was seen. A signpost!

The men tumbled ashore with such alacrity that there was later some uncertainty as to who actually made the finds – a litter of camp equipment, such kitchen refuse as bones, a large quantity of empty tins (which caused the supposition that part of Franklin's canned rations were bad) and the graves of three sailors of the *Erebus* and *Terror*. The lost ships had evidently anchored here for the winter of 1845-46. And from the quantity of scattered kit it looked as if they had sailed on in a hurry.

But sailed in what direction? There was no record under the cairn nor anywhere on the island or nearby Cape Riley. It is a mystery to this day. For what purpose had the cairn been built? It was a blank signpost. Had there been a message of intent the search might have been concluded within a year instead of a decade.

The ships sailed on westward – or tried to. The Americans took the lead. At this the British piled on all sail, for although Lady Franklin had hinted to President Zachary Taylor that his country-men might win the North-West Passage there are limits to international co-operation. But it made no difference. They all ended up faced with impenetrable ice. Barrow Strait was blocked and so was Wellington Channel.

The *Prince Albert* alone turned southward. Following Lady Jane's instructions Commander Forsyth sailed into Prince Regent Inlet, the first turn to the left off Lancaster Sound. This, less crammed with ice, was known to be a cul-de-sac, but near the southern end of it John and James Ross had found an Eskimo community in 1824, and James Ross had sledged over the Isthmus of Boothia to the ill-mapped corner that had long held Jane's imagination. Even if no land journeys had been achieved by the Franklin expedition, the Eskimos might have something to tell.

So it was a sound plan. But it failed in execution. Jane had first met Charles Forsyth when the *Beagle* called in Tasmania, and had like him. She was touched when he offered his services free for the search. But his amiable qualities did not cut much ice in the Arctic, where he had never been before, and the *Prince Albert* got only seventy miles down the Inlet.

Jane's little ship might have been successful if she had chosen the right commander. She tended to select by character rather than seamanship. This may sound amateurish but it was just this human touch that made her finally successful. For she evoked chivalry, and it was by that talisman that the secret of the North-West Passage was discovered when all else had failed.

Forsyth brought home news of the tantalising finds on Beechey Island, but nothing more. It was a heavy blow for Jane. But she quickly recovered. Although she had already spent a great deal on the *Prince Albert* she resolved to send her out again the next season under a new commander.

She chose William Kennedy, a Canadian of Orkney descent, an earnest, impulsive, deeply religious and generous-hearted man. He had not very much nautical experience, but he was backed up by a young French naval lieutenant, Joseph Réné Bellot.

The story of the second voyage of the *Prince Albert* not only conveys the chivalrous feeling and the devotion to Lady Jane that

140

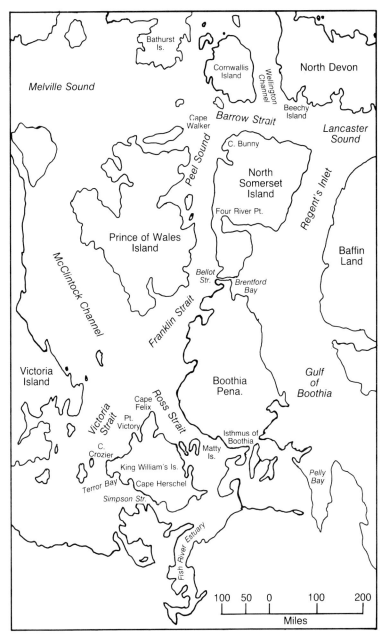

The area of the Franklin search

Sir John Franklin

Lady Franklin

H.M.S. *Erebus* and *Terror* – a mid-nineteenth century impression of the polar regions by J. W. Carmichael

characterised the whole search but also the bad luck that dogged it. Kennedy had come from Canada ready to serve in a subordinate capacity if necessary, Bellot had obtained leave and come from France, and John Hepburn, Franklin's bluejacket companion on the coastal journey of 1819-22 who had gone with him to Tasmania, had come back at the age of sixty-one to offer his services – and of course to be accepted by one who never forgot her friends. The crew were Orcadian and every one devoted to their patroness, also to whisky which they had to do without, serving under Kennedy who would allow no alcohol on board. 'No doubt this precaution will give an unprecedented lustre to our expedition,' the young Frenchman observed sadly.

Bellot kept a journal which was later published. It is charmingly revealing of life on board the little ship. They were held up for some days at Stromness and Jane came to say good-bye. She insisted that a French flag should be hoisted in honour of the second-in-command. She went through Bellot's wardrobe which she considered adequate but remarked that he still needed a mother. He warmly accepted the relationship and vowed that he would seek Franklin 'with the inexhaustible devotion of a son'. He was only twenty-five.

She was much moved at parting. 'Take care of yourself, *c'est tout ce qu'elle put me dire en pleurant. Pauvre femme!'*

Poor woman indeed. In addition to the strain of disappointment, and of refitting the *Prince Albert*, her relations with her step-daughter had come to crisis point. Eleanor had decided that her father was with God and it was a waste of money to go on looking for him. Jane had a breakdown. Sophy was very worried about her – with good reason, for Jane could never relax. As her biographer, Frances Woodward, observed, 'Each year, from 1850 to 1854, had an identical rhythm: winter, preparation; spring, departure; summer, suspense; autumn, return.' And with every return she had her passionately longing letters returned to her. How many women could stand up to that?

The *Prince Albert*, under the command of William Kennedy, was the only ship to sail for the north in 1851. The rest of the flotillas, with the exception of the Americans who had not been equipped to over-winter, were still out on the search. For the most part this was executed by tremendous sledge journeys, two hundred men fanning out from the icebound ships, charting thousands of miles of unknown coastlines but finding no clue to Franklin's whereabouts.

The *Prince Albert* did not join them. Her instructions – which as

Bellot noted had been liberally spiced by Jane and Sophy with prayers and religious injunctions to ensure that Kennedy read them – were again to penetrate Prince Regent Inlet as deeply as possible, then to strike westward overland to the unknown quarter.

Incidentally, Bellot is very interesting on the subject of religion. A Catholic among Calvinists he at first disliked the frequent services which Kennedy (not even a minister) insisted on conducting. But he soon came to appreciate their sincerity and value to morale. When, later, the captain was indisposed, and during an anxious period temporarily lost, the Frenchman led the services himself. Christian unity can never have been more evident than on that Arctic voyage of 130 years ago.

Also (one cannot resist quoting some of these touches), Bellot was delighted by Kennedy's Canadian French; the French of more than a century ago had for him '*un parfum tout particulier*'. But he was *étonné* to hear the crew discussing *Othello*. One man preferred *Macbeth*, another *Hamlet*. '*Je doute que Molière soit aussi populaire parmi les matelots français.*' Or Shakespeare among modern English seamen!

If ever an expedition deserved to succeed it was this one. And it came within a couple of hundred miles of doing so, far closer than the rest of the searching fleet. The little ship was delayed so long by the ice in Baffin Bay that she managed to penetrate only a short distance down Prince Regent Inlet before having to berth for the winter on its western side, what was called the Somerset shore. It was at that time believed that North Somerset was a continuation of Boothia, together projecting like two joined sausages 700 miles long from the continental mass, their junction being at Brentford Bay.

Kennedy's plan was to make a spring sledge journey (long before the ship could break free) southwards down the east coast of North Somerset to Brentford Bay, then across to the west coast, and south again, down the shore of Boothia, as far as they could go. If they could approach King William 'Land', which James Ross had seen on the first search expedition and which was known to sit like a cork on the estuary of the Great Fish, they would have fulfilled Lady Franklin's instructions – or very nearly. They had been made a little doubtful of their travelling ability by some hard experimental winter trips.

They had dogs, which was more than the Royal Navy and William Penny, commanding the *Lady Franklin* and *Sophia*, had. But only one man could drive them or build snow houses.

Amateur but eager, they got away on 29th March. Lady Jane had asked Bellot what names he would give to any new geographical features. He had pondered over this in his journal. But when he made an important discovery he did not recognise it as such; neither did Kennedy.

They could not find the head of Brentford Bay. The cliff-lined shores narrowed to a channel a mile wide and went on and on – then suddenly opened onto a great expanse of ice-covered water. Dimly through the haze they saw land in front. They thought that this swept round to enclose them on their right, the north. They did not realise that they had passed between Boothia and North Somerset, which is an island. The had discovered the channel which is now called Bellot Strait.

But the immediate sequel was the opposite of fortunate. There was so much they did not know that hazy day. They were in Peel Sound, the second turn to the left from the Lancaster Sound entrance. From Beechey Island the *Erebus* and *Terror* had sailed down Peel Sound to become finally icebound off Point Victory on King William Island. If Kennedy had followed his instructions – and his own original plan – and turned south, they could have solved the problem.

But they were both puzzled. Bellot to his credit wanted to stop, take observations and work out where they were. The impetuous Kennedy, no trained navigator, wanted to press on westward and cross the hazy land in front which he considered to be still part of North Somerset. Franklin could not have passed this way, he said, because the waterway was blocked to the northward. (It was not, except possibly by mirage.) Bellot did not argue. As a foreign officer he was always careful not to be insubordinate.

So they crossed Peel Sound (without realising it was Peel Sound) and then the hazy land beyond which was actually Prince of Wales Island, already explored by Ommanney and Osborn. Two months later they recrossed it to regain their base, hungry and scurvy-ridden.

When the *Prince Albert* was freed by the ice, Kennedy sailed to Beechey Island, and then home. Jane did not express her disappointment. She always had a soft spot for the terribly earnest captain. When he brought her relics from Cape Riley she wrote, 'Mr Kennedy returned with the bones, rope and sailcloth in a round basket covered with white paper like a twelfth cake'. Perhaps it was her sense of humour that kept her sane.

The period of the *Prince Albert's* voyage had been particularly hard for Jane. She was not in good health, she was almost sixty years old, and she had troubles on two fronts. One of these was the lack of success – even the lack of hopeful prospects – in the search. Austin, Kellett, McClintock, Osborn, Mecham, .Penny, de Haven – had returned with the conviction, shared by the majority of the Arctic Council and therefore the Admiralty, that Peel Sound was impassable but Wellington Channel a possibility. If Franklin had gone north from Beechey Island his ship might well have been sunk without trace in the Polar Ocean. But just possibly, some thought, he and his men had found an island rich in game and were still alive. This misty hope was almost worse than none at all. It would not have been sufficient to induce the Admiralty to send out another five ships under Captain Sir Edward Belcher, as they did. The main reason was that nothing had been heard of Captain Collinson and Commander McClure who, with the *Enterprise* and *Investigator*, had gone searching by Bering Strait in January 1850. *They* might be found if the *Erebus* and *Terror* were not. There was not much comfort for Jane in this double-purpose expedition, particularly since it was led by the reputedly most unpopular officer in the Navy, who had never been in the Arctic before.

The other front on which Jane was assailed was the domestic. Family money quarrels are best left alone by outsiders and this one was in any case to complicated to be dealt with at length. But it must be mentioned, for it was long lasting and most damaging. And at one stage it was aired in public. An anonymous letter appeared in *The Times* appealing for the preferment of the Rev. John Gell as being an indirect sufferer from the Franklin search – since money spent on it should have gone to Franklin's daughter, his wife Eleanor.

Jane continued her own appeals – to the Admiralty, to the United States, to the Emperors of France and Russia. The yearly rhythm continued: winter, preparation; spring, departure; summer, suspense; autumn, return. The Admiralty broke the pattern by announcing that, as from 31st March 1854, the names of Sir John Franklin and his men would be removed from the Navy Lists. In other words, they were written off as dead.

For a whole week Jane remained stunned as if struck by lightning. Then she reacted strongly and typically. She told the Admiralty that their decision was 'presumptuous in the sight of God, as it will be felt to be indecorous, not to say indecent (you must pardon me for speaking the truth as I feel it) in the eyes of men'. She refused to claim a widow's pension. She changed her black for brightly coloured clothes. This was defiance. As a balanced, highly intelligent woman, she had surely given up all hope that her husband was alive. It was knowledge of how and where he had died that she had been seeking, waiting for.

Before the year was out she was to receive it – incomplete and secondhand, yet proven in essentials. But before that she was to suffer other trials. In the autumn all Belcher's men came back, packed on board the *Phoenix* and *Talbot*, for on Belcher's orders H.M.S. *Assistance, Pioneer, Resolute* and *Intrepid* had been abandoned in the ice. Their officers and men brought home no news, only bitterness.

There were also carried home by the supply ship McClure and the remains of the crew of the *Investigator* – with the claim that they had discovered the North-West Passage from the east. McClure's was an extraordinary story we can no more than touch on. There was long outstanding a reward of £10,000 for the discovery of the Passage. There was also a reward for finding Franklin. Since Franklin had been looking for the Passage, any subsequent searcher might become eligible for either or both rewards. This is *not* stressed, only mentioned. There is no evidence that anyone who went to search for Franklin did so except, primarily, in response to the sacred and age-old tradition of rescue. By 1850 there was no reasonable hope of rescuing any of his men, yet the Passage remained to be discovered. By his behaviour and what one deduces of his temperament, McClure was after that at least as a second objective. He raced his commander, Collinson in the *Enterprise*, to Bering Straight. He flogged his men and his ship, the *Investigator*, into the western side of the archipelago and finally became icebound on the north coast of Prince of Wales Island, at the western limit of the waterway from Lancaster Sound. Almost certainly they would all have perished had they not been found by a sledge patrol from Kellett's *Resolute*. They were taken to her by sledge, or on foot if they could walk, then on to the Lancaster Sound ice edge, and so home.

McClure's claim that he had discovered a North-West Passage only worried Jane's clear brain in that it might make it more difficult to launch other expeditions because the intrinsically double aim was now halved. But within a month this was no longer relevant. The Admiralty received a letter which revealed the area of the Franklin tragedy.

In the spring and summer of 1854, Dr John Rae had made a

journey to complete the coastal survey. This time he was working westwards from the head of the Gulf of Boothia, which he reached overland from Hudson Bay. His purpose was purely geographical. He had informed *The Times* that there was no chance of his learning anything about the Franklin expedition. Soon after setting out he met an Eskimo who in the course of conversation recounted a story he had had from other Eskimos. Beyond the mouth of a great river, many sleeps to the westward, a large party of white men had died four years before (it was later proved to be six years – in 1848). The Eskimo had a naval officer's cap band, which Rae purchased from him.

But the cautious, unemotional Orcadian did not change his plans and go to look for the scene of the tragedy. He merely let it be known among the Eskimos that he would pay handsomely for any other relics, and continued on his way. He charted the unknown corner and made the important discovery that what had been known as King William Land was an island separated from the continent by a channel protected from heavy drift-ice.

On his return journey he bought a number of articles from the Eskimos, including Franklin's Hanoverian Order of Merit and spoons bearing the crests or initials of officers of the *Erebus* and *Terror*, Crozier's among them. He also learned the story in more detail. Many white men, all thin and hungry-looking, had been seen dragging boats down the west shore of King William Island. Later in the spring season the bodies of some forty men had been found in and about the remains of a camp on the continental shore, a long day's journey from the mouth of the Great Fish River. There were, said the Eskimos, signs of cannibalism.

To visit the place himself and look for other relics – including, perhaps, written records – Rae would have had to winter in the north. Instead he decided to write immediately to the Admiralty and to come to England with everything he had collected.

The Admiralty received his stark record on 22nd October and gave it unedited to the Press.

There was public outcry, raised chiefly by the imputation of cannibalism. Charles Dickens argued passionately against the report's veracity. Penny stated that Eskimos have no inhibitions about such accusations. They might have said what they did to distract attention from their own ill deeds. They had been bad Samaritans, only waiting until the men died to steal their belongings. Rae was blamed for giving out a story he had not confirmed. In these stormy arguments the real significance of the news was lost – the long uncertainty was over.

We know that Jane never recorded her deepest feelings. But Frances Woodward, who in her long researches into Lady Franklin, must have identified herself with her as closely as it is possible to do, states this in *Portrait of Jane*: 'There was room in her heart . . . only for a great sadness and a great relief. The end of nine years' false hopes must have meant, as well as profound pain, a release from pain'. . . . A woman would no doubt understand better than a man. Of Sophy's own feelings we know nothing. As usual she expressed only what she felt about her aunt whom she described as 'a sad invalid'. Jane was fairly often ill at this period, and before the year was out her sister Mary, with whom she had shared all the joys of youth and with whom she had always corresponded intimately, died – and there was trouble about Mary's will.

But whatever the state of Jane Franklin's mind and body she did not feel the fight was over. The third phase of her task remained. Her husband's achievement must be proved, accepted. His men had reached the continental shore and the open water that led all the way to Bering Strait. As Sir John Richardson put it in his memoir for the *Encyclopaedia Britannica*, they had 'forged the last link with their lives'. But the story could not rest only on hearsay evidence and a few pieces of crested silver. There would have to be another expedition.

The time was bad. Every ship was required for the Crimean War and public interest was in the long casualty lists from Sebastopol. The Admiralty asked the Hudson's Bay Company to send a party down the Great Fish River, and this was put in train under Chief Factor Anderson. But a naval officer could not be spared to join the party (as Jane requested) and they had not even an interpreter.

In January 1856, Jane received a letter from Anderson with an account of what he had achieved. It was not much. Conversing by sign language with the Eskimos, the two H.B.C. men had obtained a few more relics. But there was no record. Anderson suggested that anything in writing might have been destroyed because 'paper speaks to the white man'. They had not found the death camp, nor had it been possible to reach King William Island; birch-bark canoes, the best craft for the turbulent river, were not fit to cross the sea.

Jane was confirmed in her resolve to send a ship which should approach from the north as near as possible to the scene allowing a party to then explore by boat or sledge. It was her old original plan – with the difference that the location was now proved.

But what ship? The *Prince Albert* was judged unfit for further Arctic service. . . . Peace came. The Admiralty still offered nothing. But a ship offered herself. H.M.S. *Resolute*, one of the four ships that had been abandoned in the ice on Belcher's orders, had sailed unmanned a thousand miles – down Barrow Strait, Lancaster Sound, and Baffin Bay to Davis Strait where an American whaler had found her and brought her to the United States. Congress had bought her, refitted her for the Arctic, sent her across the Atlantic with an American crew and handed her back to the Admiralty. The perfect ship for the perfect gesture! But the Admiralty, in Jane's phrase, did not see the poetry in the proposal.

She believed that the American captain and crew who had brought *Resolute* home might be prepared to make the final expedition that she longed for. Captain Hartstene called on her and stayed for two or three hours (he said he could have stayed for twenty-four), but any plan they may have hatched was not approved. The truth was that the Admiralty had had enough of the Arctic, which had brought them nothing but expense and criticism.

Jane wrote to the Prime Minister, Lord Palmerston, exhorting the Government not to 'look on as unconcerned spectators'. She begged that a 'careful search be made for any possible survivor, that the bones of the dead be sought for . . . that their buried records be unearthed . . . and that their last written words be saved from destruction. . . . This final and exhausting search is all I seek'.

It was refused.

So Jane resolved to organise a final expedition herself. She was ready to spend £20,000 – though where she would have got it from goodness knows. The 177-ton steam-and-sail yacht *Fox* was on the market for £2,000. She looked for a captain. The best available man was Leopold McClintock. He had first served in the Arctic under James Ross, who thoroughly recommended him. On the Belcher expedition McClintock had commanded the *Intrepid*, had organised the sledging programmes of all the ships and had himself made a journey of 1,400 miles to the westerly limit of the islands. He had the reputation of never turning back from an unfinished task. He was both a good seaman and sympathetic. Jane liked him. She offered him the command.

He felt for her the devotion of a knight errant. Yet he hesitated. The Admiralty being ill-disposed might wreck the expedition and refuse leave; besides, he knew that she could not afford it. But Jane, when necessity demanded, could deploy more guns than the Admiralty. She approached Prince Albert through his private secretary. McClintock, who was in Dublin, received a telegram from Lady Franklin. 'Your leave is granted. The *Fox* is mine. The refit will commence immediately.'

Chivalry flowed in the veins of everyone concerned. They had need of that powerful and lubricating fuel. A luxury Victorian yacht lay in Aberdeen. Within two months at most she had to be changed into an Arctic ship. McClintock tells in *The Voyage of the Fox* how 'the velvet hangings and splendid furniture' were stripped away to be replaced by stout planking. 'The officers were crammed into pigeon-holes, styled cabins, to make room for provisions and stores. The wardroom was eight feet square. With metal-sheathed bows the elegant yacht was made to resemble "a ponderous chisel set up edgeways".'

Applications to 'serve in any capacity' poured in from every side. McClintock chose a crew of twenty-five, seventeen of them old and trusted Arctic companions. Contributions were sent in by people in every walk of life. Captain Allen Young of the Merchant Navy gave £500 and his services. All the officers served without pay. Stores and provisions were presented by firms. The Admiralty gave arms, ammunition, rockets and three tons of pemmican. A brewery gave all the beer that could be stowed. Prince Albert gave a barrel organ.

We may picture the scene as Jane and Sophy saw the ship sail off for the North-West Passage as they had watched a similar departure twelve years before. McClintock, well comprehending Lady Franklin's state of mind, tried to play down emotion. But the crew gave her three tremendous spontaneous cheers.

Then there was silence.

Jane had put a letter in the captain's hand – as she had done at the start of almost every searching voyage. But in this case it was addressed to McClintock and contained her instructions. He was to search for any possible survivors; he was to recover any records; and he was 'to confirm, directly or inferentially, the claims of my husband's expedition to the earliest discovery of the N.W. passage'.

The rest of the letter was an affectionate appeal that they should all look after themselves (as Bellot had been told to do) and an expression of gratitude and trust.

'How busy, how happy and how full of hope we all were then!'

McClintock wrote in *The Voyage of the Fox*.

But with the smile of chivalry came the evil spirit of bad luck which had haunted all the former searches. In the first season the *Fox* failed even to get across Baffin Bay. In spite of her strengthening she was no ice-ship. She was caught in the pack and drifted with it for 242 days – 1,385 miles in the wrong direction. So the first season and the first winter passed.

As soon as the ship was freed McClintock turned northwards again, and this time got through to Lancaster Sound. He visited Beechey Island to stock up with coal from the depot left there by the Belcher expedition. Although no Franklin record had been found it was now clear where he had sailed; to reach the place where the bodies had been reported he must have gone down Peel Sound. So down Peel Sound went the *Fox*, 'all of us in a wild state of excitement – a mingling of anxious hopes and fears' – for twenty-five miles. Then they came up against a wall of ice stretching from shore to shore.

It was one-year ice, not heavy. It might have scattered with a change of the wind if they had waited. But with one season lost and the second half gone McClintock could not risk waiting. He swung about, rounded the north coast of Somerset Island, sailed and steamed down Prince Regent Inlet and thrust into Bellot Strait, aiming to regain Peel Sound beyond the wall of ice.

They were half-way through the narrow waterway and could glimpse the sea beyond when they were stopped by ice and swept backwards by the powerful tide, floes surging beside them and the rocks at the cliff foot only 200 yards away.

They made a second charge, and this time got right through – but only to find another ice barrier, four miles in width. It was the end of August, the end of the season. Of necessity they retreated down Bellot Strait and made their winter quarters in Brentford Bay.

This was a bitter disappointment for all of them, for it meant that they could not reach King William Island by ship and so must make their search by long sledge journeys. For McClintock it was a double disappointment; he had nursed a secret hope to sail Lady Franklin's ship *through* the North-West Passage, following the sheltered waterway that Rae had found curving clockwise round King William Island. (Amundsen successfully followed this route in 1903-5.)

In November, George Brand, the ship's engineer, died of apoplexy, a personal and professional loss to McClintock. The young doctor, Walker, was anxious because he saw 'the seeds of scurvy' in the whole party. It was a dreary winter.

As soon as the sun returned (the coldest month as dawn is the coldest hour) the depot-laying journeys started. McClintock with Petersen, the interpreter, and another old hand sledged a couple of hundred miles down the west coast of Boothia to the Magnetic Pole where the community of Eskimos whom the Ross's had met twenty-five years before still lived. From them were obtained a silver medal which had belonged to Alexander McDonald, the assistant surgeon of the *Terror*, part of a gold chain and several buttons. All the wood and iron in the encampment came from the ships. The catastrophe had been a godsend to the Eskimos. But such information as they gave was vague – stories of bones and bodies – except for the specific mention of a great three-masted ship which had been crushed by the ice and sunk to the west of King William Island.

The search journeys proper started at the beginning of April. Young went westward across Peel Sound. McClintock and Hobson, the second-in-command, led sledge parties southward to Cape Felix, the northernmost point of King William Island. Here they parted, McClintock to the left to make a clockwise circuit of the island, Hobson to the right to examine its west coast. It deserves notice that McClintock assigned himself the route less likely to provide discoveries, leaving the more promising field to his junior whose reputation would be made by a spectacular find.

McClintock had with him the interpreter, Petersen, and two other men and two sledges, one drawn by dogs. They came on an encampment of the same Eskimo tribe they had earlier met. Here they obtained a number of Franklin relics and learned that *two* ships had been seen off the other coast. One – to the Eskimos' evident disappointment – had sunk in deep water. The other had come ashore and, they said, was still there (they must have known very well that it was not). The white men had gone away, dragging boats towards 'the great river'. An old woman said, 'They fell down and died as they walked along'.

Thus the story was building up. Many of the relics were pieces of crested silver, identifying individual officers, as had been the case in Rae's collection. Evidently the items had been divided among the seamen – for better security and to share the load. The mind's eye sees starving men eating their last scraps of food with silver forks and spoons from silver plates.

There was no written record. Petersen was told by the Eskimos that there had been many books (one wonders what word or phrase was used) but all had been destroyed by weather. An official record would be contained in something waterproof and probably buried under a cairn. They found none.

From the south coast of King William Island McClintock's party crossed the still frozen channel to the estuary of the Great Fish. They found nothing of importance there and no Eskimo to guide them. (The death camp described to Rae was never located). They crossed back to the island and started up the west coast to meet Hobson.

They were now travelling along the line that the crews must have taken, although in the reverse direction. If there was anything to be found after eleven years they would surely come upon it. But the possibly fruitful area was growing smaller with each step. They were following the shoreline where the going was easiest. The crews would probably have done the same. But if they had sledged on the ice everything would have gone into the sea.

On a low gravel ridge on the bare and windswept shore McClintock saw something round just protruding from the snow. It was the skull of a skeleton lying face downwards, scraps of uniform adhering to the bones. Beside it was a small clothes-brush, a horn pocket-comb with a few brown hairs still in it, and a notebook frozen solid. Much later, this was partially deciphered. It was Henry Peglar's record of service – the ships he had been in previous to the *Terror* – a few personal passages written backwards as if in a sort of code, and some very simple verses, probably his own. McClintock deduced from the rags that he had put on his shore-going clothes, his best suit, as if at the end of a voyage, and that the verses were of a song to entertain his companions on the journey. If that was typical of the crew they were far from despairing. But the find told nothing more substantial.

Further along the coast, at Cape Herschel, was the large cairn built by the Hudson's Bay Company surveyor, Simpson, in 1839. That would certainly have been used to cache a record. But one side had been pulled down and the centre removed. McClintock became convinced after a very thorough examination that something had been cached there, and that it had been extracted by Eskimos. The spirit of ill luck still haunted the search.

Later they came upon a boat which the men had been dragging overland. It contained two bodies and a large quantity of discarded clothing and stores – nothing more informative. But a newly built cairn contained a note from Hobson. He, coming from the north as the crews had done, had found at Point Victory 'the record so ardently sought for, of the Franklin expedition'.

It was in a metal cylinder and written on the margins of a standard naval record form. There were two entries, the second made almost a year after the first. The first was:

28 of May 1847. H.M. ships *Erebus* and *Terror* wintered in the ice in lat. 70 05N: long. 98 23W [a few miles off Cape Felix and due north of Point Victory].

Having wintered in 1846-47 [a slip for 1845-46] at Beechey Island, in lat. 74 43 28N: long. 91 39 15W., after having ascended Wellington Channel to lat. 77, and returned by the west side of Cornwallis Island.

Sir John Franklin commanding the expedition.

All well.

Party of 2 officers and 6 men left the ships on Monday, 24 May, 1847.

Gm Gore, Lieut

Chas. F. Les Voeux, Mate.

It is possible to deduce quite a lot from this note. It had been left by a reconnaissance party from the icebound ships. It told of two sailing seasons more successful than any that were made during the search. In 1845, presumably unable to pass Cape Walker or turn south, Franklin had sailed right up Wellington Channel and had found a way round Cornwallis Island before wintering at Beechey Island. Next season the ice had opened – perhaps suddenly after a storm – and provided the first opportunity to sail right down Peel Sound and its continuation Franklin Strait to King William Island. There the ships passed the second winter locked in ice. But in the spring Lieutenant Graham Gore's party went ashore to spy out the way ahead, and were encouraged. Cape Felix was only seventy miles from Cape Herschel to which Simpson had extended the map from the continental shore. The ice would loosen later in the summer. 'All well.'

They returned with their optimistic report. Within a fortnight Franklin died, and prospects changed. The ice held them all summer, perhaps damaged the ships so much that they would not have floated if released. The third winter was disastrous, with short rations, perhaps bad rations, and no doubt scurvy. In spring the decision was taken to travel south on foot, dragging boats for use on rivers. They must have been starving for if they had waited three months they could have travelled on water most of the way.

The second note was written at the start of a desperate journey. It was in the handwriting of Fitzjames, with a few words added by Crozier.

25 April 1848 – H.M. ships *Erebus* and *Terror* were deserted on 22 April, 5 leagues N.N.W. of this, having been beset since 12 September, 1846. The officers and crews, consisting of 105 souls, under the command of F.R.M. Crozier, landed here in lat. 69 37 42N., long 98 41W. Sir John Franklin died on 11 June, 1847; and the total loss by deaths of the expedition has been to this date 9 officers and 15 men.

James Fitzjames,
Captain, H.M.S. *Erebus*

and start tomorrow, 26, for Backs Fish River,

F.R.M. Crozier
Captain and Senior Officer.

As McClintock commented, 'So sad a tale was never told in fewer words'. But it was told not only in words. Skeletons and a few graves (later found) marked the trail southward to the continental shore which thirty or forty reached, thus forging the last link of the North-West Passage.

The sledge parties of McClintock, Hobson and Young met again on the icebound *Fox* in Brentford Bay. Hobson and Young were both scurvy-ridden but were soon put right by plenty of fresh food. The task now was to get back to England with the news. The engineer and chief stoker were both dead, so the captain – who had once done a course in engineering – rolled up his sleeves. 'I experienced some little difficulty in the management of the engines and boiler', he wrote. But on 9th August they got away and, after a brief stop at Godhavn to pick up mail ('It is a rather nervous thing opening the first letters after a lapse of more than two years'), they careered home with favouring gales.

Autumn had become the season when Jane was always in England, waiting for news. But in 1859 when there was news she was abroad, on doctor's orders, in the Pyrénées. So Collinson sent a telegram through the British Consul at Bayonne which she received, slightly mauled: 'Success full return of fox important letters for Lady Franclin at Bagnère Bigorre'.

One wonders what her feelings were after those fourteen and a half years. We can deduce a good deal from her behaviour. The nation revered Franklin; but there is something lacking in honouring the dead, so the homage due to him was added to what she herself had earned. Her name was in every newspaper, on all lips, and even in those early days of photography (there were no pictures in the daily Press) she was recognised everywhere she went.

The invaluable Sophy wrote: 'I am sure that if compliments addressed to her in the most heartfelt way from all quarters could turn her head my Aunt would have gone right round – but *nothing* can move her out of her calm repose.'

She was very busy, so much that Sophy was worried. 'My Aunt gets sadly worn by the quantity of work she has to go through, but really looks generally speaking very well – and people think her wonderfully improved.'

Jane entrusted the relics to the Admiralty. They were displayed at the United Services Institution. (They are now in the National Maritime Museum, Greenwich.) It was the public wish, expressed in the Press, that she should be recompensed for the fortune she had spent on the search. This she firmly rejected. But by hints dropped in the right place – which she well knew how to do – she saw to it that Parliament voted a grant of £5,000 to the officers and men of the *Fox*. She herself gave a silver watch to every member of the crew. McClintock was knighted and Hobson promoted. In those days before computer typesetting was invented, McClintock's book, *The Voyage of the Fox*, was published within a couple of months, and Jane spent the rest of her life presenting copies to kings and commoners.

But her main task was to ensure that her husband's achievement was fully appreciated. The public and the Press emotionally acknowledged it, and the Royal Geographical Society, the final arbiter in such matters, did so unequivocally in the terms of the award of their Founder's Gold Medal to the widow of Sir John Franklin, '. . . testifying to the fact that his Expedition was the first to discover the North-West Passage.' This was repeated in other words in the memorials in Wellington Place and Westminster Abbey.

Lady Franklin by her 'noble and self-sacrificing perseverance' had fulfilled her final task.

10

Aladdin's Cave

The characteristics of the three great British explorers of the golden early years of this century are often summarised in single sentences. Scott was the admirable commander, disciplined yet sensitive. Shackleton was the natural leader – sometimes leading into trouble but always out of it again. Mawson was the dedicated scientist – and largely for that reason is the least known of the three.

Douglas Mawson was born in England but brought up in Australia. He graduated as Bachelor of Mining Engineering at Sydney University. Later he became a Demonstrator in chemistry and organised a geological expedition to the New Hebrides.

Shackleton invited him to be physicist of his 1908-9 *Nimrod* expedition in the Antarcic and he at once accepted. For him there was a clear and logical answer to the question, 'Why explore?'. It offered the best opportunity for original field-work. He sledged, man-hauling, to the magnetic pole, an out-and-back journey of 1,260 miles – to make observations. He wrote the expedition's reports on physics, chemistry, mineralogy, meteorological optics, the aurora, magnetism. He proved himself a strong man who knew his own mind and capabilities.

He returned to Australia and took his Doctorate of Science. Then in 1910 he asked Scott for a passage to Adélie Land, the totally unknown country west of the Ross Sea for which the *Terra Nova* was bound. Scott could not undertake this detour but offered him a place on his expedition with a hint that he might be one of the South Pole party. This did not attract Mawson because only about 100 miles of the route was unknown. The two men parted with mutual respect.

Mawson organised his own expedition which contained fifteen scientists – almost twice as many as had ever previously been taken.

156

Douglas Mawson, D.Sc.

Lieutenant Belgrave Ninnis

Leaning against the wind while chopping ice for drinking water

Xavier Mertz, at the entrance to Aladdin's Cave

But we are not concerned with their work, not even directly with their most spectacular discovery – that description of the weather of Adélie had required another Force on the Beaufort Scale. The conventional scale rises from nought, dead calm, to twelve. Force 11 is a storm – 'Prostrates frail trees and exposed houses'. Force 12 is a Hurricane of 77 m.p.h. Mawson's addition was 'Force 13 – Adélie Hurricane – 100-200 m.p.h. – Prostrates everything'.

The *Aurora* disembarked the party in what was named Commonwealth Bay, and a base hut was built below the steep slopes of the inland ice. Only short depot-laying journeys were attempted during the winter. One main summer journey is our subject. It is of particular interest because it involved a predicament potentially present (and much discussed) on every polar expedition – what to do about a man who becomes incapacitated far from base.

This being an essentially human problem we would like to be able to picture the three men concerned. The frontispiece of Mawson's *The Home of the Blizzard* shows him as a slim young man of twenty-nine in a butterfly collar. The long, clean-shaven face, high forehead, thoughtful eyes and sensitive mouth, could well be those of a doctor, but a doctor of people (of whom he is fond) not of cold science. An Antarctic photograph roughs him up a bit; he looks amused by the ice on his whiskers.

The elder of his two sledging-companions was Xavier Mertz, a Swiss of twenty-eight, a Doctor of Law, skiing champion and mountaineer who whenever mentioned was in cheerful mood. The other was Lieutenant Belgrave Ninnis of the Royal Fusiliers, a healthy giant of twenty-three, full of the joy of life. They were officially in charge of the expedition's dogs. I do not think either had had previous experience as dog-minders; it is the label often given to good fellows with no specialist qualifications.

There were altogether five sledging parties which were to fan out between east and south from the first depot. They hoped to get away in October from the hut in Commonwealth Bay. But the average wind-speed that month was 56·9 m.p.h. so the start was delayed until 10th November 1910 when, after a feast of penguin-egg omelettes cooked by Xavier Mertz, they all drove their dogs or man-hauled their sledges to Aladdin's Cave, a depot excavated 1,500 feet up on the icecap and five and a half miles from the hut – the best they could manage in winter. There may not have been any conscious significance in the name of this most unusual depot (one of Mawson's excellent innovations, for a cave cannot be blown away or buried more than it is), but it matches what one guesses of the leader's character. It was the place from which a great wealth of discoveries were to be made, and it had an almost magical effect at the end.

Mawson's party had two loaded sledges plus an unloaded spare, and a total of seventeen dogs – all that had survived the winter. Since this route would be over much crevassed ice it was thought wise to carry the bulk of the 1,700 pounds load on the second sledge drawn by the best dogs. The weaklings drew a lightly loaded leading sledge so that if a snow-bridge gave way (almost all the crevasses were bridged at that season) the loss would be less. When eighteen days out (the loads by then being lighter) a sledge did fall through, and hung vertically. It was resurrected when Mawson had gone down on a rope, attached another rope to the tail of the sledge and so allowed the party to share the weight. He, himself, was then helped to climb out. It is rarely possible to climb out of a crevasse unaided.

Their route, says Mawson, 'led over a solid ocean rising and falling in billows 250 feet in height'. Their altitude above the real ocean was generally between 1,000 and 2,000 feet. They were travelling south-eastwards, roughly parallel with the coast. The surface was smooth except for sastrugi, the sculpted snowdrifts apparently designed by Nature to overturn sledges. These, however, reduced speed less than did numerous crevasses. One day the party covered only one effective mile, prodding out a safe way over a hidden maze of chasms. In any case (when the weather made travel possible, which was far from always) one man went in front to give the dogs something living to look at in the white desert. That stimulated their interest and made them pull better. Boredom is the worst enemy of swift icecap travel with dogs.

The men were far from bored. They were travelling through country previously unseen, daily adding to their maps a nunatak – a rock outcrop – or a glacier valley or new aspect of the coast. The danger of exploring is its magnetic pull. You must not go further than you would be able to return, and the temptation to travel on just one more day is great. But Mawson was eminently well balanced. Since the route had been so difficult that he intended to find a better way back outside the zone of the crevasses, he had left no depots. All his food was on the sledges and he knew as well as a man can calculate how far – out and back – it would take him.

If he contemplated a risk it was when, on 14th December, he

decided that the next day he would make a depot of most of their provisions and press on light and fast to make a really worthwhile eastwards achievement by linking up visually with land seen from Captain Scott's ship.

That was a particularly happy day, or most of it. For one thing it was fine and comparatively calm, the sun shining brilliantly. For another, Ninnis, who had been most depressed by a painful whitlow that kept him sleepless, had been much relieved since Mawson had lanced the finger the evening before, and had had a peaceful night. Third, they had the near prospect of turning for the hut and comfort after five weeks of hard travel.

Ninnis, still convalescent, was given the second sledge with which he would have no route-finding to worry about and the strongest dogs, which could be trusted to pull the load. Mawson took charge of the leading sledge. Mertz went out in front on skis.

He was the only one of the party who had skis, being the only proficient skier. By no means had he always been able to wear them, because of the sastrugi. But this day the surface, smooth and almost level, was ideal for langlauf. Mertz's joyousness was evident from a hundred yards or more. They had got to know this lively mountaineer on the voyage out in the *Aurora*. Up in the crow's nest he would yodel at the pack ice; now he sang mountain songs. Ninnis showed that he was feeling himself again by walking beside his sledge when, with such a good surface, he might have ridden.

Mertz held up a ski stick, equivalent to the traffic symbol of an exclamation mark, Caution! As Mawson approached the place he looked about him. But there was only the faint scar of an old snow bridge. On level ground there were few crevasses and these were most unlikely to be dangerous. He seated himself on the sledge and began to work out the last observations taken, leaving the dogs to follow the skier's track.

When he looked up again he saw Mertz stationary, staring back along the trail. At that distance his expression could not be read. But Mawson also turned. He saw nothing but the plateau.

He jumped off his sledge and ran back, thinking wildly that some unnoticed fold in the surface hid the following team. He found a great hole. Two sledge tracks led up to it, only one from it.

Waving to Mertz to bring back his sledge on which there were some coils of rope, Mawson peered down into the crevasse. Some 150 feet below there was a small ledge on which two dogs lay. One moved

159

as if it had broken its back. The other was supine, motionless. Beyond, the hole stretched down into blackness and a cold air rose from it.

All the rope they possessed, tied together, did not reach the ledge. They longed for action, however dangerous. But there was nothing they could do except call into the cavern in case Ninnis had been knocked out and might recover consciousness. They continued to call for three hours. The broken-backed dog became still.

They climbed to an eminence from which they could see the sea, hoping to reach it and find seals and penguins. But the way to the shore was steep, contorted, impassable. The sledge that had been lost with Ninnis had carried most of the man-food, all the dog-food, and the tent. On the remaining sledge was only a spare tent cover and ten days' man-food. The outward journey had occupied thirty-four days. They took observations and found that they were 316 miles from the hut – 310·5 miles from Aladdin's Cave where the first food and shelter might be found.

They returned to the crevasse and again called unavailingly into the abyss. At nine o'clock in the evening Mawson read the funeral service, the two men on the edge of the deep natural grave. Then Mertz shook Mawson's hand, said 'Thank you', and called the six remaining dogs to their feet.

The disaster had evidently been due to Ninnis being on foot whereas Mertz was on skis and Mawson on the sledge; but it was remarkable that it had happened so suddenly and silently that Mawson, only a few yards in front, had been unaware of it. The chance of the two survivors' reaching the hut depended upon speed. It may be that Mertz's brief 'Thank you' expressed impatience to be on the way.

He and Mawson hurried to their previous camp and made tent poles out of the spare sledge which they had left there. They pressed on, covering quite good distances at first. The dogs pulled until they dropped and then were used for food. Starved as the poor beasts were their flesh was far from wholesome. Both men became ill with cramps and stomach pains. Mertz was by far the worse affected. He ceased to be the cheerful, helpful companion and became a demanding, self-centred invalid. He frequently said that he must rest.

By 31st December, seventeen days after the catastrophe, they had covered over half the distance but were progressing more and more slowly. They had jettisoned everything not essential for maintaining life. All the dogs were dead. The two men had had a soup of boiled bones for Christmas dinner.

With the New Year things deteriorated further. The weather was bad. The sun, essential to give direction, let alone to cheer, was hidden. And Mertz wanted to rest almost constantly. There was no travel at all on the first two days of January. Their improvised tent was so small that only one man at a time could move in it. They had no groundsheet. Their reindeer-skin sleeping-bags, so deliciously warm when dry, had become soaked from the snow beneath and by the exhalations of their bodies. There was no comfort in camp.

On 3rd January, Mertz agreed to move, and towards evening the sun briefly appeared. But it took a long time to break camp and lash the sledge, and it was bitterly cold for emaciated bodies. Before they had covered five miles Mertz developed dysentery. Then one of his hands became frozen. He refused to believe this, saying he had always had a perfect circulation. He bit off the fleshy end of a finger before he was convinced that it had lost sensation.

The next day was 'most depressing'. The weather was bad, and Mertz said that he could not travel. The two men lay close together in their sleeping-bags. They ate little, but every ounce should have meant some progress towards salvation. Mawson spent the wasted time boiling bones but Mertz could not stomach the result. He was extremely weak and had to be helped out of his sleeping-bag when the dysentery gripped him.

There was no travel until 6th January when Mertz agreed to try to go on. The weather was comparatively fine but the surface was slippery, with awkard sastrugi. There were frequent falls – the shock of falls on tired men! After much persuasion Mertz agreed to ride on the sledge in his sleeping-bag. When lashed on he was safe, and with the wind behind Mawson could haul the load. But after only two and a half miles Mertz had an attack of dysentery and it was necessary to pitch the tent.

Mawson tried to make light conversation, urging Mertz to promise that he would make penguin-egg omelettes when they got back. But the sick man became silent and depressed. And Mawson wrote that night in his private diary, 'Both our chances are going now'. It does not seem to have ocurred to his logical mind, however, that he might leave his companion to the death that was inevitable. Mertz never spoke of this; he was no doubt too ill to realise that he was condemning his companion. Had he done so he might well have acted like Captain Oates. As for Mawson, if Ninnis had been alive, he would surely have recognised a choice of duties, but as it was he appears to have seen only one.

It was about this time that a small sea-bird visited them, a prion, Mawson thought. God knows what it was doing in that foodless desolation. It did not stay long. They watched it fly swiftly away in the direction they were trying so ineffectively to go.

'The night of the 6th was long and wearisome as I tossed about sleeplessly', Mawson wrote afterwards. His only hope rested on an agreement that they would travel next day with Mertz strapped on the sledge.

7th January dawned fine, with little wind, no snow falling, the sun shining. Mertz was got out of his bag to be ready to start when all the preparations had been made. But he had so severe an attack of dysentery that when it was over there could be no question of travel. Mawson tucked him back into his bag and got into his own to keep warm. It was hard work nursing a man in those confined conditions, and he was tired after the false early start. He lay sleepily worrying that his companion could not now even keep down the little that he swallowed.

At ten o'clock there was a rustle beside him and he found Mertz in a fit. Mawson did not specify the symptoms in his diary. But very soon the patient recovered and talked quite normally, evidently unconscious of what had happened, or of the gravity of the situation.

Apart from this sign of mental deterioration, Mertz improved during the next hour or two. He drank some cocoa without vomiting. The sun shone through the thin tent wall. But there could be no question of moving.

Late in the afternoon Mertz 'had several more fits'. He became delirious and talked incoherently and continuously until midnight.

At last he stuttered into silence and dozed off. Mawson tucked him into his sleeping-bag and slipped wearily into his own 'to get warm again and to think things over'.

One wonders what his thoughts were during the following two hours. He then reached out to touch his companion, and found him rigid.

He crouched beside Mertz and thought about him: 'Favoured with a generous and lovable character he had been a general favourite amongst all the members of the expedition. Now all was over, he had done his duty and passed on. All that remained was his mortal frame which, togged up in his sleeping-bag, still offered some sense of companionship.'

Mawson had waited 'to stand by my stricken companion and ease his sufferings as far as possible'. He was now morally free to save himself, if he could. But he suffered a reaction; he was 'nerve-worn'. He felt there was 'little hope of reaching the hut, still one hundred miles away'. Lying beside Mertz he even wondered if he could break and pitch camp single-handed.

He remained in camp for three days intending to set out only in the hope of reaching some prominent place where the diaries and scientific record would be found by a search party. Preparing for this, he reduced the load to 'the barest necessities'. He cut the sledge in half, made a mast and spar from the rails and a sail from a clothes-bag and Mertz's Burberry jacket. For the carpentry he used Mertz's knife which besides blades had a screwdriver, a gimlet and a tool for taking stones out of horses' hooves. He made a cross out of the rear halves of the sledge skis. He took Mertz out, still togged up in his frozen sleeping-bag as if in a coffin, and buried him, building a wall of snow-blocks round the grave. He read the funeral service. He lingered, making final adjustments to the marble-white tomb. He must have known that everything he did would very soon be obliterated by the wind.

These actions occupied two days and Mawson described them in some detail. He spent the third day 'in reckoning up the food remaining and in cooking the rest of the dog-meat'. One feels that he was also building up his resolve.

The climax of this chapter of his life, as he called it, was already passed. The rest is the epilogue. But in some ways this is the more interesting. Food lasts as long as will power, and there has been more than a hint of doubtfulness regarding that.

But he must have been morally strengthened by what he had done for Mertz, for as soon as he actually started out he showed certainty of purpose. He was going to reach the hut unless he was killed; he would not die passively. Yet there is a dreamlike vagueness about the narrative. He says that he developed the habit of thinking aloud. What he recorded in the evenings might be that monologue. A man can feel hopeful or despairing, careful or reckless, but he does not need to explain things to himself.

Besides suffering from starvation, he was in an unhealthy physical condition. The soles of his feet were coming off; they had to be bandaged on and covered with six pairs of socks. Boils were erupting all over his body; his fingers were festering, the nails loose; old frostbites gave trouble; his skin peeled and hair came out in handfuls. He rarely covered more than three or four miles before having to pitch the tent and patch himself up.

Travelling over the undulating frozen ocean, he came to the lip of a deep valley, the Mertz Glacier as they had named it when outward bound. Being then further inland, they had crossed with comparative ease and safety. Here it was steep and cracked into innumerable crevasses. With a detour he might have regained the safe route. Instead he plunged straight along the shortest line to Aladdin's Cave. Finding a bridged crevasse that ran in his direction he walked along it throughout its length because the snow was softer than the ice for his tender feet.

He travelled blindly through mist, snowfall and drift. Once he found himself on the very edge of a 'quarry'. He stopped short but the sledge ran past and pulled him on. He and it had a slippery tug-of-war before he got it to a safe place and pitched the tent. That night he allowed himself extra food. His tired mind decided that 'eating compensated in some measure for the sufferings of starvation'.

He descended the steepest, most dangerous slopes of the glacier through milky whiteness. He had considered waiting for better visibility. 'But delay meant a reduction of the ration and that was out of the question.' He fell up to his armpits into a covered crevasse, his legs dangling. He struggled out and carried straight on.

Next time he dropped right through a bridge. What followed is described as a sequence of thoughts and sensations with the physical subordinated as in a dream. And it shows, incidentally, that a man who has proved his ability to behave nobly does not necessarily think in a heroic vein when he believes his last hour has come.

There was no surprise or fear. He thought, 'So this is the end'. Almost simultaneously he regretted that he had not eaten all the food. Only then did he realise that he was being supported by the sledge; he does not appear to have felt any restriction from the trace rope. He saw that the crevasse was six feet wide and sheer-sided, descending into blue depths. The hole fourteen feet above him shone bright. He was conscious of cold, his loosely worn clothing being full of snow.

He began to struggle. He grasped a knot in the sledge trace and after a brief rest pulled himself up to another. He reached the top but before he could scramble out a portion of the lid broke away and he fell the full length of the rope.

Though his back might have been broken like a hanged man's neck, his next sensation was of slowly turning one way then the other. He felt that he had done all he could and regretted that he had no 'antidote' in his pocket to speed his end. . . . But he could slip out of his harness. 'I looked forward to the peace of the great release – how excited I was at the prospect of the unknown to be revealed.'

Perhaps excitement was the necessary stimulus, like the struggles that waken one from a nightmare. He called it 'the passion that burns the blood in the act of strife'. He emerged from the crevasse feet first.

Then reaction knocked him out. He lay unconscious for a couple of hours, measured by the hour-glass of the falling snow. It was a slow and painful task to pitch the tent.

There is a monotony in repetition that danger does not alleviate. Mawson was tired of crevasses. Sleepless in his sleeping-bag, he considered lying up and finishing the food as the only way of avoiding them. Then he thought of a ladder, and the idea interested him. When he started next day through the same monotonous mist and sun-obscuring snow, he was attached to the sledge by an extra length of rope with loops tied in it here and there. He had resolved 'to go ahead and leave the rest to Providence'.

Thus he crossed the dangerous area, climbing out of crevasses when he fell into them. In front of him now was a 3,000-ft climb to the high line of plateau that he had seen dimly in the distance soon after leaving the camp where Mertz died. There he had cut down his load to 'the barest necessities'. He now pruned it again, with less judgement. He abandoned his rope-ladder and his crampons, also some pairs of socks and his finnesko. The reduction in weight cannot have been much, but it may well have been a significant proportion of the whole. He carried only four or five pounds of food.

He had already been nine days on the way and the climb took eight days more. It is not surprising that the account of it is scant, for there cannot have been much to talk to himself about. 'Covered two and a half miles as the day's work', or 'I wandered through it for several hours'.

False crests had deceived but the true crest was unequivocal. There was the half-forgotten sensation of moving downhill. The sun came out, the mist lifted, and in front was the dark blue of a water sky. A black spot of rock on the white surface was a known nunatak. He knew where he was – within forty miles of the coast. 'I felt for the first time there was a really good chance of making the hut.' On his recent average, the distance would take ten days to cover. He still had twenty small chips of dog-meat and his emergency ration of raisins and chocolate, about two pounds of food altogether. In his exhilaration he covered eight miles that day.

The faster a man goes the quicker he burns up his fuel. Mawson was starving, hungry and exhausted that night. And next morning there was only disappointment, for the wind had risen and the drift was flowing like a river in spate.

He pressed on regardless, as hard as he could drive himself, uncertain of his direction, for he could not see far, and desperate for food. He had gone some five miles, head down in the drift, when he saw a black spot to his right, and turned towards it. He found a snow cairn draped in black bunting and on top of it a bag.

He opened the bag and found food. Intoxicated by 'a second miracle', he sat down in the lee of the cairn and began to eat. There was a tin containing a message written exactly six hours earlier. A search party made up of the other sledging-teams which had all returned safely to the hut had gone out to look for his trio and finally turned back at this point. The *Aurora* had arrived and was waiting only to take them home. Aladdin's Cave was 30 degrees east, 23 miles south.

Having stuffed himself, Mawson stuffed his pockets and went on at full speed, 'stimulated in body and mind'. Nothing would stop him from reaching the hut in two days. . . . Within a few miles the surface changed from snow to ice. He was frequently blown off his feet, his skeletally thin body striking the hard surface with painful force. The sledge went skidding off like a kite in the wind. He tried crawling on hands and knees, and was brushed aside. If he had kept his crampons he would have managed but without spikes on his feet he was helpless.

He had to camp – easier realised than done. As soon as he had canvas over his head he began to make crampons, using screws from the sledge-meter, the theodolite and its wooden case. This took him all night and most of the next day.

By evening the wind had dropped a little and he set out over the ice slopes with the pieces of spiked wood lashed to his feet. He covered six miles – optimistically, for the sea was in view. Then the crampons came to pieces and the wind increased. The sledge which had so often saved him from falling to the depths, skidded into a crevasse and he had great difficulty in rescuing it. With equal difficulty he camped.

Aladdin's Cave was still seventeen miles away, across the wind. He *had* to have crampons. Having already used virtually all the suitable material, it was a matter of mending rather than making, but this took as long as the original cobbling. He contrived to fix the spikes to his feet by means of soft reindeer-skin boots, and set out.

The crampons did not live up to expectation and hurt his tender feet. But he had an irresistible magnet. Far away across the universal whiteness he saw a black spot which he knew to be the beacon that marked Aladdin's Cave.

He reached it at seven o'clock in the evening, scrabbled away the snow, threw back the canvas seal of the entrance and dived into the cavern. The first things he saw were three oranges and a pineapple. This seeming magic brought before his mind's eye his warm and fertile homeland.

He sat down to patch up his crampons – hurriedly, for the hut was only five and a half miles distant and the *Aurora* would soon have to leave. He drank some hot milk and crawled out. But he did not get more than a few paces. The wind had had time to rise to a blizzard, the slope was precipitous and he could not trust his feet. He decided to wait for better weather next day.

The blizzard continued for a week. Without the complete shelter of the cave he would certainly have died. As soon as the storm eased he set out, riding on the sledge like a boy tobogganing. The wind dropped away completely and the sun came out. Commonwealth Bay was spread out below him. He saw the hut with men around it. One waved an arm. (These were men who had volunteered to wait another year in case their leader and his companions might yet return.)

He could not see the *Aurora*. She might have come closer inshore under the ice cliff, he thought.

Then he saw a speck far out to sea, a ship sailing away. . . . 'What matter!' he thought. 'The long journey was at an end – a terrible chapter of my life was concluded.'

'Aweful' would have been a more appropriate adjective than terrible. That a man should resign his life for a friend who was beyond saving and then pass through a starving icy purgatory to be reprieved wakes reverential wonder.

11

Compulsion to Live

On 8th November 1972 Marten Hartwell landed his twin-engined Beechcraft 18 at Cambridge Bay to which he had been diverted because of bad weather. He was on a commercial flight but had no passengers and planned to stay there overnight.

While settling in, he was approached by some of the hospital staff. Two patients had just been flown in by a small plane from the remote settlement of Spence Bay – an Eskimo boy with suspected appendicitis and his aunt who was in labour with complications. It would be unsafe to wait for the Pacific Western's scheduled flight at midnight. Would he take them on at once to the Stanton Yellowknife hospital?

Hartwell was unwilling, but not because he had just experienced icing conditions. He had been flying the Beechcraft for only three weeks and was not qualified to navigate by instruments alone. It would mean flying well into the night to reach Yellowknife, 530 miles away. If he undertook the flight he would be condemned by officialdom. Yet, if he refused to undertake a mercy flight, he, as a bush pilot, would be damned by everyone else.

While he hesitated he was talked to by an English nurse. Many British nurses are employed in the Northwest Territories, for one reason because they have gynaecological training, for another they have, wrote a Canadian, a special sort of determination and independence their Canadian counterparts lack. She spoke as only a nurse can – not even a doctor – when she sees the necessity. The Eskimo woman, the boy's aunt, had already lost two babies. In this pregnancy she had been fitted with a suture which tied up her womb like a balloon. Whether this should have been done for a patient who lived in so isolated a place was beside the point. She was in premature labour. If she did not reach a sophisticated hospital within a matter of hours she might die in agony.

Marten Hartwell hesitated no longer.

He took off with the Eskimo woman, Mrs Neemee Nulliayok, her nephew David Kootook, who was fourteen, and the English nurse, Judith Hill, who had accompanied them from Spence Bay settlement to Cambridge Bay. Hartwell wanted the boy, who was well enough to walk onto the aircraft, to be belted into one of the ten seats. But Nurse Hill said he would be better lying down in the gangway with his aunt who was on a stretcher.

Judith Hill sat beside the pilot in the cockpit. As they slowly climbed over the strip of frozen water, then over the white Barren Lands she produced a flask of coffee and offered a cup to Hartwell. He thanked her. She was tall, fair, strikingly good looking and twenty-seven years old. But just then he could scarcely see her face for she wore a hooded parka. She was a country girl from Devon and had emigrated to Canada three years before. She enjoyed her lonely self-reliant work in the North. But they could not hold a conversation above the noise of the engine.

When they had finished their coffee she unstrapped herself and went back to tend her patients. After a while she returned to the cockpit and they sat side by side. A flight without incident is an interval for confidence. Except for the noise Hartwell might have told her a lot about his life, which might have interested her.

He was born Leopold Herrmann, the son of an East Prussian farmer. He was a member of the Hitler Youth and was training as a fighter pilot when the war ended. He then earned a living in a variety of ways, smuggling fish into East Germany, fattening pigs for the black market, making shoes out of old tyres and cardboard, taxi driving, acting as 'chauffeur' to a business man with a private plane – he had not had a commercial pilot's licence. He had married soon after the war and his wife Emma had borne him a son in 1948.

In 1967 he sailed for Quebec leaving his family behind. His wife wrote to him saying that she wanted a divorce. In Canada he again took a variety of jobs – but always within reach of an airport where he was taking lessons to qualify as a commercial pilot. He obtained his licence at the age of forty-four, six months after leaving Germany, and celebrated the achievement by changing his name to Marten Hartwell. He also became a vegetarian. This was not a moral decision: he could not stand the smell of steaks.

He set about learning the bush pilot's trade, flying geologists, prospectors and miners from anywhere to everywhere in the Northwest Territories. It was spasmodic work at first but he finally got a permanent contract from Gateway Aviation in Yellowknife, the goldmining town on Great Slave Lake. In 1971 he met Susan Haley, a twenty-two-year-old student of ancient philosophy at the University of Alberta. They do not appear to have been together for long periods at a time but their bond was proved to be strong.

On that afternoon of 8th November 1972 Hartwell crossed the Barren Lands. Below him were a gradually increasing number of pine trees and a multitude of small lakes. There were no recognisable landmarks and in any case it was becoming dark. The magnetic compass was of no help so near to the magnetic pole. He was steering by directional giro. Individual giros vary slightly in their behaviour and he had never used that particular one before. He was also using an automatic direction finder which tunes in on ground beacons, but the call-signs were obscured by static and he could not pick up Yellowknife. He descended below the static and heard a different call-sign all too clearly, one he believed to be of Wrigley beacon which should have been far to west. He had made a mistake in indentification or direction.

He switched on a light and opened the low altitude map which showed the call-signs of all the beacons. The map fell back into its folds so that he had to open it again and smooth it out. Nurse Judith Hill was asleep at his side and he did not waken her to help him. It was 6.30 p.m., full night.

The Beechcraft hit a clump of trees on a hilltop, in that otherwise flat landscape. The wings were torn off. It cartwheeled and ended on its side.

Hartwell was pinned in his seat and was so badly shocked that he did not know at first who were the people he heard or saw about him. He saw David Kootook helping his aunt out of a rent in the fuselage. He laid her on the stretcher and covered her with a sleeping bag. Hartwell called him and asked to be helped out. His legs were locked under the seat by those of the nurse whose body hung through a hole in the cockpit, head and breast resting on the snow.

The boy could not move her alone. Hartwell struggled to help him but found he could not stand. Walking on his knees he dragged Judith Hill clear of fire danger and sat dazedly beside her listening to her heavy breathing until, after about ten minutes, it stopped. The

170

Eskimo woman died a couple of hours later.

Hartwell and David spread the engine cover and sleeping-bags (they had five) on the snow and tried to get some sleep.

Then they made an inventory of what they had with them and Hartwell assessed their position.

They were both well clad, Hartwell particularly, and the boy's garments were supplemented from the nurse's suitcase. There was a box of emergency rations intended to last two men for a week, the main items being corned beef, oxo cubes and buillon soup packets, raisins, sugar, two wax candles and some cigarettes.

There was a survival booklet and survival kit including a hunting knife, flares, a net and fish hooks, snare wire, a compass and a signalling mirror. There was also an axe. Hartwell might have drawn a rifle from the Gateway Aviation store but had not done so.

The Beechcraft had carried an E.L.T. – Emergency Location Transmitter. This is about the size of a normal transistor radio. It is powered by batteries and is designed automatically to transmit a distress signal when an aircraft crashes. This for some time could not be found but David eventually came on it in the snow. It had not transmitted on impact, and Hartwell fiddled with it for over two days before he got it to work. Even then he could not afford to keep it switched on. He determined to use it only when he heard an aeroplane. He estimated that they were between 100 and 200 miles short of Yellowknife. In fact it was 220 miles away and he was 175 miles off course.

Had they come down in the Barrens, the wreck might have been comparatively easy to see from the air. But they were among trees and shadows in a patchwork landscape of wooded ground and lakes. There was a lake in view from the hilltop they were on. It was Hattah Lake to which Hartwell had carried a team of divers who hoped to salvage silver ore that had been lost when a snowmobile went through the ice. That had been only two months before, but he did not recognise the lake.

In this lonely and difficult country Hartwell was crippled. He had broken both ankles and one knee. At first he kept on his long flying boots night and day in the hope that they would act as splints. The fractures did mend fairly well although his right leg became banana-shaped. His nose was also broken but he clicked that back with his fingers.

The boy, David, complained of pains in his back for a couple of

171

days, that was all. It was learned later that he was not an appendicitis case – he had an ulcer.

Man and boy depended entirely on each other. At first Hartwell felt that he was fantastically lucky to have an Eskimo with him. But David did not come from a nomadic tribe. He was a settlement Eskimo, his step-father a mechanic. He had none of the traditional skills of his race. Hartwell with his farming background was the more practical. But the boy was mobile and generally willing to carry out to the best of his ability what Hartwell wanted done. Most important, they kept each other company.

Colin Smith, whose *Observer* articles give the best general picture I have come across (I have relied largely on them), included some interesting touches. David was frightened of the trees. This fear may have come from ancestral memory of when the forest hid Indians on the warpath. Though only fourteen he smoked heavily. In six days he got through all the cigarettes in the emergency box and those that had been in the possession of his aunt and the nurse. Then he searched about for butts. When by way of a bedtime story Hartwell described Yellowknife with its 5,000 closely-packed inhabitants, the boy was chiefly interested in what brands of cigarette could be bought there. Latterly he liked Hartwell, a self-styled agnostic, to read aloud to him from Nurse Hill's prayer book. When they woke in the night man or boy would frequently ask the other if he was all right. It seems to have been only very rarely that they spoke of the two women whose bodies had soon been buried by snow.

It snowed heavily. Besides hampering the search for them this made it more difficult for the survivors to do essential chores. It must be hard enough to get about on two broken legs without deep snow. They boy gathered firewood and Hartwell chopped it up. His ambition was to have a huge signal-fire ready to be lit. Besides, they needed wood for cooking or at least hot drinks. But the first priority was shelter. Their first attempt – Hartwell's practical mind guiding the boy's legs and hands – was a conical tepee. But rectangular sleeping-bags would not fit together as walls so they pulled it down and made a small ridge-pole tent walled with engine tarpaulins, the stretcher and two of the sleeping-bags. They used one of the remaining three bags as a mattress. The temperature must have dropped well below zero but Hartwell's only comment on it was in a letter to his fiancée, Susan Haley: 'It's cold, you know.'

He had very soon decided that any writing should be done at once,

172

before their hands became frostbitten. On the second day after the crash – when his dazed brain had cleared, when he had seen or heard no aircraft and realised that they were unlikely to be found alive – he wrote his will, leaving half his savings to Susan Haley and half to his son, Peer Herrmann. He explained the situation. '. . . I hope this will be sufficient for the court to divide my belongings' – about $6,000. He got David Kootook to witness it.

He wrote a long statement for Gateway Aviation and letters to his son and to Susan. He kept them in Judith Hill's handbag and meant to destroy them if he was rescued. But this proved impossible. They were found by others. Parts were read at the inquest or otherwise obtained by the Press. So they ceased to be private. Some passages are revealing of the ordeal and the writer's state of mind. He began to Susan: 'I feel so sorry for you, you will have to go through such a horrible time. . . . God bless you, and may you never again fall in love with a bush pilot.' Only in an addition eight days later did he tell her that his legs were broken. He made several additions before the end.

David wrote:

To my mother and father.
Few days ago we got to Cambridge Bay. We were going to go to Yellowknife. The airplane fell. When this happened Neemee died and the nurse. The pilot's legs are broken, he cannot walk. I am all right. We fell between Yellowknife and Cambridge Bay on the hills.

In a few more days, on the 14th the pilot wants me to walk to Yellowknife, so I must try and walk. I pray to God that I will see you again. We eat all the time, the pilot and I. There is just two of us. We have white man's food [dried food]. The food is in a box. The box is just a bit bigger than my red suitcase. The weather was bad yesterday and today is foggy.

Johnny Kovalah and Lena, give them a kiss for me. We cut wood with an axe and we make fire. There is just me and the pilot here. Neemee and the nurse died when the airplane fell. There was four of us.

I will see you again in Spence Bay or in heaven. I try to pray. I do not feel cold in the daytime, only at nights. . . . Yellowknife is far away from here and I'm going to try to walk there. The pilot wants me to walk there.

I am finished writing now. I do not have any more writing paper.

David Peesurajak Kootook

173

The writing-paper had been taken from Judy Hill's suitcase. Hartwell used her fountain pen until the ink froze. They may not have spoken of her but at one time or another they used a number of her possessions.

David was wrong in writing that the pilot wanted him to walk to Yellowknife – 220 miles away – but Hartwell did frequently urge him to go to the lake and fish. The pilot spent most of the eight daylight hours in a seat which had been taken from the aircraft. When he had finished chopping wood he sat and stared at the lake, more and more obsessed by the thought of plump trout swimming about under the ice. Even a settlement Eskimo who had never had to fend for himself in the wilds could fish through the ice.

But could he get there? Hartwell was convinced that he could for he believed that the lake was only four miles away. The boy was unwilling to try, perhaps mainly from his unreasoning fear of the trees. He was eventually persuaded to make several attempts, we cannot know with how much determination, and he ate four of the six tins of corned beef on these journeys. To be fair, the task was impossible for him. The lake was actually twelve miles distant and in the soft, undrifted snow of the woods he would have had to wade thigh deep.

Shortly after the crash they had shared a feast of a whole tin of corned beef and some rice. But after that the seven-day emergency rations were strictly conserved and they tried to live off the country. Following the instructions in the survival booklet they set snares. There were tracks on the snow, probably of hares or foxes, but they caught nothing. The boy gathered lichen from dead branches. This they first added to their soups, then boiled alone. The booklet also told them that the inner bark of trees was nutritious. They tried this well boiled, but their bowels rejected it exactly as it had come in. One wonders about David's ulcer. He only once complained of cramp pains and stilled them by eating snow.

His condition deteriorated faster than that of Hartwell. His attempts to reach the lake – however far he got – must have taken it out of him. On the first attempt he was only away for three hours and returned saying that he was frightened.

After considerable persuasion he agreed to try again – if he was paid. Amazed, Hartwell promised him five dollars a trout, cash down. The boy set off with net, hooks, axe, sleeping-bag and his little red suitcase. He came back in the middle of the night saying that he

174

had been walking in circles. It transpired that he had placed the compass on the axe-head to read it.

Again he tried, and came back without his sleeping-bag and suitcase saying he had left them beside the carcass of a caribou which he had found. Hartwell sent him back for his belongings, telling him to eat his fill and bring all the meat he could carry. After fifty-one hours David returned with sleeping-bag and suitcase, saying that he could not find the dead caribou. He was all in, so Hartwell did not chide or question. But he added to his letter to Susan, 'Boy no good. No more food. See you in heaven'.

Hartwell had another reason for being disheartened by the boy. He had asked him whether he had ever heard stories among his people of the dead being used for food in times of starvation. David said 'No', but he used to be told as a child that if he did not go to bed the white men would come and eat him. Hartwell then asked him bluntly if he was prepared to eat the bodies of the women. David said he was, but not his aunt because she had been good to him. So things remained, neither of them doing anything about it.

A helicopter thundered right over their camp without seeing it. The air search had been intensive, costing a million dollars, but it had not covered their area. On 27th November it was called off. Susan Haley, who had acted throughout as a volunteer spotter, was told that she might as well go home and cry.

The next day Hartwell and David shared the last piece of candle. He had written to Peer, who was doing his military flying-service in Germany: 'When you receive this letter I will be dead. . . . Please forgive me my sins. I love you, my only son.' And he made a last addition to his letter to Susan: 'Still alive but David gave up. He might die tomorrow and I two or three days later. No good at all. Lived for a while on lichen. My legs don't carry me yet. Amen. Poor Susan. I love you.'

Hartwell told the Eskimo boy to go and cut flesh from the dead bodies. 'Shut up,' David said. 'I'm going to die.'

Until then Hartwell had shown courage, getting about on his knees or on makeshift crutches. He never mentioned pain in what he wrote. But he could not perform this final act himself. Watching the boy evidently dying seems to have numbed his will to live. He tried to devise a way of hanging himself. If they had had a rifle it might then have been fired.

He did a curious thing. He shared the nurse's emergency drugs

175

with David, each of them choosing the ampules blind. One at least was a tranquilizer and another to stop bleeding. It made no difference one way or the other.

On 1st December the search was resumed as a result of energetic representations made by Professor Haley, Susan's father.

David died that night. Hearing him gasping Hartwell tried artificial respiration and gave the kiss of life. But the boy had not in him the wherewithal to live. He was wasted to skin and bone and in his stomach there was only some moss bark and pine needles.

When he was alone Hartwell's urge to live revived. He struggled to the nearest tree that had dead lower branches and therefore lichen, cut a bundle of wood and crawled back. This took about two hours. Then he made a fire, melted snow and boiled up the handful of lichen. Obtaining that minimal nourishment had exhausted him. Without another source of food he would die.

He took the 'intellectual' decision to live on the dead bodies. He told Colin Smith (more than four months later): 'The first day I did not take much nor the second. I had a little bit of it in my hand and I held it for what seemed like hours. I thought you have to do it. When I did it I could feel myself going to be sick and had to force it down. I thought I was finished as a human being. I cried out to the bush for help.'

It took a couple of days to get over this physical and mental revulsion. Even after that, though he ate a lot, he had to shut his eyes when he went to get more. He went only to the nurse. He never touched the boy or the Eskimo woman.

Six days after the boy's death a Canadian Armed Forces Hercules plane flew over the tent. The crew were not looking for him. They were on a routine flight and were sixty miles off course. Hartwell switched on his E.L.T. They heard it, turned and flew round the hill until they had exactly located the site.

Thirty-two days after the crash Hartwell was rescued by parachutists and a helicopter. The first parachutist to reach him held out a hand. Hartwell did not take it. He sat, expressionless, in the seat outside the tent. At last he said, 'You are welcome here in the camp of a cannibal.'

I chose this Arctic incident, although it is not concerned with exploration, because after considerable research I have found it to be the only frank, unequivocal and sufficiently explicit record of cannibalism by a sensitive, civilised man. And I suppose the steps from the last mouthfuls of rations and forage to the first mouthful of a dead companion are much the same whether that man is an explorer or a bush pilot.

Eating human flesh in such circumstances is not against the law of either man or the Christians' God, but it is subject to a taboo that embraces equally the religious and the atheist, the criminal and the law-abiding. In this case one cannot help suspecting that the final decision resulted from having no witness rather than – as he stated later – from a suddenly resurrected will to live. But Hartwell stood up squarely to the consequences. He made a full statement to the Royal Canadian Mounted Police, which was kept secret until the inquest in March. He refused to attend the inquest on the grounds that he had nothing more to tell and his presence would only increase the drama and pain for the families. (Incidentally, the parents of Judith Hill behaved admirably. They approved the Press report on which I have mainly drawn – there were plenty of Press reports.) Hartwell retired among trappers and such people who did not ask questions or, still worse, stare. His only defence was to exclaim that those who have not been faced with the choice of eating human flesh or dying should not judge. He did not marry Susan Haley. As soon as he was given back his licence, which was withdrawn, he became a bush pilot again.

I have tried in this book to include all the special knowledge or personal experience I could, but I have to admit that I have never eaten man, only man's best friend. I found him, sentiment apart, very much the same as what you get from the family butcher.

I did, however, once come within talking range of being eaten. On one journey with Gino Watkins we became desperately short of food. He asked me whether if he died I would eat him. I made a non-committal joke of it.

'Well, you'd better make up your mind because I'd eat you,' Gino said, for once sharply.